Best of the Best from

QVC

Cookbook

Favorite Recipes from Viewers, Hosts, Employees and Friends

Best of the Best from
QVC
Cookbook

Favorite Recipes from
Viewers, Hosts, Employees
and Friends

■ ■ ■

edited by
Gwen McKee and Barbara Moseley

illustrated by Tupper England

QUAIL RIDGE PRESS
Preserving America's Food Heritage

ISBN 1-893062-33-3

Printed in Canada
Book design by Cynthia Clark • Cover photos by Greg Campbell
Inside photos courtesy of QVC, Inc., Gwen McKee, and Tara Logan-Elinski

First Printing, February 2002 • Second, September 2002

Library of Congress Cataloging-in-Publication Data
Best of the best from QVC cookbook : Favorite recipes from viewers, hosts,
    employees and friends / edited by Gwen McKee and Barbara Moseley.
       p. cm. —
    Includes index.
    ISBN 1-893062-33-3
    1. Cookery. I. McKee, Gwen. II. Moseley, Barbara. III. QVC (Firm)

TX714.B448 2002
641.5—dc21   2001059421

On the cover: Queen Anne's Lace Cake (p. 198), Frosted Roll-Out Sugar Cookies (p. 246),
Cilantro Chicken (p. 147) with Grill Thrilled Vegetables (p. 111) and Brown Rice Casserole (p. 134),
Shrimp Lauren Ann (p. 162), Spinach Ranch Roll-Ups (p. 27), Marble-ous Meatloaf (p. 177),
Delightfully Light No-Bake Cheesecake (p. 221), Little Bits of Heaven Ice Box Rolls (p. 32),
Chocolate Chip Tiramisu (p. 279)

QUAIL RIDGE PRESS
P. O. Box 123 • Brandon, MS 39043
e-mail: info@quailridge.com • www.quailridge.com

Table of Contents

In mid-March, there may still be a tad of snow beneath the trees, but according to BEST OF THE BEST editor Gwen McKee, the entrance to QVC is always impressive and welcoming, no matter the season.

Preface

$\mathcal{W}$hen QVC approached Quail Ridge Press about coordinating a contest cookbook for their viewers, I was immediately excited! My first thoughts were that this would be a connection to all those people on the other end of the TV cable who watch and love QVC and feel a part of it. Now they would have a chance to actively participate by sending in a favorite recipe to be published in a special cookbook written by them and for them. I loved it!

The book was QVC's Executive Vice President, Darlene Daggett's idea, and she got enthusiastic support right from the beginning. Since Quail Ridge Press' slogan is "Preserving America's Food Heritage," and because the BEST OF THE BEST STATE COOKBOOKS have been so popular with viewers, the same friendly, easy-to-use format was the style of choice. QVC in Pennsylvania, Quail Ridge Press in Mississippi, and QVC viewers all over the country began collaboration on a labor of love . . . *Best of the Best from QVC Cookbook*.

Early in 2001, we began formulating the contest rules and forms so we could send them out with Quail Ridge Press' new *Recipe Hall of Fame Quick & Easy Cookbook*. Contestants could also obtain order forms online or by calling the QVC operators. When the first entries arrived, we were so excited to see that not only were people sending in delicious recipes, but many of them had delightful personal stories that often revealed family traditions related to the recipes. I read each one several times, realizing right away that it was going to be hard not to include them all. We expected hundreds of recipes . . . we got thousands! Our testing committee, headed by Barbara Moseley, (BEST OF THE BEST and RECIPE HALL OF FAME co-editor) and me, worked in our own kitchens, but had to bring the dish for the entire committee to evaluate. Lunches at Quail Ridge Press were always exciting and delicious. Some of the recipes were tested again by people in different locations who would know more about that particular recipe. Before any decisions were made, there was "a whole lotta cookin' goin' on."

The criteria for judging was based on taste and ease of preparation, with points given for originality, and most importantly, an emphatic "Yes!" had to be answered to the question, "Would you prepare this recipe again?" We used a four-star evaluation system, and in the end, only the three- and four-star recipes made the book.

We included some excellent recipes, photos, and sometimes a little commentary from QVC hosts and other QVC employees that we thought you might enjoy. More than just outstanding recipes, I wanted the book to give viewers some idea of what QVC is really like behind the scenes. Since I have appeared often with my BEST OF THE BEST STATE COOKBOOKS, I get asked all the time: "What's it like?" "Is it scary being on camera?" "Are the hosts really that friendly?" And my favorite, "Is it live?" Oh, yes! It's live, and that's what makes it exciting! And as far as scary goes, yes, my adrenaline always rises to the occasion, but I just talk to the host and imagine a roomful of friendly people—I don't let myself think that there are millions of people in the room!

As for the hosts . . . they are friendly, warm, and genuine, both on and off the air. They care about doing the best job they can of helping the vendors to sell their products. I wish everyone could meet the helpful producers and coordinators and studio operations people . . . I just love them all. QVC is terrific, and I feel privileged to have been associated with them since December of 1996, when they discovered our first BEST OF THE BEST STATE COOKBOOK.

There are so many people who helped in the development of this book. At QVC, in addition to Darlene Daggett and her assistant, Lorianne DeVita, I wish to thank Karen Fonner, Rachel Stevenson, Doug Thompson, Anne Luttrell, Mary Harlyvetch, Rebecca Helmeczi, Abby Schaefer, Holly Rutkowski, Patsy Sanborn, Geraldine Bowden, Carolyn Hendrickson, and Elizabeth Brubaker for their gracious assistance. Thanks also to Bobbi Cappelli for recipe testing and advice (she, her daughter, Holli, and her staff are responsible for showing my recipes on camera so beautifully that you can almost taste them). In August, QVC sent Tara Logan, Paul Schneider, Eric Godfrey, Mark Goodwin, Paula Bower, and Jill Bauer to our offices and my home to film and help out with testing and sampling recipes—they were so delightful, helpful, . . . and fun! At Quail Ridge Press, everybody was willing to put on a new hat to do whatever needed doing. Special thanks to Terresa Ray, Sheila Williams, Cyndi Clark, Annette Goode, Jimmie Saucier, Christy Campbell, Gordon Denman, Keena Grissom, Leona Tennison, Dawn Macke, and especially Barbara Moseley, my co-editor and best friend.

I save a very special thanks to all the contestants who sent in their recipes, whether they ended up in the book or not . . . they're all winners. These people were gracious in sharing their recipes and the family traditions that go with them. The message woven throughout was that shared food is shared love. Thank you, QVC viewers across America, for joining QVC and Quail Ridge Press in helping to Preserve America's Food Heritage.

Always my best,
Gwen McKee

Foreword

By Darlene Daggett, QVC's Executive Vice President

Dear Friends,

Gwen and I have been pen pals—make that e-mail pals—for quite some-time now. It wasn't until a few weeks ago that we had the opportunity to sit down finally, meet face to face and talk about our newest venture, *Best of the Best from QVC Cookbook.*

Before we talked about business, we talked about kids, grandkids, life in the kitchen, and how hot it gets in Mississippi in the summertime! God bless Gwen. She said that if I could find a few days in my schedule, she might even be able to teach me how to golf. I told her it would probably take half a lifetime given my swing.

Darlene is all smiles when it comes to talking about family—her husband and four adorable children as well as her extended QVC family.

I've always loved spending time in the kitchen. There is something very true about it being the heart of the home. Homework gets done at the kitchen table. Family and friends gather there, and life's celebrations and most important conversations take place there. Regardless of the size of your home, try to have a party without people in the kitchen—it's virtually impossible! Perhaps it is because it is the place where we are most comfortable with ourselves, and the conversation and laughter flows a bit easier.

I've been a cookbook junkie for quite some time and have collected more than my share over the years. A while back, my husband tried to put me on cookbook probation. He told me if I retired today and cooked new and different meals for the rest of my life, I couldn't put a dent in all the recipes on my shelves. He was probably right, but cookbook collecting isn't a practical pursuit, it is one of passion. You can never have enough. Ask anyone who loves cooking, and they will wax eloquent about their favorite recipes, their favorite books, and if you're a really good friend, they may even show you their spattered and worn three-ring binder where they've been glueing some of their all-time favorite recipes from magazines and newspapers over several decades.

Webster has a few definitions for the word "recipe." Most of the time it is associated with good things to eat. If you take a little bit of culinary license, you can come up with the answer to a question that I am asked more often than any other: "Why is QVC so successful?" The answer is quite simple. It's all about PEOPLE. Always has been . . . always will be.

So in keeping with our newest venture in BEST OF THE BEST, I thought I would give you QVC's Secret Recipe:

- Start with plenty of committed people who have a passion for what they do;
- Fold in a vendor community that loves to excite and delight the customer;
- Sprinkle in plenty of good information, neighborly charm, and a little laughter;
- Serve with trust and a warm smile!

Stirrin' it up in the kitchen,
Darlene

Lorianne DeVita (Darlene's Assistant),
Gwen and Darlene

Visitors from all over the world utilize this Tour Entrance where the QVC Studio Tour
is a must-see tourist attraction. Also the entrance for the gift shop and live studio
audience shows, it is highlighted by a huge hanging shipping box reminding
visitors that their contents are always BIG on Quality, Value, and Convenience, and
always fun to receive.

Refreshing Almond Fruit Tea

Southerners like tea, and this is the easiest and best-tasting fruit tea I have made. Using instant tea is a time-saver, and the vanilla and almond flavorings add a refreshing zest. I am an elementary school librarian, and this always makes a hit at faculty potlucks, as well as family get-togethers.

5 tablespoons unsweetened instant tea	1 (12-ounce) can frozen pineapple-orange juice, undiluted
4 cups water	1–3 teaspoons vanilla extract
1 cup sugar	1–3 teaspoons almond extract
1 (12-ounce) can frozen lemonade, undiluted	Additional water

In a gallon container, stir tea, water, and sugar together. Add lemonade and pineapple-orange juice. Mix well. Add vanilla and almond extracts to taste. (My family likes 1½ teaspoons of each.) Add enough water to make one gallon. Refrigerate.

Note: Sweetened instant tea may be substituted for the unsweetened, just omit the sugar.

Betty Lou Wright (Goodlettsville, Tennessee)

Sonya's Famous Lemonade

1 lemon-lime seltzer water	12 lemons
1 (1-liter) bottle regular seltzer water	1½–2 cups sugar, divided
	½ cup pineapple juice (optional)

The trickiest part is that you have to take your time and open the tops on the seltzer water nice and slowly (they tend to fizz over). Then you squeeze the lemons to make 1½–2 cups juice. Add the sugar, but not all at once (about ½ cup per one bottle of seltzer water). When you stir it, it will get very foamy. Gradually add the rest of the sugar until it slows down the foam. Then add the rest of the seltzer water and pineapple juice. Now you will have the BEST LEMONADE in town.

Sonya Baggett (Hyattsville, Maryland)

Mommy, Daddy, and Baby-Makes-Three Juice

Here is my simple, yet special recipe that's inspired by a mommy's never-ending quest for healthy treats. My three-year-old son and I have a ball juicing our concoctions. It's the only way I can get him to eat carrots and fresh fruit. He helps me put the fruit in the juicer and turns it on by flipping the switch. It's safe and fun, and the drinks are super delicious.

2 carrots	**1 banana**
3 golden apples	**2 cups ice**
2 slices golden sweet pineapple	

Juice the peeled carrots, apples, and pineapple in a juicer. Pour in blender; add peeled banana and ice and blend till ice is crushed. Delicious! Sometimes I put in strawberries, mango—any fruit in season. Mommy and Baby love the fun, fruity veggie drink and so does Daddy.

Lena McIlwain, QVC Host (West Chester, Pennsylvania)

I made it myself and it's gooooood!

Host Lena McIlwain enjoys photography, scrapbooking, gardening, and reading. She has also been inspired by her husband to become an avid sports fan. But her favorite pastime is being a mom to her son, Brandon. Here she gets a little help from Brandon in the kitchen.

King's Clam Dip

This recipe was handed down to me by my mother who got it from my grand-mother. This is my 10-year-old son's favorite food and is also a favorite of mine.

1 (8-ounce) package cream cheese	1/4 teaspoon garlic powder
1 (6.5-ounce) can minced clams (reserve juice)	1 tablespoon Worcestershire sauce
	1 cup cottage cheese

With electric mixer, beat the cream cheese and clam juice until creamy, adding only a little juice at a time until reaching the right consistency. With mixer, mix in the garlic powder and Worcestershire sauce. Add the cottage cheese to cream cheese mixture, mixing with a spoon. Drain extra juice off clams and stir clams into mixture. Serve with potato chips, crackers, or veggies. Refrigerate leftovers. Tastes even better the next day!

Note: You can use more or less garlic powder, Worcestershire sauce, and cottage cheese according to your taste. For a less clammy dip, use 2 bricks of cream cheese and some extra cottage cheese.

Rachel Stephens (Eugene, Oregon)

Cheesy Cajun Crawfish Dip

4 tablespoons butter	3/4 cup cream
1 green onion, finely chopped	1/4 cup white wine
2 tablespoons flour	8 slices American cheese
1 tablespoon minced garlic	2 slices Swiss cheese
1/4 teaspoon hot sauce	1 pound crawfish tails, chopped
1 teaspoon cayenne	small

Microwave butter and green onion on HIGH, covered, for 2 minutes. Stir in flour, garlic, hot sauce, cayenne, cream, and white wine. Add American and Swiss cheeses. Stir until melted. (May have to be put back into microwave to melt.) Add chopped crawfish tails; cook 8 minutes on MEDIUM. If crawfish are already cooked, you can shorten time. Serve with crackers or veggie sticks. Keeps several days.

Judy Thornton (Ethel, Mississippi)

Corned Beef Rye Dip

1 (8-ounce) package cream
  cheese, softened
1 (16-ounce) carton sour cream
1 packet Italian dressing mix
1 tablespoon prepared white
  horseradish

½ pound deli-style shaved corned
  beef
1 round loaf rye bread
1 loaf unsliced rye bread, cut into
  chunks

Beat cream cheese, sour cream, dressing mix, and horseradish until
well blended. Fold in corned beef. Refrigerate for at least 1 hour to
allow flavors to blend.

Scoop out a hole in the top of the round rye loaf and cut chunks
out of scooped-out bread to use with dip.

Place bread bowl on large tray or platter. Place dip in bread bowl.
Surround bowl with rye bread chunks. You can place bread bowl on
decorated wreath for holiday presentation.

Anna Nahajewski (Tampa, Florida)

3-Minute Low-Fat Black Bean Dip

1 (8-ounce) bar low-fat cream
  cheese
1 cup black beans, cooked (or
  canned)

1 cup salsa
Whole wheat pita bread

Combine first 3 ingredients in food processor. Serve on toasted pita.
Yields 12 (¼-cup) servings.

Nutrition Facts: Serving size 1(96g); Calories 192; Fat Cals. 36; Total Fat 4g or 7%; Saturated Fat
1g or 3%; Cholesterol 12mg or 4%; Sodium 602mg or 25%; Total Carbohydrate 32g or 11%;
Dietary Fiber 7g or 26%; Sugars 3g; Protein 11g.

Mark Goodwin, QVC Executive Chef Manager
(West Chester, Pennsylvania)

 QVC adds more than 250,000 new customers each month.

Always-a-Hit Pizza Dip

1 (8-ounce) package cream
  cheese, softened
1 (8-ounce) carton sour cream
  (may use light or reduced-fat)
1 tablespoon garlic powder
1 (14- to 16-ounce) jar or can
  pizza sauce

1½ cups mixture of shredded
  mozzarella and Cheddar cheese
Pepperoni slices
Tortilla chips

Preheat oven to 350°. In mixing bowl, combine cream cheese, sour cream, and garlic powder. Mix into a paste. Line bottom of baking dish with cream cheese mixture. Smooth pizza sauce over all. Layer cheeses on top of pizza sauce. Place slices of pepperoni on top of cheese, being sure to cover entire baking surface, as pepperoni will shrink during baking. Bake uncovered for 30 minutes at 350°. Serve hot with tortilla chips. Serves 4–6.

Christa Pitts, QVC Host (West Chester, Pennsylvania)

"My first on-air experience with a cooking show was one to remember. I love to cook and felt that cooking during a broadcast would be fun. However, I neglected to realize that there is a definite "system" to cooking during a live show. As I began my cookware presentation/demonstration, I realized in a panic that I had never learned the set-up of the kitchen for the cook show. I was standing there talking to the camera but I had no idea how to proceed with cooking this dish and demonstrating the cookware at the same time. While I was talking, the line producer was telling me the order of ingredients for the meal, the floor manager was writing me notes about what to do next, and the person in charge of food preparation was utilizing his own version of sign-language to help me show-off the cookware. After what seemed an eternity, the demonstration ended, and I escaped from the kitchen a much wiser cook."

Prior to joining QVC, Christa Pitts (recipe on opposite page) worked in sales and marketing for ATI in Kennesaw, Georgia, and for Aramark Uniform Services. While at Aramark, she received recognition for outstanding sales performance. Christa's hobbies include cooking, traveling, reading, investing, and spending time with her family.

South of the Border Dip

Being raised in a border town (bordering Mexico and New Mexico), I grew up loving and eating authentic Mexican foods. My family loves dips, so I came up with this recipe with a truly Mexican flair. Whenever I serve it at get-togethers, it's the first thing to go.

1 (15-ounce) can chili (no beans)
1 (4-ounce) can diced green chiles
1 (8-ounce) block sharp Cheddar cheese

1 (8-ounce) block Monterey Jack cheese

In a large frying pan, mix the chili and the diced green chiles; heat over a medium flame. Cube the cheeses and add to the chili mixture. Stir constantly until all the cheese is melted. Pour into a large dip bowl and serve immediately with corn chip scoops or tortilla chips. Also good to put in tacos in place of the sour cream.

Michelle Weidner (Las Vegas, Nevada)

Cheese-Crab Fondue

My family loves this treat—especially at holiday times. Very festive, fun, and tasty. Also good served hot over English muffins for a light supper.

1 (8-ounce) package cream
  cheese
1 (5-ounce) jar sharp cheese
½ cup light cream
½ teaspoon garlic salt

1 teaspoon Worcestershire sauce
Dash cayenne
1 can flaked crab meat
French bread cubes

In double boiler, melt cream cheese and sharp cheese. Add light cream, garlic salt, Worcestershire sauce, and cayenne; mix until smooth. Add crab meat. Keep warm in fondue pot. Serve with French bread cubes.

Leilani Dwigans (Danville, California)

Crab Cheesecake

This has become my price of admission to potluck get-togethers.

1 cup saltine cracker crumbs
3 tablespoons butter, melted
2 (8-ounce) packages cream
  cheese, softened
¾ cup sour cream, divided
3 eggs
2 teaspoons grated onion

1 teaspoon lemon juice
¼ teaspoon seafood seasoning
2 drops hot sauce, or to taste
1 cup crab meat
Paprika and seafood seasoning for
  garnish

Combine cracker crumbs with butter. Press into bottom of 9-inch springform pan. Bake 10 minutes at 350°. Remove from oven; cool on rack. Reduce heat to 325°.

Beat cream cheese and ½ of the sour cream until smooth. Add eggs one at a time and beat slowly, until just combined. Add remaining ingredients, except reserved sour cream, crab meat, and garnish, and beat until blended. Fold in crab meat. Pour over crust. Bake 35–45 minutes. Cool on wire rack. Spread remaining sour cream on top. Sprinkle with paprika and seafood seasoning. Refrigerate overnight.

B. J. Bennett (Lacey, Washington)

Peppery Pimento Cheese

*My children, Terry and Amanda, always say, ". . . needs more pepper, Momma," so
don't skimp on the pepper—this makes the difference.*

1 (1-pound) block sharp
   Cheddar cheese, grated
1 (4-ounce) jar sliced pimentos,
   undrained

1 cup mayonnaise
½ teaspoon salt
1½ teaspoons black pepper—no
   less

Mix all ingredients. Serve on crackers.

Annette Goode (Richland, Mississippi)

Pimento Cheese Dressing

*I got my recipe from an old notebook of my mother's. During the Depression, the
President set up community centers to help people learn different things. Cooking
classes were one thing they offered. People learned to use different foods and different ways to make them go further to feed their families. This recipe is one of
those. I collect cookbooks and I have never seen it anywhere. I am 75 years old
and grew up in those times.*

½ pound Hoop cheese*
1 egg, well beaten
3 tablespoons sugar
2 heaping tablespoons flour
2 teaspoons salt

3 tablespoons water
1 stick butter or margarine
1 (4-ounce) jar chopped pimentos
½ cup milk
3 tablespoons vinegar

Mix first 8 ingredients together in a double boiler and cook, stirring
constantly, until cheese is melted and mixture is thick. It will thick-
en very quickly. Add milk and stir well; then add the vinegar and
stir well. Remove from heat and pour into a bowl.

This dressing can be used for sandwiches or on crackers (and
good on broccoli or cauliflower). Delicious warm or chilled.

*Hoop cheese is red waxed wedges of yellow Cheddar cheese.

Dorothy W. Cooley (Meridian, Mississippi)

Company's Coming Cheeseball

Our family never has a get-together without serving this cheeseball. The jalepeños and hot sauce add just the right kick to jazz up any party.

1 (8-ounce) package cream
  cheese
½ cup sour cream
8 pieces cooked bacon, crumbled
½ cup diced green onions

10 stuffed green olives, chopped
1 jalapeño pepper, diced
Dash of hot sauce
1 cup shredded Cheddar cheese,
  divided

Mix all of the ingredients together with ½ cup cheese. Roll into a ball and wrap with plastic wrap. Refrigerate for at least 2 hours. Coat outside of cheeseball with remaining cheese. Serve with assorted crackers or raw vegetables.

Donita Coleman (Fishers, Indiana)

So Good Hot Cheese Squares

Every time I bring this appetizer to an occasion, I get requests for the recipe. My mother-in-law gave it to me and she is a wonderful cook. It tastes so good, I usually double the recipe.

8 ounces Cheddar cheese
8 ounces hot pepper cheese

4 eggs, slightly beaten

Grate cheeses together and add beaten eggs. Pour into greased 8x8-inch pan. Bake at 375° for 30 minutes. Cut into squares. Freezes well.

Note: When doubling, use a 9x13-inch pan.

Debbie Swencki (Racine, Wisconsin)

 With $143 million in sales, the week ending December 2, 2001, was QVC's largest sales week in history.

Jivey Chivey Cheese Puffs

1 (3-ounce) package cream cheese
1 egg
1 teaspoon chopped chives
½ cup shredded Cheddar cheese
4 slices bacon, cooked crisp and
  crumbled
Salt and pepper to taste
1 package frozen puff pastry,
  thawed
1 egg yolk mixed with 1 tablespoon
  water

Combine cream cheese, egg, chives, Cheddar cheese, bacon, salt and pepper. Chill.

Roll out pastry to an equal thickness; cut into 9 squares. Place 1 tablespoon or so of cheese mixture in middle and fold over into a triangle. Press edges with fork to seal (can dab a bit of water on edges to seal better). Brush each with yolk/water mixture. Place on cookie sheet. Bake at 400° for 12–15 minutes, or until lightly browned.

Peggy Smith (Wilmington, Delaware)

Shrimp Pesto Nibblers

I created this appetizer one year for our annual Gelsomini Christmas Extravaganza and it has been a hit ever since. Simple and delicious!

8 small (6- to 7-inch wide) flour
  tortillas
4 tablespoons pesto
1 pound pre-cooked shrimp,
  tails removed
2 cups shredded Monterey Jack
  cheese
1 small can chopped black olives

Cover a large cookie sheet with tin foil and coat with nonstick spray. Evenly space 4 tortillas on the sheet. Cover each tortilla with 1 tablespoon pesto. Layer shrimp, cheese, and olives on top of pesto, equally dividing each between the 4 tortillas. Top each with another tortilla and spray top lightly with nonstick spray.

Bake at 350° for about 20 minutes, or until tortillas are lightly browned and cheese is melted. Let set for 5 minutes, then cut each tortilla into 4–6 wedges and serve hot.

Pamela Gelsomini (Wrentham, Massachusetts)

Shrimp LeJon

This has become one of my favorite (and best-received) finger-food appetizers at dinner parties that my wife and I throw. It's easy to make, and the combination of flavors from the bacon and horseradish is unmatched by anything else I've tasted. I always use straight ground horseradish instead of the creamed variety (it tends to be a little hotter).

16 jumbo shrimp, peeled and deveined

Fresh horseradish, grated
8 strips bacon, cut in half

Gently cut each shrimp lengthwise, about ¾ of the way through, creating a pocket in them. Fill the pocket with horseradish. Wrap filled shrimp with half a strip of bacon and secure with a toothpick.

These may be grilled, broiled, or sautéed in a skillet or on a griddle. Cook them until the shrimp is cooked through and coral colored.

Bob Bowersox, QVC Host (West Chester, Pennsylvania)

Bob Bowersox appeared on the first QVC broadcast in November, 1986. These days you're likely to find him hosting his signature show, "In the Kitchen with Bob." A cookbook inspired by Bob's show sold 156,000 copies on its launch date, a record for first-day sales by a single retailer. He's always cookin' up somethin' good.

"In the Kitchen With Bob" is often on location, like here in Scituate, Massachusetts. While Bob is showing one product, Gwen is putting the finishing touches on the next to be shown. A hand-held camera can get up close to capture those delicious details of the dish being shown.

Shrimp Stack with Remoulade

REMOULADE SAUCE:

1 stick butter or margarine, melted
1/2 cup mayonnaise
1/4 cup ketchup
4 tablespoons chopped onion
1 tablespoon chopped garlic

2 tablespoons Worcestershire sauce
3 tablespoons creole mustard
2 tablespoons lemon juice
1/4 teaspoon thyme
1 boiled egg
Salt to taste

Combine all ingredients in food processor and process until smooth. Set aside.

3 (8-ounce) packages cream cheese, softened
1/2 teaspoon garlic powder
1/2 teaspoon onion powder
1 teaspoon Worcestershire sauce

1 pound shrimp, boiled in seasoned water and peeled
1 small bell pepper, chopped
1 bunch green onions, chopped

Combine cream cheese, garlic powder, onion powder, and Worcestershire. Spread on serving platter. Top with Remoulade Sauce, then shrimp, bell pepper, and onions. Serve with snack crackers.

Judy Thornton (Ethel, Mississippi)

Magical Shrimp Rounds

Whenever I take these shrimp rounds to parties, they turn into "magical" shrimp rounds because they disappear before your eyes.

2 large English cucumbers (long)
1 (8-ounce) package cream
cheese, softened
1 (6-ounce) can tiny shrimp,
drained

Salt, pepper and garlic powder
to taste
Paprika

Slice cucumbers and drain on paper towel. Let set for a couple of hours. Mix cream cheese and shrimp in a bowl. Add seasonings to taste. Spread shrimp mixture on cucumber rounds. Sprinkle with paprika. Refrigerate until ready to serve.

Note: Works with 3–4 regular cucumbers. Also good on celery or crackers.

Kristina Presentati (Magalia, California)

Hawaiian Chicken Biscuit Cups

What a simple and easy appetizer that everyone really loves! Also good for a woman's luncheon or shower.

1 (8-count) can flaky biscuits
2 cooked chicken breasts (can be
leftover chicken), cubed or cut
into small pieces

½ cup barbecue sauce
1 (11-ounce) can pineapple tidbits
or chunks, drained

Separate biscuits into thirds. Put divided pieces into a sprayed mini-muffin tin. Mix chicken with barbecue sauce and fill each tin with a portion of the mixture. Top each with some of the pineapple. Bake in preheated 350° oven about 10–12 minutes. Makes 24 appetizers.

Pam MacIver (Prescott, Arizona)

 QVC employs over 12,000 people worldwide. From the representatives who take your calls to the people who pack your purchases, everyone on QVC's staff is focused on achieving the goal of 100% customer satisfaction.

Chinese Meatballs

Can be served as a main dish, too!

1–1½ pounds ground round	1 teaspoon dry mustard
1 cup finely crushed gingersnaps	1 teaspoon salt
1 egg, slightly beaten	¼ teaspoon pepper
3 tablespoons soy sauce	¾ teaspoon garlic powder
1 (8-ounce) can crushed pineapple, drained (reserve liquid)	

Combine all ingredients (except reserved pineapple juice), mixing well. Shape into approximately 70 small meatballs. Bake in pre-heated 350° oven for 20–25 minutes, turning once. Drain, put into a chafing dish, and set aside.

SAUCE:

1 cup ketchup	2 tablespoons brown sugar
¼ cup soy sauce	Reserved pineapple juice
½ teaspoon dry mustard	

In a small saucepan, blend Sauce ingredients together and heat to boiling. Pour over meatballs. Serve warm.

Phyllis Schierloh (Loveland, Ohio)

Lady Tsen Mei Wings

My mother was the first Chinese woman to star in movies in this country. Her name was Lady Tsen Mei—this was her recipe! We always have these on Chinese New Year.

2 cups soy sauce	3 tablespoons five-spice powder*
¼ cup thinly sliced fresh ginger	2 pounds chicken wings, or more
4 large garlic cloves, minced	

Mix all ingredients except chicken wings in a saucepan and bring to a boil. Simmer, covered, 5 minutes. Place disjointed wings in a baking dish with enough soy mixture to keep from sticking. Bake in a 350° oven until done, about an hour or more. (You can also do baby back ribs the same way.) Place soy mixture in a jar to cool. Can be refrigerated up to 8 weeks. Skim off any grease and ginger before keeping. Just add new ginger before using again.

*Five-spice powder is a combination of equal parts Szechwan (or black) pepper, star anise (or anise), cinnamon, cloves, and fennel, all ground.

Merritta M. Dane (Naples, Florida)

Chinese Chicken Wings

Very easy and sooo good.

3 pounds chicken wings, cut up
4 eggs, beaten
Salt
Pepper

Garlic powder
2–4 cups of cornstarch
1–1½ sticks margarine

Dip chicken wings in beaten eggs. Place dipped wings on plate; season with salt, pepper, and garlic powder to taste. Roll seasoned chicken wings in cornstarch. Cook wings in margarine until golden brown. Place wings in a jellyroll pan (cookie sheet with sides).

SAUCE:
½ cup sugar
½ cup vinegar
4 tablespoons ketchup

1 tablespoon soy sauce
¼ cup chicken broth

Mix all ingredients together and boil till sugar melts. Pour Sauce over chicken wings. Bake at 350° degrees for 1½ hours, turning several times.

Debbie Swencki (Racine, Wisconsin)

Pistachio-Stuffed Mushrooms

20 medium mushrooms
3 tablespoons minced onions
7 tablespoons butter, divided
⅓ cup dried bread crumbs
¼ cup chopped pistachio nuts

2 tablespoons chopped fresh
  parsley
¼ teaspoon marjoram
¼ teaspoon salt

Clean and remove stems from mushrooms. Chop stems and sauté along with onions in 3 tablespoons butter until tender. Add bread crumbs, pistachios, parsley, marjoram, and salt. Mix well. Fill caps with heaping amount of mixture. Place on cookie sheet; drizzle with remaining melted butter. Bake 5–7 minutes at 350°.

Debbie L. Dean (Cross Lanes, West Virginia)

Spinach Ranch Roll-Ups

I make this recipe for every party or BBQ. It always receives great praises, especially from those who do not like spinach.

1 (8-ounce) package cream cheese
1 (8-ounce) carton sour cream
¼ cup mayonnaise
1 package ranch-style dressing mix
1 bunch green onions, chopped
1 (10-ounce) package frozen chopped spinach, cooked and squeezed dry

1 can sliced water chestnuts, drained, chopped
2–4 tablespoons chopped canned jalapeño peppers
¼ cup chopped pine nuts or pecans
1 dozen flour tortillas

In food processor, mix cream cheese, sour cream, mayonnaise, and package of dressing. Process until thoroughly mixed and creamy; transfer to medium-size bowl. Then add remaining ingredients, except tortillas, and mix well. Spread enough mixture on a tortilla to cover. Roll up in foil; refrigerate for at least 4 hours.

Remove foil; slice (about ½ inch thick) and serve on a small platter. You can also freeze these, then thaw 2 hours before serving. (Pictured on cover.)

Chila Robles (Oxnard, California)

Portobello Delicioso

One day my mom was visiting from Florida and she was tired and didn't want to go out for dinner. I asked her what ingredients she liked and I just put this together. Now, whenever we entertain, this is our specialty. Once I used anchovies and bacon instead of the sausage. It was also a hit. Enjoy!!!

1 head garlic
1 tablespoon olive oil
2 ripe tomatoes, peeled and
    seeded
½ pound spicy Italian sausage

4 large portobello mushrooms
½ cup port wine
½ pound blue cheese
Crushed black pepper

Preheat oven to 350°. Cut garlic head in half and pour the oil onto the cloves. Wrap in foil and bake for 50–60 minutes, or until just golden. Meanwhile, seed and chop the tomatoes. Cook the sausage in a pan until browned all over; drain. Remove stem from mushrooms and, using a spoon, remove the gills, being careful not to break the mushrooms. Add the whole mushrooms to the pan of sausage; then add the port. Cover and cook for 5 minutes, or until mushrooms get a little soft.

Take the cooled garlic halves and squeeze out the cloves. Chop them, being careful not to get any of the paper, and add to the blue cheese. Add a bit of crushed black pepper. Fill the caps with the blue cheese mixture and top with the sausage and add any remaining wine liquid. Top with the chopped tomato, place on baking sheet, and bake for 5–7 minutes, or until hot. Let set for 1 minute before serving so it will not fall apart. Serve cut into wedges.

Barry Sercus (Phoenix, Arizona)

 QVC, Inc. was founded in 1986 by Joseph Segel, founder of The Franklin Mint, and the company established a new record in American business history for first full-fiscal-year sales by a new public company, with revenues of over $112 million.

Fried Walnuts

I serve these every Christmas.

6 cups water
4 cups walnuts
¹/₂ cup sugar

Oil (for deep frying)
Salt

In a 3-quart saucepan, heat water to a boil. Add walnuts. Boil 1 minute. Drain and rinse walnuts under hot water. Drain. In a large bowl, stir walnuts and sugar till coated. Heat 2–3 inches of oil in frying pan. Fry walnuts, stirring constantly for 5 minutes. Remove from oil; put on wax paper, or something they won't stick to. Sprinkle with salt. Store in an airtight container.

Virginia Arbogast (Champlin, Minnesota)

Glazed Spiced Nuts

I like to fix these around the holidays. They are a big hit and I always have to make more. Enjoy!

¹/₃ cup sugar
¹/₂ stick unsalted butter
¹/₄ cup fresh orange juice
1¹/₂ teaspoons salt

1¹/₄ teaspoons cinnamon
¹/₄ teaspoon cayenne pepper
¹/₄ teaspoon ground mace
1 pound unsalted mixed nuts

Preheat oven to 250°. Line jellyroll pan with foil. Cook sugar, butter, orange juice, salt, cinnamon, cayenne, and mace over low heat until butter and sugar melt. Increase heat to medium and add nuts; mix well.

Spread in single layer on pan. Bake 1 hour, stirring every 15 minutes. Transfer nuts to sheet of foil; separate nuts and let cool. Store in airtight container. If they get sticky, reheat in low oven until crisp, about 20 minutes.

Gail Sipple (Folsom, California)

Decades-in-the-Making Snack Mix

I have truly been working on perfecting this recipe since 1963. I've had many batches that were either too bland or seasoned too much. Two years ago, I finally got it just right for my family's taste. This is it!

THE SEASONING:

3 tablespoons lemon juice
2½ sticks margarine
10 teaspoons seasoned salt
9 teaspoons garlic powder

1 teaspoon garlic salt
1 teaspoon onion salt
3 tablespoons plus 1 teaspoon
   Worcestershire sauce

Place all ingredients in a small saucepan and melt over medium heat.

THE MIX:

1 (17-ounce) and 1 (12-ounce)
   box crisp cereal squares
9 cups round oat cereal

7–8 cups mixed nuts
1 (15-ounce) bag pretzel sticks,
   broken in half

Combine all ingredients into a very large roasting pan (or make in 2 batches). Spoon the melted ingredients from the saucepan over the dry mix in the roasting pan(s). Mix well. Bake at 250° for 45 minutes, stirring every 15 minutes. Remove from oven and cool. Store in airtight containers.

Mary F. Guertin (Bourbonnais, Illinois)

The letters "QVC" are in and on the huge wall that greets you upon entering. Here Justan Pratt issues a badge to Tara Logan. You must have special badges to enter certain doors, and whether you're there to go on the air or not, there's a good chance you'll be on camera when you're in the building. QVC takes security seriously.

Little Bits of Heaven Ice Box Rolls

I was 12 years old when I went with a friend to her aunt's house for a picnic, and her aunt served these rolls. I was so crazy about them that I kept asking her to get the recipe from her aunt. She finally did and I have been making these for my family for about 42 years. Every time I serve these to someone, they rave about them and want the recipe.

2 packages yeast
1/2 cup lukewarm water
3/4 cup shortening
1 cup boiling water
1 cup cold water

1 cup sugar
1 teaspoon salt
2 eggs, beaten
6 cups flour

Dissolve yeast in lukewarm water in a cup or small bowl. Put shortening in large mixing bowl. Add boiling water to melt shortening. Then add cold water, sugar, salt, yeast dissolved in lukewarm water, and beaten eggs. Add flour and mix well. Cover with greased wax paper and a damp dishcloth and place in ice box for 8–10 hours before using.

When making rolls, flour surface of dough (dough will be sticky) and hands lightly, and take small pieces (about the size of a walnut) and shape into rolls. (Be careful not to make the rolls too large because they will not bake all the way through before they become too brown on the outside.) Put in greased pan to rise for 2–3 hours in warm place before baking. Bake at 425° till brown (11–16 minutes). I use a 7x11-inch pan to make a dozen.

Dough keeps up to a week in refrigerator if dampened cloth is put over bowl. No kneading necessary. Makes about 3 dozen. (Pictured on cover.)

Linda Welsh (Muskegon, Michigan)

Editors' Extra: Try using less sugar. Either way, these are wonderful little pop-in-your-mouth rolls.

 So what does QVC stand for? Quite literally, it represents Quality, Value, and Convenience.

Fiesta Cornbread

1 package yellow cornbread mix
1 package Mexican cornbread
  mix
1 pound ground beef, cooked and
  drained
1 (8-ounce) package shredded
  Colby and Monterey Jack cheese,
  divided

1 can Mexican-style tomatoes
1 can ranch-style beans
1 can corn with red and green
  peppers
Picante sauce

In a mixing bowl, combine mixtures of yellow and Mexican cornbread as directed on packages. Put half the combined cornbread batter in a deep cast iron skillet. Add ground beef. Spread about 4 ounces of the cheese on top of the ground beef layer. Open and drain tomatoes, beans, and corn, layering one on top of the other. Take the remainder of the corn bread batter and spread it to cover the top. Add the rest of the cheese and cook for 30 minutes at 400°. Cool and serve. Top each slice with picante sauce or other salsa of your choice.

Bobbye Fussell (West Monroe, Louisiana)

Sweet Onion Cornbread

2 sweet onions, chopped
$\frac{1}{2}$ cup butter
3 cups corn muffin mix
2 eggs
$\frac{2}{3}$ cup milk
1 (14$\frac{1}{2}$-ounce) can cream corn

4 drops hot sauce
2 cups sour cream
$\frac{1}{2}$ teaspoon salt
$\frac{1}{2}$ teaspoon dill weed
2 cups grated Monterey Jack
  cheese

Sauté onion in butter. Beat muffin mix, eggs, milk, cream corn, and hot sauce. Spread in buttered 9x13-inch pan. Add sour cream, salt, dill, and half of cheese to onion mixture. Spread over batter, then sprinkle with remaining cheese. Bake, uncovered, at 425° for 30 minutes.

Lynda Paviolo (North Huntingdon, Pennsylvania)

Great Garlic Cheese Bread

Something a little different, this bread gets people's attention. I have taken it to many gatherings, and everyone wants to know who made the bread. What a great way to meet new people at social events!

1 large loaf French or sourdough bread	2–3 cloves garlic, crushed
½ pound rope or shredded provolone cheese	¼ cup half-and-half
	1–2 tablespoons minced parsley

Slice bread into 1- to 1½-inch slices, cutting all the way through. Combine the remaining ingredients. Mix well. Spread between slices. Wrap loaf lightly in foil and leave venting at top of foil. Bake in preheated 400° oven 20–25 minutes. Serve warm.

Carol Murray (St. Louis, Missouri)

Special Hushpuppies

My mother would fix fried fish and hushpuppies for all our northern neighbors who had never had fried fish, much less hushpuppies. My job was to chop the onions and tomatoes. My mother and I used this time to talk . . . very special time.

1 cup plain flour	1 egg
2 cups yellow cornmeal	¾–1 cup milk
2 teaspoons baking powder	1 cup finely chopped tomatoes
1 teaspoon salt	½ cup finely chopped onions

Mix flour, cornmeal, baking powder, and salt. Sift together. Beat egg; add to milk. Pour into flour mixture. Add tomatoes and onions to flour/milk mixture. Mix well. Batter should be thin.

Drop into hot oil by tablespoon. Fry till brown. Will float to top when ready to flip over.

Kay Hobbs (Tallahassee, Florida)

Raisin Cinnamon Crescent Rolls with Custard Cream

This is one of my family's all-time favorites. I hope you enjoy my recipe as much as we do.

1 (8-count) can refrigerated crescent rolls	2 tablespoons sugar, divided
½ cup raisins, divided	2 teaspoons ground cinnamon
	3 tablespoons butter, melted

Heat oven to 350°. Separate crescent dough into 4 rectangles. Roll or press each rectangle to measure 7x5-inches. Sprinkle 2 tablespoons raisins, 1 teaspoon sugar and ½ teaspoon cinnamon evenly over top of each rectangle. Starting with the 5-inch side, roll up, seam-side-down and cut each roll into 4 (1½-inch) slices. Place the 16 rolls, cut-side-down, spaced equally apart, in a 11x7x1½-inch glass baking pan. Drizzle melted butter over rolls.

CUSTARD CREAM:

2 large eggs	2 cups whipping cream, divided
1 cup sugar	6 whole red maraschino cherries
2 teaspoons vanilla extract	with stems

In a 2-quart mixing bowl mix eggs, sugar, and vanilla. Beat on high using an electric mixer for 1 minute. While mixer is still running, slowly pour in 1¼ cups whipping cream and continue beating on high for an additional minute. Carefully pour over rolls.

Bake at 350° for 30–35 minutes or until top is golden brown and custard is almost set. Remove from oven and let cool for 15 minutes. (Custard will continue to set while cooling.)

In a 1-quart mixing bowl, add remaining ¾ cup whipping cream and remaining 2 teaspoons sugar. Beat on high, using an electric mixer, till soft peaks form, 2–3 minutes. Refrigerate until ready to use.

To serve, cut dessert into 6 equal pieces. Serve warm. Spoon into dessert bowls. Top each serving with an equal amount of whipped cream. Place a maraschino cherry in the center of whipped cream on each serving. Serves 6.

Gloria Herdman (Pomeroy, Ohio)

Swedish Tea Log

My mother and I made this recipe for special Christmas gifts. We did not have money when I was growing up, so we gave these Tea Logs as Christmas gifts. I am an 81-year-old great-grandmother and still bake these at Christmas. My mother came up with the recipe experimenting while making bread. I am teaching my great-granddaughter how to make these.

1 package dry yeast	$\frac{1}{2}$ cup evaporated milk
$\frac{1}{4}$ cup warm water	1 egg
$2\frac{1}{4}$ cups sifted flour	$\frac{1}{4}$ cup raisins
2 tablespoons sugar	$\frac{1}{2}$ cup brown sugar
1 tablespoon salt	$\frac{1}{2}$ cup chopped pecans
$\frac{3}{4}$ cup butter, divided	

Soften yeast in $\frac{1}{4}$ cup warm water. Sift together flour, sugar, and salt. Add $\frac{1}{2}$ cup butter and cut until particles are fine. Mix together evaporated milk, egg, and raisins. Mix yeast mixture with flour mixture; add milk mixture and mix well. Refrigerate this overnight.

Cream together $\frac{1}{4}$ cup softened butter, brown sugar, and pecans. Take dough out of refrigerator and divide into thirds. Roll out one part at a time on floured surface to a 12x6-inch rectangle. Spread each rectangle with $\frac{1}{3}$ filling ingredients; roll dough and seal sides. Place on cookie sheet lined with aluminum foil. Make cuts along outside edge of each roll 1 inch apart to within $\frac{1}{2}$ inch of center. Turn cut pieces on side. Repeat with remaining dough. Let rise in warm place until light, about 1 hour. Bake in 350° oven until golden brown (about 20 minutes.) Frost while warm.

FROSTING:

2 tablespoons butter	$\frac{1}{2}$ teaspoon vanilla
1 cup powdered sugar	1–2 tablespoons evaporated milk

Melt butter; add sugar and vanilla. Add enough milk for spreading consistency.

M. Ruth Probst (Cayuga, New York)

Delicious Lite Coffee Cake

I wanted to make a delicious, yet heart-smart cake for a loved one. I came up with this—now it's everyone's favorite!

1 box yellow low-fat cake mix	¼ cup olive oil
1 cup lite sour cream	½ cup skim milk
1 package instant coconut pudding	½ cup sugar
	1 cup chopped walnuts
Egg beaters (equal to 4 eggs)	2 teaspoons cinnamon

In large bowl, mix first 6 ingredients. In a separate bowl, mix sugar, nuts, and cinnamon. Place ½ the batter in greased 9x13x2-inch pan, top with ½ sugar mixture, then pour in remaining batter. Top with remaining sugar mixture. Bake at 350° for 35–40 minutes.

Katie Vattilano, QVC Employee (West Chester, Pennsylvania)

Pecan Crusted Overnight French Bread

This can be made for a large group by doubling or tripling the recipe—as long as you can refrigerate all of it overnight.

½ cup butter, melted	1 teaspoon vanilla
½ cup pancake syrup	1 tablespoon cinnamon
1 cup chopped pecans or walnuts	Dash nutmeg
2 eggs	1 loaf French bread, sliced into
½ cup half-and-half	enough slices to fit pan
3 tablespoons sugar	(about 16)

Mix butter and syrup. Pour on shallow pan or cookie sheet. Sprinkle nuts over syrup mixture. Mix eggs, half-and-half, sugar, vanilla, cinnamon, and nutmeg. Dip bread in mixture until good and moist. Place bread on syrup mixture; cover and store in refrigerator overnight.

Next morning, bake in 350° oven for 30 minutes, or until golden brown.

Rose Gundy (Richland, Washington)

Peach-Pecan Biscotti

So good to dunk in coffee or hot chocolate!

1 cup dried peaches, cut into small pieces	2 large eggs
½ cup orange juice	1 teaspoon vanilla
Rum (optional)	2 cups flour
1 stick unsalted butter, softened	2 teaspoons baking powder
¾ cup sugar	1 cup chopped pecans

Put peaches in small saucepan with enough orange juice to cover them. Bring to a boil. Add a splash of rum. Cover. Set aside for ½ hour.

Cream butter and sugar. Add eggs one at a time. Stir in vanilla. Add flour and baking powder slowly, being gentle. Drain fruit in a colander. Stir fruit and nuts into dough. Spoon onto parchment-covered cookie sheet in 2 long strips, flattening to ¾ inch deep with spatula. Bake at 350° for 30 minutes.

Remove from oven and cut in 1-inch strips, turning each strip on its side. Return to oven for 10 more minutes. Repeat this process, flipping strips to other side for 10 more minutes. If you want a softer biscotti, eliminate the second turning. Cool and enjoy.

Monica Roche (Chicago Ridge, Illinois)

The QVC Local (see opposite page).

Surprise Breakfast Pastries

I recently had a sister family reunion. They all were surprised at what a good cook their baby sister turned out to be. Try this recipe and you'll think I'm a good cook, too. People are so surprised that the pastry is a giant flaky biscuit! These are great with a cup of coffee when the guests arrive.

2 (8-count) cans giant-size biscuits

Flatten each biscuit to a 4-inch circle.

FILLING:

2 (8-ounce) packages cream cheese, softened	**½ stick butter**
½ cup powdered sugar	**½ cup coconut**

Mix ingredients with hand mixer till smooth (no lumps).

SYRUP:

¾ cup maple syrup	**1 cup dark brown sugar**
1 stick butter	**¾ cup chopped nuts, your choice**

Mix ingredients and melt in microwave. Pour into bottom of a 9x13-inch pan and 8-inch cake pan. Place 3 tablespoons filling on half of the biscuit circles. Fold over and pinch sides of biscuit together. Place pastries on top of syrup in pans. Bake at 350° for 25 minutes.

Diane Buckner (Longview, Washington)

QVC's 45-foot long, state-of-the-art, mobile studio, the QVC Local (shown left) boasts one of the world's largest U.S. road maps on its bright orange and yellow exterior. Inside the air-conditioned cruiser, there are fully equipped broadcast technical rooms, a lounge for hosts and guests, and a wardrobe and make-up room. Since its first road trip, "the big orange bus," has logged over 350,000 miles in all 50 states (it's even been shipped to Alaska and Hawaii!).

Mom Barnes's Delicious Apricot Bread

This recipe was my mother's and is approximately 80 years old. She was an excellent cook and baker, which incidentally was her maiden name—Baker. It's the greatest!

1 cup dried apricots	½ cup orange juice
1 cup sugar	2 cups sifted flour
2 tablespoons margarine or butter, softened	2 teaspoons baking powder
	¼ teaspoon baking soda
1 egg	1 teaspoon salt
¼ cup water	½ cup chopped nuts

Soak apricots for 30 minutes in very warm water. Drain and cut into ¼-inch pieces. Set aside. Mix sugar, margarine, and egg together. Stir in water and orange juice. Combine dry ingredients; add sugar and egg mixture. Blend in chopped nuts and chopped apricots. Let stand 20 minutes. Pour into greased and floured loaf pan. Bake 55–65 minutes at 350°.

Lois J. Myers (Sault Ste. Marie, Michigan)

Nutty Orange Cranberry Bread

4 cups flour	1½ cups orange juice
2 cups sugar	2 eggs, beaten
3 teaspoons baking powder	2 cups whole berry cranberry sauce
1 teaspoon baking soda	
2 teaspoons salt	1 cup chopped walnuts
½ cup softened margarine	

Sift together flour, sugar, baking powder, baking soda, and salt. Cut in margarine until mixture resembles coarse cornmeal; set aside. Combine orange juice and eggs; pour into dry ingredients, mixing slightly to dampen. Fold in cranberry sauce and nuts. Spoon into 2 greased 9x5-inch loaf pans. (Spread corners and sides slightly higher than middle.) Bake at 350° for 1 hour. Let set for 15 minutes; then remove from pans and let cool. Store leftover bread well wrapped in refrigerator.

Betty J. Bancroft (Miamisburg, Ohio)

Nana's Nana Bread

My mother, Gladys, was always "Nana" to my son Dylan, who has been blind since the age of two. The smell of this bread baking always reminds us of how blessed we were to have our wonderful Nana.

1 stick butter or margarine,
  softened
1 cup sugar
2 eggs, beaten
4 very ripe bananas

1 cup flour
Dash of salt
1 teaspoon baking soda
1 cup chopped nuts (optional)

Preheat oven to 375°. Cream butter and sugar; add beaten eggs. Mix well. Add bananas, one at a time, and beat well. Add dry ingredients; blend well. Add nuts. Spoon into a greased 9x5-inch loaf pan, or two small loaf pans. Bake at 375° for 15 minutes. Lower heat to 350° and continue baking for 35–45 minutes, depending on size of pan. When cool, remove from pan. Cool completely and wrap in plastic wrap.

Wilma Hunt-Jones (Irvine, Kentucky)

Blueberry-Lemon Muffins

I made these often for my family of 12. My children are grown now but still talk about these muffins. I am from Salzburg, Austria, and I love to cook.

2 cups all-purpose flour	**1 egg**
1 cup sugar	**^{2}/$_3$ cup milk**
1 tablespoon baking powder	**3 tablespoons lemon juice**
1 teaspoon salt	**1 teaspoon vanilla**
6 tablespoons butter, cut in pieces	**1^1/$_2$ cups blueberries**

Preheat oven to 400°. Generously coat standard-size 12-cup muffin pan with nonstick cooking spray. Mix flour, sugar, baking powder, and salt. With pastry blender (or knife and fork), cut in butter until mixture resembles fine crumbs. Lightly beat egg, milk, lemon juice, and vanilla in a small bowl. Stir egg mixture into flour mixture until just blended.

Fold berries into batter. Divide batter among prepared muffin cups. Bake in 400° oven for 20 minutes, or till toothpick comes out clean. Enjoy!

Gertraud Casbarro (Summerville, South Carolina)

Editors' Extra: These make great pop-in-your-mouth mini-muffins. Bake about 12 minutes.

Gram's Delicious Ginger Puff Muffins

A Sunday morning favorite! This recipe has been on a card in my grandmother's recipe box so long that the card is yellowed and crumbling and full of molasses stains. Gram was proud of this original muffin. So am I!

1 egg	¹/₂ cup boiling water
¹/₂ cup sugar	¹/₂ teaspoon ground ginger
¹/₂ cup dark molasses	¹/₂ teaspoon ground cinnamon
1¹/₂ tablespoons butter	¹/₄ teaspoon salt
¹/₂ teaspoon baking soda	1 heaping cup flour

Break egg into bowl; add sugar, molasses, and butter. Stir. Dissolve baking soda in the boiling water and add to mixture. Sift ginger, cinnamon, salt, and flour. Add to mixture and mix well. Bake in a greased (12-cup) muffin tin at 350° for 18–20 minutes. Great served hot with butter. Also good frosted with chocolate icing.

Anne Paris Davison (Baltimore, Maryland)

Hint of Orange Moist Bran Muffins

2¹/₂ cups flour	2 cups buttermilk
1¹/₂ cups sugar	2 eggs, slightly beaten
2¹/₂ teaspoons baking soda	¹/₂ cup vegetable oil
³/₄ cup boiling water	1 cup currants or raisins (optional)
2 tablespoons frozen orange juice concentrate	Ground walnuts or pecans (optional)
3 cups all-bran cereal, divided	

Combine flour, sugar, and baking soda. Add boiling water and orange juice concentrate to 1 cup all-bran cereal; mix well. Add this mixture to dry ingredients along with the remaining 2 cups cereal, buttermilk, eggs, and oil; mix well. Add currants and nuts, if desired. (May add an additional ¹/₄ cup cereal if batter is too thin.) Spoon into greased muffin tins, ²/₃ full. Bake at 350° for 15–20 minutes. Muffins may be frozen.

Helen Stamatelatos (Carlsbad, California)

Green Tomato Raspberry Jam

This jam is better than any I've tasted; it looks and tastes like raspberry jam. People always have end-of-garden green tomatoes, and this recipe takes care of them. It makes a much-appreciated gift.

5 cups ground green tomatoes
2 tablespoons lemon juice
5 cups sugar

1 large and 1 small box raspberry
or strawberry gelatin

Put green tomatoes and lemon juice in large kettle. Boil for 1 minute. Add sugar and gelatin and boil for 5 minutes. Put in jars and hot water bath for 10 minutes, or freeze. Makes about 5 pints. Does not have to be refrigerated.

Beverly N. Clark (Gooding, Idaho)

Apple Pie Pancakes

3 cups flour
2 teaspoons baking powder
1 teaspoon baking soda
½ cup plus 2 tablespoons sugar
1 teaspoon apple pie spice
2 eggs

2 cups milk
½ cup butter, melted
1 teaspoon vanilla
2 large Granny Smith apples,
peeled and finely chopped

Combine flour, baking powder, baking soda, sugar, and apple pie spice. Whisk together eggs, milk, butter, and vanilla. Combine wet and dry ingredients. Stir in apples. Drop batter by ¼ cup onto greased griddle. Cook until golden on each side. Makes 42 pancakes, enough for 8–10 people; halves easily.

Diane DiSalvo (Boynton Beach, Florida)

Blueberry Yogurt Pancakes

This is one of my daughter's favorites! Toni, my wife, has moved us into healthier thinking these days, and the yogurt really makes a nice addition to the flavor. The blueberries should be big and juicy.

1 cup flour
1 tablespoon sugar
1 teaspoon baking powder
$^1/_2$ teaspoon baking soda
$^1/_4$ teaspoon salt
$^1/_8$ teaspoon ground nutmeg
1 egg

$^1/_2$ cup plain yogurt
$^1/_2$ cup milk
2 tablespoons vegetable oil
$^3/_4$ cup fresh or frozen (thawed) blueberries
Butter or margarine
Maple syrup

Stir together the flour, sugar, baking powder, baking soda, salt, and nutmeg. In a second large bowl, beat the egg with yogurt and milk; beat in the oil, then add flour mixture a little at a time. Stir until just combined. Fold in blueberries.

Cook on preheated griddle, first on one side until covered with bubbles, then flipped and browned on the other side. Serve at once with butter and syrup. Makes 1 dozen (4-inch) pancakes.

Bob Bowersox, QVC Host (West Chester, Pennsylvania)

People find it fascinating to watch all the goings-on required to put on a live television broadcast, like here in downtown West Chester. Host Bob Bowersox always invites people from the audience to participate—and they love it!

Refrigerator Waffles

This batter will keep up to one month in your refrigerator.

1 package dry yeast (scant
  tablespoon)
2½ cups warm water
1 tablespoon sugar
¾ cup powdered milk
⅓ cup oil

½–1 teaspoon salt
½ teaspoon baking soda
2 large eggs
1 tablespoon vanilla
3 cups flour

Dissolve yeast in warm water. Let stand 5 minutes. Add remaining ingredients and beat with mixer on low speed until smooth. Refrigerate in 2-quart (no smaller, as it grows!) covered container 8 hours, or overnight.

Stir before using. Bake in waffle iron according to manufacturer's directions.

Natalie Leon Golankiewicz (Pittsburgh, Pennsylvania)

Eggs Benedict Souffles

I've been watching QVC for 12 years. I can't stand or walk, and I use a motorized wheelchair to get around. I brought four shoe boxes of recipes, and shelves of cookbooks to the retirement home. I enjoy cookbooks as much as novels (I like those, too). Here's one of my favorites.

4 eggs
¼ cup whipping cream
1 teaspoon salt
Dash pepper
¾ cup finely diced cooked ham

½ cup shredded Swiss cheese
1 envelope hollandaise sauce mix
4 English muffins, split, toasted,
  and buttered

Beat together until frothy eggs, whipping cream, salt and pepper; stir in ham and cheese. Pour into 4 well-buttered custard cups. Bake at 250° for 50–60 minutes, or until knife inserted in center comes out clean. Prepare sauce as directed on envelope. Remove eggs from custard cups, turning upside down on English muffins. Serve topped with hot hollandaise sauce. Makes 4 servings.

Lois M. Day (Escondido, California)

Breakfast or Brunch Surprise

1 (6-ounce) can chunk ham
½ cup chopped bell pepper, or
  1 (4-ounce) can green chile
  peppers
¼ cup chopped onion (optional)

1 (15-ounce) can yellow or white
  hominy, drained
4–6 eggs, beaten
Salt and pepper to taste

In skillet, sauté ham, pepper, and onion for a few minutes, until tender. Add hominy and heat. Add beaten eggs, and salt and pepper to taste. Stir until done. Serves 3–4 as main dish or 5–6 as side dish.

Note: Sliced tomatoes or salsa would be good with this dish. I have used green or red salsa instead of chopped bell peppers.

Rowena Cates (Hobbs, New Mexico)

Bacon and Cheese Garlic Grits

I am a newly retired teacher of 36 years who recently began to enjoy cooking. I am repeatedly asked to bring this dish to covered-dish dinners and family gatherings. My mother told me that I cook with too much spice and garlic. She thought my children would never enjoy "regular" food, and she was right!

1¼ cups quick cooking grits
3½ cups water
3 tablespoons onion flakes
1 stick real butter
1½ rolls garlic cheese
4 slices bacon, crisply cooked

¼ teaspoon garlic salt
¼ teaspoon seasoned salt
1 teaspoon seasoned pepper
2 eggs
1 cup milk
½ cup grated American cheese

Cook grits in boiling water, adding onion flakes, butter, cheese rolls, crumbled cooked bacon, and seasonings for 5–7 minutes, until grits are done. Beat eggs well in small bowl. Add milk to eggs and beat well. Mix this mixture with the prepared grits. Pour into a 9x13-inch glass casserole sprayed with nonstick coating. Bake about 40 minutes in a 350° oven, then sprinkle with grated cheese and continue baking until cheese has melted.

Marion Gaffney (Jackson, Tennessee)

Mom's Sausage Roll

I got this recipe 30 years ago from a friend. Shortly after, I added more ingredients to it, making it my own special sausage roll. My family and friends always request that I make this. My three children dubbed it Mom's Sausage Roll.

1 package pizza dough	Salt
2 pounds hot sausage (bulk)	Pepper
1 (8-ounce) can mushrooms,	Garlic salt
drained	Oregano
3 eggs, divided	Parmesan or Romano cheese

Let pizza dough rise in plastic bag, 6–8 hours. Roll out dough like a pie shell. Fry sausage until cooked thoroughly; drain. Sprinkle sausage all over pizza dough. Add mushrooms on top of sausage. Mix 2 eggs, salt, pepper, garlic salt, and oregano together and spread over and into sausage. Sprinkle top with Parmesan or Romano cheese. Roll up and put on a cookie sheet, seam-side-down. Beat remaining egg and spread all over sausage roll. Bake at 350° for 40–45 minutes, or until golden brown.

Patricia Firsching (Whitesboro, New York)

Killer Pizza

I make this often for my son and his friends and there are never any leftovers. They call it "Killer Pizza."

1 pound hot sausage	6 large eggs, beaten
1½ cups hot salsa	½ teaspoon salt
1 (14½-ounce) can sliced white	½ teaspoon pepper
potatoes, drained	Paprika
1 (8-ounce) package shredded	
Cheddar cheese	

Preheat oven to 350°. Brown and crumble sausage in large skillet. Drain. Press into a 10-inch, deep-sided pie pan. Spread salsa over sausage, then layer potatoes over salsa. Layer cheese over potatoes. Pour beaten eggs, seasoned with salt and pepper, over cheese. Bake 35 minutes, or until top is golden brown. Garnish with paprika. Cool and cut into wedges. Serves 8.

Note: Cuts easier after being refrigerated; reheat in microwave.

Glenda L. Latusek (Morgantown, West Virginia)

Breakfast Pizzazz Pizza

1 package refrigerated crescent rolls	1 cup shredded Cheddar cheese
1 pound regular or hot sausage	5 eggs
1/2 medium-sized onion, chopped	1/4 cup milk
2 cups frozen hash browns	Salt and pepper to taste
	3 tablespoons Parmesan cheese

Separate rolls and place in ungreased 12-inch pizza pan. Place points in center of pan and press over bottom of pan and up the sides, forming a crust. Fry sausage; place on paper towels to remove grease. Put sausage in crust and add potatoes, onion, and cheese. In separate bowl, beat together eggs, milk, salt and pepper. Pour into crust; sprinkle with Parmesan cheese. Bake at 375° for 25–30 minutes. Serve with fruit.

Jeroline Stockdale (La Mesa, California)

Yum Yum Pizza Loaf

. . . and it is yummy! This has been a family favorite for 25 years!

1 loaf frozen bread dough	1–2 cups spaghetti sauce
1 small onion, chopped	2 cups shredded Cheddar cheese
2 cloves garlic, chopped	2 cups shredded mozzarella or Monterey Jack cheese
1 tablespoon olive oil, more or less	Chopped mushrooms (optional)
1 1/2 pounds ground beef or ground turkey	

Cover dough with wet cloth and place dough in warm spot to rise. Sauté onion and garlic in small amount of oil. Add ground meat and cook until done. Add spaghetti sauce, a little at a time, being careful not to let it become runny.

Grease cookie sheet with olive oil. On a floured board, roll out dough into a square shape. Using a slotted spoon, scoop meat mixture down center of bread dough. Cover with cheese. Add mushrooms, if desired. Fold ends of dough over meat mixture and pinch together to seal. Bake at 375° till brown.

Ginny Gallant (Mashpee, Massachusetts)

Grilled Cheese Delight

This is a family favorite passed down from my German heritage. It's a great alternative to fish during Lent. This sandwich was a staple during the days of meatless Fridays.

2 ripe tomatoes, diced
1 medium onion, diced
3–4 heaping tablespoons
   mayonnaise

8–12 slices bread
Butter
4–6 slices Cheddar cheese, or
   cheese of choice

Mix tomatoes and onion; then add mayonnaise to a chunky thickness (not soupy). Prepare 2 slices of bread by buttering 1 side of each piece. Add cheese to other side and place in frying pan. Then spoon filling on top of cheese. Top with other slice of bread. Grill both sides until cheese is melted and bread is browned. Repeat with each sandwich and enjoy!

Linda M. Harris (Silverdale, Washington)

Lisa Robertson loves to taste the goodies, sometimes popping on camera to share her enthusiastic response with viewers.

Lisa's Open-Faced Sandwiches

6 eggs, hard-boiled
6 green onions, chopped
1 green pepper, chopped
1 small can chopped black olives
¹⁄₂ pound shredded cheese

¹⁄₈ cup oil
1 (8-ounce) can tomato sauce
8–10 sourdough buns, cut in half
  and buttered lightly

Finely chop eggs; add onions, pepper, black olives, cheese, oil, and tomato sauce. Mix thoroughly. Cover top of each bun half with egg mixture. Place on lower rack in oven, under broiler. Watch carefully. Remove from oven when slightly brown. Let stand for 5–10 minutes before serving.

Lisa Robertson, QVC Host (West Chester, Pennsylvania)

Shown here proudly with nephew, Jack, Lisa enjoys reading science fiction, watching Star Trek, shopping, and dining out. Lisa, a former Miss Tennessee, was raised in Collegedale, Tennessee, which she said, "once had a traffic light."

Hot and Hearty Sandwich Loaf

1½ pounds ground chuck	1 loaf French bread
1 medium onion, chopped	Parmesan cheese
Salt and pepper to taste	1 (8-ounce) package Cheddar
1 small can black olives	cheese
1 (10-ounce) can tomato paste	1 large tomato, thinly sliced

In skillet, break up ground chuck with onion, and brown until completely done. Remove from burner. Add salt and pepper, black olives, and tomato paste. Mix until combined.

Split French bread lengthwise. Lay foil on a cookie sheet. Place bread on top of foil. Spread ground chuck mixture evenly on both halves. Sprinkle both halves with Parmesan cheese. On the top side of bread, sprinkle Cheddar cheese over meat. On the bottom half, add tomato slices to cover meat.

Bake at 325° until cheese is bubbly and bread is light brown (about 25 minutes). Be careful not to brown bottom of bread too much. Remove from oven. Place cheese side on top of tomato side. Let cool 5 minutes. Slice into 2-inch slices. Serve with tossed salad and French fries. Serves 10–12. Enjoy!

Jennifer J. Davis (Chester, West Virginia)

Soups, Chilies, and Stews

This is one of the distribution lines that thousands of QVC packages pass through on a daily basis. In the U.S. alone, QVC can pack approximately 300,000 packages daily for delivery via UPS or the U.S. Postal Service.

Creamy Chicken Vegetable Soup

2 tablespoons butter or
  margarine
$\frac{1}{2}$ cup chopped onion
1 clove garlic, minced
2 cups water
2 medium potatoes, peeled, diced
2 (10-ounce) packages frozen
  mixed vegetables
1 pound boneless, skinless
  chicken breasts, cubed

$\frac{1}{3}$ cup dry white wine
1 ($14\frac{1}{2}$-ounce) can diced
  tomatoes, drained
1 ($10\frac{3}{4}$-ounce) can cream of
  chicken soup, undiluted
5 drops hot sauce
$\frac{1}{2}$ teaspoon ground black
  pepper
1 cup evaporated skim milk

Melt butter in large saucepan; add onion and garlic. Cook, stirring constantly, until tender. Add remaining ingredients, except milk. Bring to a boil; cover, reduce heat, and simmer 25 minutes, stirring occasionally. Stir in milk and heat through. Yields 2 quarts.

Vivian Levine (Oak Ridge, Tennessee)

Turkey Rice Soup

My family and I have visited the Amish area of Pennsylvania on four occasions. We have loved our visits and especially enjoyed the food. Our last visit was Thanksgiving, and as it was cold, our favorites at the restaurants soon became the wonderful soups. This particular recipe is my own version of a chicken-rice soup that we enjoyed. I changed a few ingredients and the method of cooking to fit my busy lifestyle.

1 cup chopped onion
1 cup chopped celery
$\frac{1}{2}$ cup chopped carrots
$3\frac{1}{3}$ quarts water
3 cups cooked, chopped turkey
  or chicken

1 cup brown rice, uncooked
$\frac{1}{2}$ teaspoon pepper
1 teaspoon celery salt
$3\frac{1}{2}$ tablespoons chicken base
1 teaspoon parsley

Combine all ingredients in crockpot. Cook on MEDIUM 8 hours or longer. Makes 1 gallon of soup.

Robbie Wagner (Hesperia, California)

Beefy Cheesy Tortellini Soup

1 pound ground sirloin
2 small to medium onions, diced
2 stalks celery, cut into chunks
1 tablespoon olive oil
4 beef bouillon cubes
1 package dry onion soup mix
1 (11½-ounce) can vegetable juice
1 (11-ounce) can tomato sauce

1 (11- to 12-ounce) can Italian-style stewed tomatoes
3–4 cans water
2 tablespoons brown sugar
1 small package frozen cheese tortellini
1 (4- to 5-inch) stick pepperoni, cut into slices

In a large Dutch oven, brown ground sirloin, onions, and celery in olive oil. Add bouillon cubes, dry onion soup mix, vegetable juice, tomato sauce, stewed tomatoes, water, and brown sugar. Bring to a boil, then lower heat and let simmer for 30–45 minutes.

About 15 minutes before serving, return soup to boil and add the frozen cheese tortellini and sliced pepperoni. Stir; return to simmer, cooking until the tortellini is done (about 8 minutes).

Cut string beans or sliced carrots may also be added when you are browning the ground sirloin to make a heartier soup. Serve this with a good bread. Freezes well and is always a good leftover.

Mary A. Durfee (St. Albans, Vermont)

The Information Services Department provides research and information on a large variety of topics related to the many and varied business interests of the QVC staff. Part of its mission is to support the numerous contests and sweepstakes sponsored by QVC including the QVC/Quail Ridge Press recipe contest.

Beer Cheese Soup

This is great on a cold winter day.

4 chicken bouillon cubes
1 can beer
1 quart water
1 cup chopped celery
1 cup diced onions
1½ cups diced potatoes

1 (20-ounce) package frozen
   broccoli, carrots, and
   cauliflower
2 cans cream of chicken soup
1 (1-pound) package processed
   American cheese, cubed

In a large stock pot, dissolve bouillon in water and beer. Bring to a simmer, then add celery, onions, and potatoes. Cook 15 minutes. Add frozen mixed vegetables. Cook 5 minutes longer and then add soup and cheese. Cook until heated through and cheese is melted. Serves 8–10. Can be frozen for later use.

Ann E. Dierksen (Topeka, Kansas)

Broccoli, Ham, and Cheese Soup

2 tablespoons butter
2 tablespoons oil
1 small onion, diced
¼ cup flour
16 ounces heavy cream
1 cup water

1 (16-ounce) package frozen
   chopped broccoli
1 pound ham chunks
1 pound shredded Cheddar cheese
Salt and pepper to taste

In Dutch oven, melt butter with oil; add onion and sauté 2–3 minutes. Stir in flour and sauté until flour mixes with butter and begins to brown (about 4–5 minutes). Add heavy cream and water, then broccoli and ham. Slowly add cheese, 3 or 4 batches at a time, stirring frequently. Simmer on medium to low heat until all the cheese is melted and soup is thick and creamy. Add salt and pepper to taste. Serves 6.

Rebecca Stanford, QVC Employee (San Antonio, Texas)

Dilly Cucumber Soup

You'll love it!

1 quart buttermilk
3 cups lemon yogurt
Juice of 1 lemon

Salt and pepper to taste
2 teaspoons dill weed
2 cucumbers, grated

Mix buttermilk, yogurt, lemon juice, salt and pepper, and dill weed in large bowl. Add grated cucumber and stir. Refrigerate 1 hour. Serve cold.

Nancy Davis (Gladstone, Oregon)

Cabbage-Beef Comfort Soup

Great on a cold winter day.

1 large onion
1 large green pepper
2 stalks celery
2 cloves garlic
Oil or margarine
1½ pounds ground beef
1 (46-ounce) can tomato juice
1 (12-ounce) can vegetable juice
2 (14½-ounce) cans diced
tomatoes

6 beef bouillon cubes
1½ cups hot water
1 small cabbage, chopped
1 teaspoon dried basil
1 teaspoon marjoram
Pepper to taste
2 (15½-ounce) cans kidney beans,
undrained

Chop and sauté onion, green pepper, celery, and garlic in small amount oil or margarine. Brown ground beef; drain. Combine with sautéed vegetables. Add tomato and vegetable juices, tomatoes, bouillon (dissolved in hot water), cabbage, herbs, and pepper. Bring to a boil, then simmer for about 1 hour. Add kidney beans with juice and simmer another 15 minutes. Freezes well.

Molly Ingle (Canton, North Carolina)

Roasted Sweet Potato and Squash Soup

The great thing about this recipe is that THERE IS NO CREAM and you would never know it! Everyone who has ever eaten this soup could not believe it was made without cream. Amazing! My husband talks about this soup whenever the subject of food comes up with anyone. He brags about it and I love it!

3 big sweet potatoes	**2 tablespoons olive oil**
1 (1½-pound) butternut squash	**6 cups chicken broth**
1 medium onion	**Nutmeg, salt, and white pepper**
1 tablespoon chopped fresh sage	**Sour cream**
1 tablespoon chopped fresh thyme	

Peel potatoes and cut into 1-inch squares. Cut squash in half, take out seeds, peel, and cut into 1-inch pieces. Peel and chop onion. Preheat oven to 425°. Combine potatoes, squash, onion, sage, and thyme in a large bowl. Add olive oil and toss to coat the vegetables well. Spread mixture on a large baking sheet in a single layer. Roast for about 40 minutes, stirring vegetables 2 or 3 times while cooking (they should be caramelized).

Remove vegetables from oven and put about half into a food processor fitted with a metal blade. Add 2–3 cups of the broth and process until smooth. (I start with 2 cups and then see how it goes. I add more broth as I process the veggies until the mixture has the consistency of sauce or gravy. It should be thicker than cream but not too thick to pour smoothly.) Transfer this mixture to a large stockpot and repeat with the other half of the vegetables.

When all vegetables are puréed and in the stockpot, add a pinch of nutmeg, salt, and white pepper. Bring soup to a simmer over medium heat. Add any remaining chicken broth, if you need to. Adjust seasoning to taste. Serve in bowls with a little plop of sour cream on top and a sprig of thyme. This soup is great to freeze. Adjust the seasoning when you reheat the soup.

__Melanie McCausland, QVC Associate Producer__
__(West Chester, Pennsylvania)__

Tipsy Sweet Onion Soup

My family craves entreés with sweet, flavorful onions. They are easy to grow and very easy to cook with. This is my family's favorite soup recipe.

¼ cup unsalted butter
5 large sweet onions, chopped
5 cups chicken broth
½ cup celery leaves
1 large potato, peeled and cubed
2 teaspoons sugar
1 cup Chardonnay or white
   Zinfandel wine

1 tablespoon white wine or
   balsamic vinegar
1 cup fat-free half-and-half
2 tablespoons fresh parsley,
   chopped
1 teaspoon each of salt and white
   pepper

Heat butter in stockpot, add onions, and cook and stir for 5 minutes. Add broth, celery leaves, and potato; bring to boil. Reduce heat to simmer and cover, simmering for 30 minutes.

    Purée mixture in blender and return to stockpot. Blend in sugar, 1 cup wine, and vinegar. Boil and reduce heat to a simmer for 5 minutes. Stir in half-and-half, parsley, and seasonings. Heat thoroughly, but do not allow to boil.

Elaine Sweet (Dallas, Texas)

Editors' Extra: For quicker prep, microwave the potato, halve it, and scoop out baked potato into soup—no need to cook it as long, and no need to purée in blender.

Terrific Taco Soup

This has been in my family for years, passed down from generation to generation.

1 pound ground beef	1 can ranch-style beans
1 small onion, minced	1 can whole-kernel corn
1 small can green chiles	1½ cups water
1 can stewed tomatoes	1 package ranch dressing mix
1 can Mexican-style stewed tomatoes	1 package taco seasoning mix

Brown beef, onion, and chiles. Add remaining ingredients and bring to a boil. Simmer 20 minutes. Great with cornbread! Serves 6.

Donna Smith (Denison, Texas)

Editors' Extra: We like to crush a few corn or taco chips in each bowl with a sprinkle of grated Cheddar cheese. Yum!

Hot Dog Soup

My sister taught me how to make this quick and easy recipe about 30 years ago. My children always enjoyed it and are now making it for their families.

1 pound hot dogs	1–2 tablespoons butter
5–7 medium potatoes	Salt and pepper to taste
½ medium onion	8 ounces frozen corn

Cut hot dogs in ¼-inch pieces. Peel and dice potatoes. Cut onion into small pieces. Put this in a 3-quart saucepan. Cover with water. Add butter and salt and pepper. Cook till potatoes are tender, about ½ hour. When potatoes are done, add frozen corn. Let cook 3–4 minutes more. Enjoy!

Susan Crostley (Lehighton, Pennsylvania)

 QVC created its own unique packaging for fine jewelry to better protect merchandise while in transit from QVC to the customer.

Sausage, Potato, Broccoli Soup

Comfort food is what it is! This recipe makes a huge pot, and is even better the next day.

2 pounds bulk sausage
4 large baking potatoes
1 (1-pound) block processed
   cheese, cubed
4 cans cream of mushroom soup

4 (14½-ounce) cans chicken
   broth
1 (20-ounce) bag frozen chopped
   broccoli
Salt and pepper to taste

Brown and drain sausage. Scrub potatoes and cut into bite-size pieces. Cut cheese into large chunks. Put sausage, potatoes, and cheese into 8-quart stockpot.

In large mixing bowl, combine soup and chicken broth. Pour into stockpot. Cook until potatoes are almost tender, stirring often so it doesn't stick to bottom. Add broccoli and continue to cook till vegetables are tender and soup is hot. Season to taste. Recipe can be halved easily.

Nancy Blazon (Cantonment, Florida)

Italian Sausage Soup

1½ pounds Italian sausage
1½ cups chopped onion
½ cup chopped celery
2 cloves garlic, minced
3 tablespoons olive oil
1 cup tomato paste
2 cups chopped canned tomatoes

6 cups chicken broth
½ teaspoon oregano
½ teaspoon basil
2 bay leaves
¼ teaspoon thyme
3 tablespoons sugar
1–2 cups small shell pasta

In same pan, brown meat and sauté onion, celery, and garlic in olive oil until soft and clear. Add tomato paste and cook 5 minutes, stirring often. Add all other ingredients except pasta and simmer for 30 minutes. Add pasta and simmer until pasta is cooked.

Dorothy Tannahill Moran (Portland, Oregon)

New Orleans Style
Chicken and Sausage Gumbo

This recipe was handed down to me from my grandmother, who would kill me if she knew I was giving out the family's secret gumbo recipe! This is my favorite dish.

1½ cups flour
1½ cups olive oil
1 cup chopped onion
½ cup chopped green pepper
½ cup finely chopped celery
5 garlic cloves, finely chopped
4 boneless chicken breasts, cut in squares
1 pound Andouille sausage (or Polish sausage)

8 cups chicken bouillon or water
1 bay leaf
Salt and red and black pepper to taste
1 (10-ounce) box frozen okra (optional)
1 pinch of thyme
Minced parsley

First have all your chopped vegetables ready. Then make a roux with flour and olive oil. Cook and stir over medium heat, using a tall 6- or 8-quart pot.

Cook and stir about 15 minutes. When roux is brown (don't let it burn), add all your chopped vegetables. Now add your cut-up chicken and sliced sausage. Then add your bouillon (or water) slowly. Then put in one bay leaf and seasonings. Add the okra at the end (or leave it out if you like). Then add thyme and parsley. Cook over slow fire for 2½ hours.

Serve over hot steamed rice along with potato salad. Serves 8–10.

Suzanne Kuhnle (Slidell, Louisiana)

Mock Crab Chowder

1 onion, chopped
4 stalks celery, cut up
2 tablespoons margarine or
  butter
2 cans cream of potato soup

1 quart whole milk
1 pint half-and-half
1 pound imitation crab, cut in
  bite-size pieces
Salt and pepper

Sauté onion and celery in butter or margarine until soft. Add soup, milk, and half-and-half to pot. Heat thoroughly and add crab meat. Salt and pepper to taste.

Colleen Batty (Buellton, California)

Alaskan Seafood Chowder

Living on Kodiak Island, I've learned to create recipes with all the seafood available to us.

1 small onion
1 clove garlic
4 tablespoons oil
1 pound halibut chunks
½ pound shrimp
½ pound scallops
1 (8-ounce) package cream
  cheese, softened
2 cups heavy cream combined
  with 1 cup milk

1 (15-ounce) can carrots, drained
1 (15-ounce) can corn, drained
1 (15-ounce) can peas, drained
4 (10¾-ounce) cans cream of
  potato soup
2 (10¾-ounce) cans cream of
  mushroom soup
Salt and pepper to taste
Red pepper to taste

Chop onion and garlic. Sauté in oil. Remove onion and garlic from pan. Fry seafood in seasoned oil. In meantime, combine cream cheese with cream and milk in large saucepan. Add vegetables and soups. Heat and stir until smooth; add seafood. Salt and pepper to taste. Sprinkle lightly with red pepper. Serve in bowls. Salad and dinner rolls complete this meal.

Sharon A. Walberts (Kodiak, Alaska)

Grandmother's Clam Chowder

On Sundays after we all got back from church, my grandmother made this special chowder; she always served it with homemade biscuits or chowder crackers.

¹/₄ pound slab bacon or salt
  pork, chopped
1 large onion, diced
4 stalks celery with leaves,
  chopped
4 carrots, peeled and thinly sliced

6 medium potatoes, peeled and
  cut into small cubes
4 cups chicken stock
Fresh parsley, chopped
Salt and white pepper to taste
2 quarts diced clams with juice

Sauté first 3 ingredients until tender and onions are transparent. Drain off extra bacon grease. Add carrots and potatoes. Next add chicken stock and simmer until potatoes and carrots are tender, adding parsley and salt and pepper to taste. Add clams and clam juice to chowder, heating until chowder is bubbly. Serve with biscuits or chowder crackers. Enjoy!

Helen Zavesky (Redding, Connecticut)

Cheesy Chowder

My best friend's mom, Rita, would make a big batch of this chowder when we would visit on the weekends. A late night chat over chowder was always fun.

1 cup chopped potatoes
¹/₂ cup chopped carrots
¹/₂ cup chopped celery
¹/₂ cup chopped onion
¹/₂ cup chopped green pepper
4 tablespoons butter
3 cups chicken stock

2 cups milk
¹/₂ cup flour
1 teaspoon parsley
Dash white pepper
3 cups shredded sharp processed
  American cheese

In large saucepan, cook vegetables in butter and chicken stock about 20 minutes, or until tender. In separate bowl, whisk milk and flour; add parsley, pepper, and cheese. Stir mixture into vegetable broth mixture. Cook and stir until thick and bubbly. Can be made ahead and reheated.

Dawn Tomaschefsky, QVC Employee (San Antonio, Texas)

Veggie Chili

This is a wonderful entreé for vegetarians (and everyone) on those cold winter evenings. You can make it as spicy as you want just by using hotter green chiles and adding more chili powder. Because the tofu has been frozen, thawed and crumbled, it has more of a "meat" consistency.

1 package firm tofu, freeze in original package
1 pound fresh mushrooms, sliced
½ cup chopped onion
1 clove garlic, chopped
3 tablespoons butter
2 (4-ounce) cans chopped green chiles
2 (15-ounce) cans tomato sauce

1 (15-ounce) can pinto beans
1 (15-ounce) can kidney beans
1 (10-ounce) box frozen corn niblets
1 (5-ounce) can whole small black olives
Salt, pepper, chili powder, cumin to taste
½ cup shredded Jack cheese

Thaw frozen tofu, drain, and crumble. Sauté mushrooms, onion, and garlic in butter. Mix together all ingredients, except cheese, in large pot and simmer 30 minutes. If too thick, add water. Add cheese, heat 5 more minutes. Serve with crackers or cornbread.

Liz Hochevar (Arvada, Colorado)

From the top of the stairs above the living room, this quiet view of the sets and cameras and cables is evidence that the action is presently going on elsewhere.

Chili Quick

I always think of my late mother-in-law when I make this chili. Of all the recipes she gave me, this is our favorite. I know this sounds too easy to be good, but it is delicious.

1 pound ground beef
1 (14½-ounce) can diced
  tomatoes
1 (10-ounce) can diced tomatoes
  with green chiles
1 (16-ounce) can baked beans with
  onions, liquid included
1 (1¼-ounce) package dry chili
  mix

Brown ground beef in large saucepan; add remaining ingredients. Simmer for as little as 15 minutes and serve. It's good to serve alone or on top of macaroni. Grated cheese on top is nice.

Dannie Anderton (Germantown, Tennessee)

Jerry's Colorado Kickin' Chili

I started with my mother's delicious recipe and gave it a little bit of a "Colorado kick."

2 pounds ground beef
1 medium white onion, chopped
1 small can diced jalapeños,
  hot or medium
2 large cans hot chili beans
2 regular cans kidney beans
1 (29-ounce) can tomato sauce
6 tablespoons chili powder, or
  less
3 tablespoons white vinegar
1 tablespoon ground cumin
3 tablespoons red pepper flakes

Brown ground beef with onion and diced peppers. Drain and set aside. Next, combine all the remaining ingredients into a 5-quart crockpot; mix well. Add ground beef mixture to this and stir well again. Cook for 6–8 hours on LOW.

Jerry D. McMillian II (Golden, Colorado)

Spicy Chicken Chili

After getting married, I realized that I was overweight and unhealthy. I love to cook, but so many of my favorite recipes are loaded with fat and empty carbohydrates. I started "tweaking" my favorites so they would fit into my new lifestyle, and found that many times the recipes are better without the extras! I hope you enjoy this lite version of my Texas chili!

2 pounds cooked chicken breasts, cubed
1 medium yellow onion, finely minced
3 cloves garlic, minced
¼ cup red chili powder
1 teaspoon paprika
½ teaspoon ground black pepper
1 teaspoon creole seasoning

½ teaspoon oregano
1 teaspoon cumin (comino)
2 (10-ounce) cans tomato sauce
1 can water
1 can each, whole pinto beans, black beans, light red kidney beans, all rinsed and drained
1 can yellow corn, drained

In large stockpot, combine chicken, onion, garlic, spices, tomato sauce, and 1 can water. Bring to boil over medium heat; reduce and simmer for 1 hour. Add beans and corn; continue to simmer for 30–45 minutes. Serve with cornbread, over rice, inside tortillas, or by itself. Very low-fat and healthy!

Carrie Falquist (Vancouver, Washington)

Mock Oyster Stew

This is an exceptionally good dish, especially when you don't have (or can't eat) oysters and have plenty of summer squash.

4–5 yellow squash
2 tablespoons butter or
  margarine
1/8 teaspoon celery salt
1/4 teaspoon paprika

1/2 teaspoon salt or to taste
1/4 teaspoon black pepper or to
  taste
1 (12-ounce) can evaporated
  milk

Wash and slice squash. Place into saucepan. Add enough water to stew. Add remaining ingredients, except milk. After squash is done, mash well with potato masher or hand blender, then add milk. Reheat, but do not boil. Serve hot with saltines. Very good!

Willena Lowman (Valdese, North Carolina)

Italian Zucchini Stew

My grandmother came from Avellino, Italy (near Naples). This is one of many country dishes she taught me to make. We always have enough for everyone coming in the door—the smell while cooking tickles their taste buds.

2 tablespoons olive oil
1 medium onion, chopped
3 cups zucchini, cut into thin
  slices
2 white potatoes, peeled and
  thinly sliced
1 (16-ounce) can tomato sauce
1/2 can water

1/4 teaspoon onion powder
1 teaspoon garlic powder
1/4 teaspoon salt or to taste
1/2 teaspoon pepper
2 tablespoons chopped fresh basil
1 pound cooked Italian sausage or
  smoked sausage, sliced
  (optional)

Heat olive oil in large skillet over low heat; add chopped onion and sauté for 4 minutes until tender. Stir in zucchini and potatoes and cook for 5 minutes over medium heat. Add tomato sauce, water, onion and garlic powder, salt, pepper, and basil. Simmer for 20 minutes until tender. Add sausage in last 8 minutes of cooking. Serve with Loccatelli cheese and, of course, Italian bread.

Mary Roberto (King of Prussia, Pennsylvania)

Arkansas Red Stew

This recipe originated, as best I can tell, with my grandmother's grandmother in Kentucky around 1850. My grandmother was born in 1882 in Kentucky and moved with her parents by covered wagon to northern Arkansas in 1889. Before canned tomato juice, my ancestors used to take overripe tomatoes and mash them through a sieve. Also, Grandma said instead of store-bought browning sauce, they used beef blood and salt pork cooked down to a thick paste. I remember my grandmother cooking this stew for me when I was a kid and sick in bed . . . it was the only thing that tasted good to me.

1 (3-pound) pot roast (or stew meat)
1 (16-ounce) can stewed tomatoes
1 (46-ounce) can tomato juice, or vegetable juice
3 ribs celery with tops, cut
1–2 medium turnips, chunked, to taste
2 onions, chunked

3 carrots, chunked
¼ medium cabbage, chopped
1 teaspoon sugar, or to taste
2 beef bouillon cubes dissolved in 3 ounces hot water
1 tablespoon browning sauce
7 sprigs parsley
1 cup red wine
3 medium potatoes, cut small
3 large cloves garlic, minced

Cut roast in large chunks with all fat removed. Place meat in very large heavy pot and brown. When brown, add tomatoes, tomato juice, celery, turnips, onions, carrots, and cabbage. Bring to boil, then turn down to simmer. Let cook for 10 minutes; add sugar and bouillon. Simmer on low for 2½–3 hours, then add browning sauce, fresh parsley, red wine, and potatoes. Cook until potatoes are done, about ½ hour. Add garlic during last 15 minutes of cooking.

Serve with French bread, tossed green salad, buttered fine noodles, and a nice Merlot wine.

Note: Add a little cilantro for a spicier taste, but only if you like cilantro.

Steve Beeler (Flagstaff, Arizona)

 The hallmark of QVC merchandise is quality and variety at good value. More than 100 experienced, informed buyers comb the world to launch at least 250 new products each week—about 15% of the 1,680 products offered each week on QVC are new.

Crockpot Mulligan Stew

My mom and I created this as a recipe needed for my Girl Scout cooking badge 30 years ago. It has been a great favorite with my family, especially the men! I still get requests to make this when I see my brothers at holiday gatherings.

2 pounds beef, chuck or round,
   cut into 1-inch cubes
½ cup flour
3 tablespoons vegetable oil
2 cans tomato soup
2 soup cans water
3 stalks celery, chopped

1 (1-pound) bag carrots, peeled
   and cut into 1-inch pieces
1 cup pearl onions, or 1 cup
   chopped onion
6 potatoes, peeled and cut in half
2 bay leaves
Salt and pepper to taste

Dredge beef cubes in flour to coat. Heat oil in large skillet. Add beef cubes and cook until brown.

In crockpot, add remaining ingredients and browned beef cubes. Set crockpot on HIGH until stew starts to steam, then turn crockpot on LOW and cook for 4–6 hours. Salt and pepper to taste. This stew is great with crusty bread. Serves 4–6.

Rosemary Stevens (Katonah, New York)

Father Fred's Stew

This is a very special recipe that has been passed down through our family for many years. The dish was created by my husband's cousin, Father Fred, who after many years of service to his community as a Roman Catholic priest, has chosen to live out his life as a cloistered monk. My husband's mother treasured this recipe and always made this meal whenever we would come to visit—we always looked forward to this delicacy.

1½ pounds stew beef
4 potatoes
4 carrots
1 onion
1 (8-ounce) can tomatoes

1 can cream of celery soup
½ cup red wine
3 bouillon cubes
Salt and pepper to taste

Cut beef, potatoes, carrots, and onion into bite-size pieces. Combine all ingredients in a large casserole dish. Cover, and cook for 4 hours at 300°. Serves 6.

Kathleen Arbuthnot (Morgantown, West Virginia)

One-Pot Slow-Cook Sauerbraten Beef Stew

My husband of Polish and Slavic descent loves this German dish and thinks I have slaved for hours in preparation.

1½–2 pounds chuck roast
2 tablespoons olive oil
1 small onion, diced
1 (8-ounce) box frozen sliced
  carrots
1½ teaspoons dill weed
⅛ teaspoon garlic powder

⅛ teaspoon beef bouillon
2–3 potatoes, sliced
1 can stewed tomatoes
1 bag/can sauerkraut
1 cup any carbonated soda
1 cup water

Brown roast in large frying pan in olive oil; cook 5 minutes each side. Place in slow cooker adding onion, carrots, and all spices. Top with potato slices, then stewed tomatoes and drained sauerkraut. Pour soda and water over all. Cook in slow cooker on MEDIUM for 6–8 hours. Gently stir before serving.

Linda L. Abramowitz (Glens Falls, New York)

Product Coordinators such as Carrie Lynch work behind the scenes, escorting featured items between Product Central, where two of every product is stored, to Product Prep, where it is readied for its on-air appearance, and finally to the set. Product Coordinators are responsible for getting the right product to the right place at the right time.

Sweet & Sour Beef Stew

1½ pounds beef stew meat,
    cut into 1-inch cubes
2 tablespoons cooking oil
2 medium carrots, shredded
1 medium onion, sliced
1 (8-ounce) can tomato sauce
½ cup water

½ cup packed brown sugar
¼ cup vinegar
1 tablespoon Worcestershire sauce
1 teaspoon salt
1 tablespoon cold water
2 tablespoons cornstarch
Rice or noodles, cooked

In a 3-quart saucepan, brown half the meat at a time in hot oil; drain. In same saucepan, combine meat, shredded carrots, sliced onions, tomato sauce, water, brown sugar, vinegar, Worcestershire, and salt. Cover and cook over low heat until meat is tender, about 1½ hours. Blend 1 tablespoon cold water with cornstarch. Add to stew; cook and stir until thickened and bubbly. Serve over rice or noodles.

Janice Richard (Simi Valley, California)

Campfire Oven Stew

This is one of our family favorites that we have used for at least 40 years. We used to cook this recipe over a campfire in a Dutch oven when our children were camping with us. It is equally good baked in the oven or in a slow cooker.

3 tablespoons flour
1 teaspoon salt
2 pounds stew meat, cubed
2 tablespoons salad oil
12 very small onions
2 stalks celery, cut into 2-inch
    pieces
3 medium carrots, cut lengthwise
    in quarters

6 small potatoes, peeled, chunked
1 can tomato soup
1¾ cups water
1 teaspoon salt
Dash of pepper
2 whole cloves
1 small bay leaf
1 cup frozen peas

Combine the flour and salt. Roll meat in flour and salt mixture, then brown in the hot oil. Place in 3-quart casserole dish. Add all vegetables except peas. Set aside.

In saucepan, combine and heat remaining ingredients (except peas) and pour over meat-vegetable mixture. Bake, covered, at 350° for 1 hour and 45 minutes. Add peas and cook 10 minutes longer.

D. Arlone Larsen (Grand Junction, Colorado)

Fernando's Louisiana Chicken Stew

6 split chicken breasts, skinned
1 teaspoon paprika
1½ teaspoons salt, divided
1 teaspoon black pepper, divided
¼ cup oil
⅔ cup all-purpose flour
1 large onion, chopped, divided
3 cloves garlic, finely chopped, divided
1 quart plus 1 cup water, divided

10 medium red potatoes, peeled and halved
6 carrots, peeled and cut into 1- or 2-inch pieces
1 medium bell pepper, chopped
1 teaspoon celery seed
¼ cup finely chopped fresh parsley
1 teaspoon hot sauce

Season chicken with paprika, ½ teaspoon salt, and ½ teaspoon black pepper. In nonstick or lightly greased skillet, brown chicken on medium heat. While chicken is browning, start making the roux. In 2-quart saucepan, heat oil on medium heat; add the flour, ½ teaspoon black pepper, ½ teaspoon salt, 1 tablespoon onion, and 1 tablespoon garlic. Continue stirring until the mixture becomes medium to dark brown. When roux reaches this stage in color, add 1 quart of tap water. Stir until all lumps are gone.

In a Dutch oven or large stew pot, combine chicken, potatoes, carrots, bell pepper, and remaining seasonings. Pour roux into stew pot, adding 1 additional cup of water. Bring to a boil and simmer for 2 hours. As stew cooks, you may need to add more salt and pepper. Always season to taste. Serve over steamed long grain rice (not minute rice). Serves 6.

Fernando P. Augustine (Hot Springs, South Dakota)

Pork and Mushroom Stew

2 small onions, chopped
2 large fresh bell peppers,
    chopped
2 stalks celery, chopped
3 fresh garlic cloves, minced
½ cup vegetable oil
1½ pounds fresh mushrooms,
    sliced

½ cup margarine
2 pounds boneless pork chops,
    cubed
1 pound bulk Italian sausage
1 (29-ounce) can tomato sauce
2 (29-ounce) cans whole
    tomatoes
Salt and pepper to taste

Sauté onions, peppers, celery, and garlic in oil. Sauté sliced mushrooms in separate skillet in margarine. Brown cubed pork and Italian sausage in skillet; drain well. Place sautéed mushrooms (margarine and all), sautéed vegetables, browned pork and sausage, tomato sauce, and tomatoes in large stockpot. Salt and pepper to taste. Simmer 2–3 hours on low heat. Serve alone or on top of cooked pasta. Serves 8–10.

Florence Coleman (Marcy, New York)

Lights, camera, action! If you were doing a live presentation, you would see lights, cameras, and monitors! Be sure to look for the camera with the red light— you provide the action!

Crab Pasta Salad

There's never any left when I take this to a family gathering.

1 cup sweet, mayonnaise-type
  salad dressing
½ cup zesty Italian dressing
2 tablespoons grated Parmesan
  cheese
1½ cups imitation crab meat,
  chopped

1 small green pepper, chopped
1–2 tomatoes, chopped
1 small onion, chopped
1½ cups corkscrew noodles,
  cooked and drained

Combine salad dressings and cheese; mix well. Add remaining ingredients. Refrigerate for a few hours before serving.

Marlene Svasek (Columbus, Nebraska)

Yummy Seafood Pasta Salad

This is one of my "concoctions" that turned out right. My family (Rick, Brian, and Aaron) really enjoys it and it has become a staple at our house for summer meals. My co-workers at QVC like it, too!

1 pound small shell pasta
1½ cups mayonnaise
¾ cup chili sauce
1 tablespoon parsley, chopped
1½ teaspoons lemon juice
2 teaspoons horseradish, or to
  taste
Salt and fresh ground pepper to
  taste

Hot pepper sauce, if desired
1 pound imitation crab meat,
  chopped
¼ pound cooked shrimp, chopped
4 ribs celery, chopped
1 onion, chopped
Seafood seasoning to taste

Cook pasta according to package directions. Cool. Add to dressing mixture of mayonnaise, chili sauce, parsley, lemon juice, horseradish, salt, pepper, and hot sauce, if desired. Mix in seafood, celery, and onions. Refrigerate and allow flavors to blend. Sprinkle with seafood seasoning. Enjoy!

Jaye Ann S. Hostetler, QVC Employee (West Chester, Pennsylvania)

Pasta Primavera Salad

So easy and delicious. Using bought spaghetti sauce makes putting this salad together a snap!

8-ounces tri-colored pasta
½ cup frozen, chopped broccoli
½ cup Italian dressing
½ cup spaghetti sauce
¼ teaspoon sugar
¼ teaspoon garlic powder
¼ teaspoon Italian seasoning

3 scallions, sliced
1 (16-ounce) can diced tomatoes, drained
½ cup chopped cucumber
½ cup chopped black olives
Romano cheese (optional)

Cook pasta per package directions. Add chopped broccoli during last 3–4 minutes. Drain and rinse with cold water. Set aside.

In a large bowl, mix Italian dressing, spaghetti sauce, sugar, garlic powder, and Italian seasoning. Add all other ingredients and toss well. Cover and refrigerate 2 hours, or until well chilled. If desired, sprinkle with Romano cheese just before serving. Serves 6.

Margaret Glassic (Easton, Pennsylvania)

Belvidere Pasta Salad

This recipe has been well received at graduation and anniversary parties. Good any time!

2 cups curly noodle pasta, cooked
1 cup diced cooked turkey or chicken
1 cup chopped celery
1 onion, chopped

½ green pepper, diced
1 package dry ranch dressing
1 cup mayonnaise
1 teaspoon garlic salt
⅓ cup Italian dressing

Mix all ingredients well. Chill.

Linda Lehman (Belvidere, Illinois)

Merchandise is selected based on product uniqueness, quality, demonstrability, timeliness, and appeal. QVC is one of only a handful of retailers with its own in-house quality assurance program and warehouse quality control.

Lite Pasta Salad

A very colorful, quick, and easy recipe my grandmother taught me long ago. She liked it because it feeds quite a few people and is great leftover.

12 ounces bow tie pasta
1 cucumber
1 sweet red pepper
2 cups shredded carrots
1 (16-ounce) can whole pitted
  black olives

1 (8-ounce) bag shredded
  mozzarella cheese
2½ cups lite Italian dressing

Cook bow tie pasta, drain, and let cool. Cut up cucumber and red pepper however you like. Mix all remaining ingredients together, then place in refrigerator and let chill for about 1 hour. Serve and enjoy.

Joanie Gowell (Grand Forks AFB, North Dakota)

Robusto Spaghetti Salad

I can never make enough of this pasta salad (or enough copies of the recipe)!

1 pound thin spaghetti or
  linguine, broken into quarters
2 tablespoons vegetable oil
1 (6-ounce) jar green or black
  olives, drained
1 small onion
1 green pepper
1 cup shredded Cheddar cheese

2 tomatoes
3 small pickling cucumbers (or 1
  regular)
1 large (16-ounce) bottle of robust
  Italian seasoned salad dressing
Salt, pepper, and seasoned salt to
  taste

Cook spaghetti and drain. Mix with oil so it doesn't stick together. Let set in large bowl to cool. In food processor, finely chop olives, onion, and green pepper. Mix with spaghetti; add Cheddar cheese, mixing until blended well.

Chop tomatoes and cucumbers into bite-size pieces. Toss with spaghetti mixture. Pour salad dressing over all, season, and mix well. Let set in refrigerator overnight, tossing once in a while so that the flavors blend. Keeps for several days in refrigerator.

Lorraine M. Saulnier (Clarksburg, Massachusetts)

My Best Macaroni Salad

I've been cooking since I was tall enough to reach the stove. My mother and grand-mother were both skilled in the kitchen and it rubbed off. I love to cook for friends and family. I always get many requests for this recipe. Enjoy!

1 (1-pound) box medium shell macaroni

4 hard-cooked eggs, peeled and chopped

1 small jar green olives, drained (reserve 1 tablespoon juice)

1 small jar sweet pickles, drained (reserve 1 tablespoon juice)

2 cups salad dressing (sweet mayonnaise-style)

2 tablespoons parsley flakes

1 tablespoon celery seed

5 drops yellow food coloring (optional)

Paprika

Cook shells according to package directions. Rinse with cold water till cool enough to handle. Place in large bowl. Add chopped eggs. Slice olives in half and add to mixture. Chop sweet pickles into small pieces and add to mixture. Toss to mix.

In separate bowl, combine salad dressing and both olive and pickle juices. Add parsley, celery seed, and food coloring, if desired. Stir till well blended. Add dressing mixture to shell mixture and gently combine till the shells are well coated. Place in serving bowl and dust with paprika to taste. Chill for 2 hours before serving.

Melody Black (Johnstown, Pennsylvania)

The "Burbs" Patio Salad

This is an excellent salad to serve on a warm summer day . . . even better the next day, if there is any! Enjoy!

DRESSING:

¾ cup salad dressing
2 tablespoons soy sauce
1 teaspoon dark, hot mustard

¼ teaspoon garlic powder
White pepper to taste

Blend all ingredients together.

SALAD:

2 (4-ounce) cans shrimp, rinsed and well drained
1 (16-ounce) can bean sprouts, rinsed and well drained
1 cup canned baby peas, well drained
1 stalk celery, chopped
½ cup chopped green pepper
1 small onion, chopped

1 cup sliced and halved water chestnuts, well drained
1 (4½-ounce) can sliced mushrooms, well drained
1 or 2 boiled eggs, chopped (optional)
5 ounces vermicelli, snapped into 3-inch strips, cooked, drained

Mix all, except vermicelli, together. Add cooled vermicelli last, and toss all together. Add Dressing and toss again. Refrigerate to chill thoroughly. Serve on lettuce leaves with dark rye bread and a glass of wine or raspberry lemonade. Serves 6–8.

Doris J. Reid (Brown Deer, Wisconsin)

Nutty Chicken Salad Confetti

A very colorful and tasty salad, people always love this.

1 (10-ounce) can honey roasted peanuts
2 packages dry ramen noodles, broken up
1 small head cabbage, chopped
1 red pepper, chopped

1 green pepper, chopped
3 stalks celery, chopped
3 chicken breasts, cooked and chopped
1 bottle poppy seed dressing

Combine all ingredients. Let stand a few hours before serving.

Sharee Plumer (Council Bluffs, Iowa)

Lois' Sevenoaks Chicken Salad

If you're going to make chicken salad, don't put too many fillers—make chicken salad! This is superb!

3 large chicken breasts with ribs
½ medium onion, peeled
1 tablespoon Cajun seasoning
Juice of ½ lemon
⅓ cup Italian salad dressing
1 cup chopped celery

1 (2½-ounce) package slivered almonds
¾ cup mayonnaise
¼ cup sour cream
Fresh cracked black pepper to taste

Boil chicken breasts in water to cover with onion and seasoning; cook about 45 minutes. Cool chicken and cut with scissors, placing in flat casserole dish (discard onion and broth). Sprinkle chicken with lemon juice and salad dressing. Cover and refrigerate overnight, or at least a couple of hours.

Remove chicken to bowl. Add remaining ingredients. Mix and serve on Romaine lettuce leaves with grapes, sliced tomatoes, and crackers.

Lois McKee (Baton Rouge, Louisiana)

The QVC Studio Tour allows visitors to view sets and sites—like this product warehouse—from above. Though QVC is not located in a metropolitan city (Philadelphia and Wilmington are closest), it is listed on highway signs as an attraction, and so is easily found.

Chinese Chicken Salad

DRESSING:

¹/₃ cup vegetable oil
¹/₄ cup red wine vinegar

¹/₈ cup sugar
¹/₈ cup soy sauce

Mix all ingredients and set aside. Pour over chicken mixture when ready to serve.

SALAD:

1 package ramen noodles
1 pound boneless, skinless
  chicken breasts, cut into
  bite-size pieces
1 tablespoon vegetable oil

2 tablespoons sesame seeds
¹/₂ cup sliced almonds
¹/₂ head green cabbage, shredded
5 green onions, chopped

Cook noodles as directed (without seasoning packet) and drain. Spray large nonstick skillet with cooking spray; heat on high until hot. Add chicken and stir-fry until chicken is light brown (with no pink). Remove from skillet and set aside.

Add vegetable oil to nonstick skillet and heat on medium-high. Add noodles, sesame seeds, and almonds and cook till golden brown. In large bowl, combine cabbage, onions, chicken, noodles, seeds, and almonds. Mix everything together. Pour Dressing on top and mix again, coating entire salad.

Leah Williams, QVC Host (West Chester, Pennsylvania)

"My first week on the air at QVC included an hour of "Now You're Cooking." I had come to QVC from sister station Q2 where I was NEVER called upon to cook . . . with good reason . . . I could barely boil water back then. My cooking hour featured a variety of essential kitchen items including a nonstick muffin pan. I started my muffin pan presentation well enough. I mentioned how heartbroken one would be having baked the perfect muffin only to find that it couldn't be easily removed from the pan. I described the horrors of muffin tops severed from their bottoms trapped in a "non" nonstick pan. I was ready for the crowning moment of my presentation . . . "the demo." I had a pan full of golden brown muffins in front of me. And with a grand gesture, I picked up the pan, flipped it over with all my might, and watched muffins go flying across the counter and onto the floor! Although it wasn't the smooth, flawless demonstration I was going for, it WAS an effective example of just how "nonstick" that pan was. It also cinched my fate, that cooking would not be my area of expertise on QVC! Fortunately, in real life, I'm a much better cook today."

When Program Host Leah Williams (recipe on opposite page) says "go for your dream, because it can happen," she's not kidding. Leah moved from California, to New York, to Pennsylvania in less than a year to reach her goal of becoming a QVC Host.

Chunky Chicken Salad

This was the first chicken salad recipe that I tasted when moving to the South from New England. My friend who shared it with me is no longer around, but I love this recipe and think of her often when I serve it for a church gathering or luncheon.

1 chicken, boiled and deboned	⅓ cup mayonnaise, or to taste
1 (8-ounce) can crushed pineapple	Salt and pepper to taste
2 or more stalks celery, finely chopped	1 cup finely chopped pecans

Dice chicken and set in bowl. Add crushed pineapple, celery, and mayonnaise; season with salt and pepper. Add chopped nuts, then chill at least 4–5 hours. Stir again before serving. Delicious!

Ella F. Smith (Spartanburg, South Carolina)

Chicken Fruit Salad

I served this to my investment club and they just loved it.

1 cup mayonnaise
¹/₄ cup honey
¹/₂ teaspoon ground ginger
3 cups cubed, cooked chicken
1 large can mandarin oranges,
   drained
1 cup grape halves

1 large can pineapple chunks,
   drained
1 cup chopped, unpeeled red apple
1 cup chopped, unpeeled yellow
   apple
1 cup walnut or pecan halves
Lettuce leaves

In large mixing bowl mix first 3 ingredients. Add chicken and drained fruits. Lightly fold in nuts. Refrigerate for 1 hour. Serve on lettuce leaf.

Rendy Perkins (Glasgow, Kentucky)

Pot O' Gold Chicken Salad

In 1998, my parish pastor was in charge of sandwiches for National Prayer Day. He asked for five volunteers of which I was one. I wanted to come up with something healthy and refreshing. I get rave reviews with this recipe.

1 whole roasted chicken, skinned
   and deboned (store bought)
1 stalk celery
2 green onions
12 dried apricots

³/₄ cup golden raisins
³/₄ cup dried cranberries
1 carrot
³/₄ cup honey-roasted sunflower
   nuts

Using food processor, separately chop all ingredients except nuts. In large bowl, mix chopped ingredients with sunflower nuts.

DRESSING:

1 cup low-fat mayonnaise
1 teaspoon garlic powder
³/₄ teaspoon cayenne pepper
1 (8-ounce) can crushed pineapple
   (in own juice), undrained

1 teaspoon curry powder
1 cup fat-free sour cream
1 tablespoon lemon juice

In separate bowl, mix Dressing ingredients; pour over chopped ingredients. Mix well and chill at least 3 hours. Serve with crackers or use as filling for sandwiches. I use croissants.

Cheryl M. Lafferty (Incline Village, Nevada)

A+ Hot Potato Salad

Anytime my mother and I get together, one of us has to make this! Her recipe has no amounts, but I'm a foods and nutrition teacher and more precise than she is, so this is how I make it. Enjoy!

7 cups peeled and cubed potatoes
1 pound Swiss cheese, cubed
2/3 cup mayonnaise

1 teaspoon garlic salt
1 (10-ounce) jar olives, chopped, drained

Cook potatoes in a small amount of boiling, salted water, covered for 18–20 minutes, or until tender. Drain.

Grease a 9x13-inch baking pan. Mix all ingredients in a large mixing bowl and transfer to baking pan. Bake at 350° for 35–40 minutes.

Shari Woodruff (Middlebury, Indiana)

Jane's Potato Salad

This was my mother-in-law's family recipe. Their mother made this as early as the 1930s (or so I was told). It is by far the best potato salad recipe ever!

12–15 medium red potatoes
1 bunch celery, cubed
1/4 head cabbage, finely shredded
6 hard-boiled eggs, chopped
1/4 cup vinegar
2–3 tablespoons sugar

1 (10-ounce) jar famous sandwich spread
1 tablespoon mayonnaise (or more to make creamy)
1 tablespoon heavy cream
Salt to taste

Boil potatoes, cool, and dice. Add celery, cabbage, and hard-boiled eggs. Mix gently and set aside. Warm the vinegar and sugar on the stove on low heat until sugar dissolves. Add vinegar/sugar mixture and famous sandwich spread; let cool. Add mayonnaise and heavy cream. Toss the dressing and ingredients gently. Add salt to taste. Refrigerate.

Joanne Ridley-Pacicca (Syracuse, New York)

Party Potato Salad

I've been making this potato salad for 40 years, and it's still the dish I'm usually asked to bring to potlucks.

3 pounds potatoes, whole,
   unpeeled
3$\frac{1}{4}$ teaspoons salt, divided
4 eggs
1 cup thinly chopped green
   pepper
$\frac{3}{4}$ cup thinly sliced celery

$\frac{1}{2}$ cup finely chopped onion
2 cups salad dressing or
   mayonnaise
$\frac{3}{4}$ cup milk
3 tablespoons yellow mustard
$\frac{1}{4}$ teaspoon pepper

Cook whole unpeeled potatoes in water to cover till fork tender, adding 2 teaspoons salt to cooking water. Cool to room temperature.

While potatoes are cooking, hard-boil the eggs, then cool quickly in ice water to avoid green edge on yolks.

Peel cooled potatoes, cut into 1-inch pieces, and place in large bowl. Peel and chop eggs and add to bowl with potatoes. Add green pepper, celery, and onion.

In separate bowl, whisk together salad dressing, milk, and mustard. Season potato mixture with remaining 1$\frac{1}{4}$ teaspoons of salt and the pepper. Add dressing and mix well. Refrigerate for at least 1 hour before serving to allow flavors to blend. Serves 10.

Theresa R. Powers (St. Clair Shores, Michigan)

 QVC is the leader in electronic retailing reaching approximately 96% of all U.S. cable homes and nearly 16.2 million satellite homes.

Garlic-Roasted Potato Salad with Balsamic/Bacon Vinaigrette

3 pounds baby red potatoes, halved
1 cup olive oil, divided
6 ounces garlic, minced, divided
Seafood seasoning
1/2 pound bacon, crisped and roughly chopped, fat reserved and kept warm

1 large red onion, 1/2 inch dice
1 large bell pepper, 1/2 inch dice
1 bunch parsley, minced
5 hard-boiled eggs, roughly chopped
1/4 cup balsamic vinegar
Salt and pepper to taste

Preheat oven to 350°. Toss potatoes with half the olive oil, half the garlic, and sprinkle with seafood seasoning. Roast on well-oiled cookie sheets until cooked through and golden brown. Let cool until warm enough to handle.

Combine remaining ingredients (including reserved bacon fat) with roasted potatoes. Season with salt and pepper to taste. Let mixture marinate at room temperature for 20 minutes. Taste. If too dry, toss in extra oil and vinegar. Adjust seasoning, if necessary. Serve warm or at room temperature.

Noah Staitman (Van Nuys, California)

Sassy Spinach Salad

SALAD INGREDIENTS:

2 bunches fresh spinach
2 slices bacon, cooked, chopped
2 hard-boiled eggs, sliced
1 large cucumber, peeled and
  very thinly sliced
1/2 cup walnuts or pecans

2 oranges or grapefruits, peeled
  and sliced
1/2 cup grated cheese, any type
1/2 cup garbanzo beans
1/2 cup black olives
Salt and pepper

On a large platter, place washed spinach, torn into bite-size pieces. Sprinkle or arrange remaining salad ingredients on top of spinach. Salt and pepper to taste.

DRESSING:

1 package dry salad dressing
  mix, your favorite flavor
1/3 cup canola oil
1/3 cup non-fat yogurt
1/3 cup vinegar

1/3 cup water
1 clove crushed garlic
1/4 teaspoon hot sauce
1 teaspoon sugar

Combine Dressing ingredients and mix in blender. Pour Dressing over the spinach salad about 10 minutes before serving. Toss right before you serve.

Mary McKee (Colorado Springs, Colorado)

Almost all video footage, meaning any part of the show that isn't live, is edited in Post Production where they also produce demonstration tapes for products that are difficult to demonstrate in the studio, such as snow shovels, gas grills, or toy airplanes. QVC promotions, which are like commercials for upcoming shows that air only on QVC, are also edited here.

Dress Yourself Spinach Salad

1 pound fresh spinach
1 pound bacon, fried crisp,
  crumbled
1 handful fresh bean sprouts
1 cup fresh, sliced mushrooms

1 small onion, chopped
7 eggs, hard-boiled and chopped
1 can water chestnuts, sliced or
  chopped

Combine all ingredients. Refrigerate while making Homemade French Dressing.

HOMEMADE FRENCH DRESSING:
$1/2$ cup vegetable oil
$3/4$ cup sugar
$1/3$ cup catsup
$1/4$ cup vinegar

1 teaspoon Worcestershire sauce
1 medium onion, finely chopped
1 teaspoon salt

Mix all ingredients well. Serve Dressing along side of salad; let each individual dress their own.

Doris Drake (South Bend, Indiana)

Post Audio and Dubbing is where all the audio work is completed. In this department, program hosts' and announcers' voices are recorded for promotions that run on air. Copies of videotapes are also made in this department.

"Dark Lettuce" Salad

I could never get my children to eat spinach until I started making this. I told them it was dark lettuce! Today, they ask for it by name, "Hey, Mom, can you make the dark lettuce salad?"

DRESSING:

2 tablespoons sugar
½ teaspoon thyme
½ teaspoon salad seasoning
½ teaspoon garlic powder

½ cup mayonnaise
2 tablespoons oil
1 tablespoon vinegar

Whisk all dressing ingredients together until smooth, preferably one day before you plan on serving salad. Cover and refrigerate. You may want to double these ingredients if serving on individual plates.

1 bag spinach, washed, dried, and chilled
3 hard-cooked eggs, chopped
1 small red onion, sliced into very thin rings

6–8 slices bacon, cooked crisp, crumbled
1 cup thinly sliced mushrooms

Put salad ingredients together in large bowl and toss with Dressing, or divide spinach onto individual salad plates and top decoratively with remainder of ingredients by "dividing" the plate into four sections (visually) and placing each topping separately at 12, 3, 6, and 9 o'clock, as if on a watch dial. Pass Dressing for each person to add to their own salad. This is a wonderful first course with slices of dark pumpernickel or rye bread.

Janet Venditti (Pittsburgh, Pennsylvania)

Editors' Extra: This Dressing is so good, you can use it on any green salad.

 Of all the orders placed with QVC, more than 90% are shipped within 48 hours from distribution centers that have a combined floor space of 2.7 million square feet (the size of 60 football fields).

Layered Salad Deluxe

Unfortunately, I can't claim this recipe as my own. My mother is the entertainer in the family. She's the one I go to for the "showstopper" on the table.

1 pound fresh spinach, torn
1 red onion, sliced in rings
6 hard-cooked eggs, sliced
½ cup chopped celery
1 pound bacon, cooked and
  crumbled (reserve some for top)
1 (8-ounce) can water chestnuts,
  drained
1 (10-ounce) package frozen peas,
  thawed

1 cup salad dressing (sweet
  mayonnaise-type)
½ cup sour cream
½ (0.4-ounce) package buttermilk
  salad dressing mix
6 ounces shredded Cheddar cheese,
  for topping

Layer first 7 ingredients in large, tall, glass bowl. Combine remaining ingredients, except reserved bacon and Cheddar cheese. Spread dressing on top of salad; seal to edge of bowl. Cover tightly and refrigerate overnight. Toss gently and top with reserved bacon and Cheddar cheese.

Kim Parrish, QVC Host (West Chester, Pennsylvania)

Kim Parrish loves being in the kitchen with her mom, Kathryn, who is always stirring up something delicious!

Nutty Sesame Salad

This is my version of a recipe given to my mom by a neighbor who got it from a chef in Key West, Florida. I experimented with a few changes and we really like the results.

DRESSING:

6 tablespoons vinegar
6 tablespoons sugar
½ cup sesame oil

½ teaspoon salt
Seasoning from ramen noodle soup
  package

Place vinegar, sugar, sesame oil, salt and seasoning packet in a bottle; shake well and refrigerate.

SALAD:

1 pound Chinese cabbage, cut
  into bite-size pieces
1 pound bok choy (using white
  center and leaves), cut into
  bite-size pieces

1 can sliced water chestnuts,
  drained
1 bunch green onions, chopped
1 green bell pepper, chopped

In a large bowl, place Chinese cabbage, bok choy, water chestnuts, green onions, and bell pepper; toss.

TOPPING:

1 ounce sesame seeds
1 cup cashew halves

Noodles from ramen noodle soup
  package

Spray a skillet with cooking spray. On medium heat, sauté sesame seeds, cashew halves, and broken pieces of the soup noodles till golden. Set aside till cooled.

Sprinkle cooled Topping onto Salad and toss. Remove Dressing from refrigerator and shake till sugar is dissolved. Pour over Salad and Topping; toss well. Salad will last for several days; just toss before serving. Keep refrigerated.

Sonya Bynum (Florahome, Florida)

 As of October 2001, QVC reaches over 138.3 million cable and satellite homes throughout the world.

Crispy Green Maple Salad

DRESSING:

¼ cup rice wine vinegar
½ cup canola oil
½ cup maple syrup

½ teaspoon dry mustard
1 shallot, minced
Salt and pepper to taste

Mix all ingredients together in a jar.

½ pound bacon, fried
2 medium Vidalia onions, thinly
   sliced
1 small head Boston lettuce
½ bag baby spinach

¾ cup halved pecans
¼ pound fresh Romano cheese,
   thinly sliced with vegetable
   peeler

Fry bacon till crisp; remove and cut into thirds. Caramelize onion slices in bacon fat. Assemble lettuce and spinach in large bowl. Top with pecans, bacon strips, cheese strips, and caramelized onion slices. Pour Dressing over all.

Ardis R. Miller (Weymouth, Massachusetts)

Calypso Cornbread Salad

1 (8-inch) pan baked cornbread,
   crumbled
1 (14-ounce) can kidney beans or
   chili beans, drained
1 cup chopped tomatoes
1 pound bacon, crisp-cooked,
   crumbled

1 cup chopped red or green bell
   pepper
1 bunch green onions, chopped
   (or 1 medium onion)
1½ cups mayonnaise
½ cup pickle relish and juice

Place all ingredients, except mayonnaise and pickle relish, in medium-size bowl. Mix mayonnaise and relish; pour over salad ingredients and toss to coat. Refrigerate.

Jeroline Stockdale (La Mesa, California)

Creamy Bean Salad

2 (10-ounce) packages frozen
  French-style green beans
1 small onion, chopped
1 cup sour cream

½ cup mayonnaise
1 tablespoon vinegar
Salt and pepper

Cook green beans in salted water. DO NOT drain. Let cool in refrigerator.

In a separate bowl, mix onion, sour cream, mayonnaise, and vinegar. Add salt and pepper to taste. Drain beans and place in a 1-quart casserole dish and pour sour cream mixture over beans. Chill until ready to serve. Serves 6.

Liz Williams (Sebring, Ohio)

June's Summer Salad

3 (15-ounce) cans three bean
  salad, drained
1 (16-ounce) can garbanzos
  (chick peas), drained
1 cup chopped celery
1 cucumber, peeled, seeded, and
  chopped

1 yellow pepper, chopped
1 orange pepper, chopped
½ cup chopped onion
½ cup sliced black olives

Mix all the ingredients except black olives in a large bowl with cover.

DRESSING:
1 cup oil
1½ cups vinegar
2 cups sugar

2 teaspoons salt
½ teaspoon black pepper

In a medium bowl, mix oil, vinegar, sugar, salt, and black pepper until sugar is dissolved. Pour over bean mixture, mixing well. Place black olives on top. Cover and refrigerate overnight.

June Denor (Kewaskum, Wisconsin)

Springtime Salad

1 can tiny peas, well drained
1 can French-cut string beans, well drained
1 small jar pimento, drained

1 small green pepper, diced
1 small onion, diced
4 stalks celery, diced

Mix together in bowl.

DRESSING:
½ cup salad oil
1 tablespoon water
1 teaspoon salt

½ cup vinegar
½ cup sugar
Dash paprika

Mix Dressing ingredients separately, then pour over drained vegetables. Marinate overnight in refrigerator, covered. One hour before serving, drain off excess dressing.

Can be increased by adding 1 more can of string beans, but DO NOT increase marinating sauce.

Jean Michael (Coopersburg, Pennsylvania)

Pea-Cheesy Salad

Can be made the night before or the morning of serving.

3 (16-ounce) cans peas, drained
4 stalks celery, chopped
½ medium red onion, finely chopped
1 (4-ounce) can chopped black olives, drained

1 cup sweet relish
¼ cup mayonnaise or salad dressing
6 hard-boiled eggs, chopped
12 slices American cheese
Salt and pepper to taste

In bowl, add peas, celery, onion, olives, relish, and mayonnaise. Stir carefully so as not to mash peas. Add eggs. Stack cheese in layers of 4 (to give them thickness), then cut them into cubes. Stir into mixture. You may need to add more mayonnaise to your desired taste. Salt and pepper to taste. Serve chilled.

Variations: Add finely chopped carrots or a can of rinsed and drained kidney beans.

Tina Flohr (Lake Stevens, Washington)

Classic Cauliflower Salad

Thanks to my cousin, I have been enjoying this wonderful recipe for many years. Everybody loves it.

1 head lettuce, cut up
1 head cauliflower, cut up
1 red onion, thinly sliced

1 pound bacon, fried crisp, drained, and crumbled

Layer lettuce, cauliflower, onion, and bacon in large bowl.

SALAD DRESSING:
1 cup salad dressing
⅓ cup Parmesan cheese

¼ cup sugar
Salt and pepper to taste

Mix salad dressing, Parmesan, sugar, salt and pepper and put on top of salad. Refrigerate for several hours. Toss before serving.

Diana Holt (Breckenridge, Missouri)

Butter Cream Apple Salad

When I first made this salad in 1975, my five-year-old daughter said, "Well, it doesn't look like much, but it surely tastes like a whole lot more."

⅓ cup self-rising or plain flour
¾ cup sugar
½ pint whipping cream (not whipped topping)
1 large can crushed pineapple, drained

½ stick margarine
4–5 medium sweet apples, peeled and chopped
1 cup chopped pecans
Maraschino cherries

Sift flour and sugar into top of double boiler; gradually stir in whipping cream, then crushed pineapple. Stir and cook over boiling water for 3 minutes. Add margarine, stir, and set aside.

In casserole dish, mix the apples and pecans; pour pineapple mixture on top, stirring lightly. Decorate top with cherries. Refrigerate. Can be made the day before.

Lynne Harris (Brookings, South Dakota)

Anaheim Orange Fluff Salad

Great tasting! Compliments almost any dinner, especially holiday venues.

1 small package orange gelatin
1 small package vanilla pudding
  (not instant)
1 small package tapioca pudding
  (not instant)

2 cups water
1 small can mandarin oranges,
  drained
1 medium container whipped
  topping

Put gelatin and puddings in a pot. Add 2 cups of water; cook until mixture begins to boil and thicken. Remove from heat. Let mixture set and cool down. Then add oranges and whipped topping to mixture. Blend thoroughly and refrigerate. Enjoy!

Rosalie McDonald (Anaheim Hills, California)

Tomato Aspic

Makes a lovely, refreshing change of pace, and the taste will surprise everyone.

1 (3-ounce) package lemon
  gelatin (sugar-free, if desired)
1¼ cups hot water
1 (8-ounce) can vegetable
  cocktail juice
1 tablespoon vinegar
Dash salt and pepper

⅓ cup chopped celery
⅓ cup sliced black olives
⅓ cup chopped pecans
1 teaspoon Worcestershire sauce
Leaf lettuce, parsley, pimento-
  stuffed olives for garnish

Mix gelatin, water, vegetable juice, vinegar, and salt and pepper. Chill in bowl until slightly thickened. Add celery, olives, pecans, and Worcestershire sauce. Pour into mold and refrigerate.

When set, unmold onto plate lined with leaf lettuce; top with fresh parsley and chopped, pimento-stuffed olives.

Judy Wilson (Seneca Falls, New York)

 QVC's worldwide corporate headquarters, more commonly known as Studio Park, sits on 84 acres of land in West Chester, Pennsylvania, and the building is roughly the size of 15 football fields.

Berry Easy Gelatin Salad

Only takes three minutes to prepare . . . what a blessing!

2 small packages raspberry or
  strawberry gelatin
2 cups of boiling water
2 cups applesauce

2 (10-ounce) containers frozen
  raspberries, or 1 bag frozen
  raspberries (or strawberries)

In your actual serving bowl, add the boiling water to gelatin. Stir till gelatin is dissolved. Blend in, by hand, the applesauce, then the frozen berries. Refrigerate till firm. Garnish with whipped cream, if desired.

Anne Marie Scobie (Walton, New York)

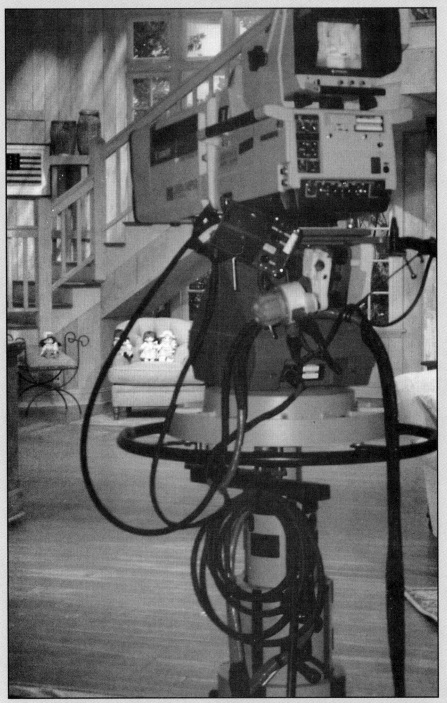

These robotic cameras do most of the camera work, but real people operate them from the Control Room. Crews move cables, walls, tables, etc., to get the cameras into the right position. Earphones keep the cast and crew in constant touch with the Control Room. Hand-held cameras are used for close-up shots of the products.

Texas Bean Bake

I am the wife of a retired USAF fighter pilot. We have had many potluck dinners from this lifestyle, and this recipe is an all-time favorite.

1 (28-ounce) can pork and beans
1 can lima beans, drained
1 can kidney beans, drained

½ pound bacon
1 pound ground beef
1 onion, chopped

Mix beans in large casserole dish. Cut bacon into pieces and fry; drain fat. Brown hamburger and onion. Add bacon and beef mixture to beans.

SAUCE:
1 cup ketchup
1 tablespoon prepared mustard
½ cup brown sugar
2 tablespoons vinegar

¼ cup molasses
Several dashes Worcestershire
   sauce

Mix Sauce ingredients well and add to the beans. Bake at 350° for 1 hour.

Julie Stine (Del Rio, Texas)

Bari's Baked Beans

½–1 pound bacon
⅔ cup dark brown sugar
1 cup chili sauce
½ bunch scallions, sliced (green
   and white part)
1 bell pepper, thinly sliced or
   diced

1 can French-style green beans,
   drained
1 can pork and beans, drained
1 can red kidney beans, drained
2 cans chili with beans

Dice bacon and sauté in 4-quart roaster until crisp but not charred. Drain. Add brown sugar and melt on medium heat. Add chili sauce, scallions, and bell pepper. Stir. Add canned beans and chili. Cook on high for 15 minutes, then simmer for at least 2 hours (or bake in oven for 1 hour at 350°). Stir occasionally; do not let bottom burn. Freezes well. Tastes even better if prepared the day before and reheated.

Bari G. Hill (Mesa, Arizona)

Perry County Green Beans

3 (9-ounce) packages frozen
  French-style green beans
3 tablespoons butter
1 (10¾-ounce) can cream of
  mushroom soup
1 (3-ounce) package cream
  cheese, softened
1 teaspoon dried onion flakes

1 (8-ounce) can sliced water
  chestnuts, drained
¼ teaspoon garlic salt
¼ teaspoon pepper
1½ cups shredded Cheddar cheese
1 (2¼-ounce) package slivered
  almonds
Paprika

Cook green beans according to package directions; drain. Melt butter in Dutch oven; add soup and cream cheese. Cook over low heat, stirring constantly, until cream cheese is melted and mixture is smooth. Remove from heat. Stir in green beans, dried onion flakes, water chestnuts, garlic salt, pepper, and shredded cheese.

Spoon into lightly greased 1¾-quart casserole dish. Top with almonds and sprinkle with paprika. Bake, uncovered, at 375° for 45 minutes. Serves 8.

Lyn Wallace (Elliottsburg, Pennsylvania)

Marion's Green Bean Casserole

My mom always made this at Thanksgiving, Christmas, and Easter. She is now gone, and I have carried on the tradition with my family.

1 (16-ounce) package frozen
  green beans
4 tablespoons butter, divided
2 tablespoons flour
1 teaspoon sugar
1 teaspoon salt

¼ teaspoon pepper
1 tablespoon chopped onion
1 cup sour cream
½ pound sharp Cheddar cheese,
  grated
2 cups crushed cornflakes

Cook beans till tender; drain and set aside. Melt half the butter in saucepan. Blend in flour, sugar, salt, pepper, and onion. Stir in sour cream gradually until thickened. Fold in beans until coated. Pour into greased casserole dish. Spread grated cheese over top. Melt remaining butter and combine with crushed cornflakes (zip-lock bag works great). Spread crushed cornflakes evenly over top of cheese. Bake at 350° for 30–45 minutes.

Lisa Genthner Gunn (Waldoboro, Maine)

Moosie's Potato Surprise Patties

My Grandma Yetta used to make her own version of potato knishes that were fried in pure chicken fat. You could smell them before you got to her front porch. They were a taste sensation. I kept trying to duplicate that amazing woman's recipe, updating it healthier (baking, not frying). The addition of the cauliflower taste is so delicious. When they are baking, the entire house smells scrumptious. Everyone who has tried these always says, "You should enter them in a cooking contest." Thank you, QVC, for the opportunity. Enjoy!

10 medium potatoes, cut and
  peeled
1 stick butter or margarine
Salt and pepper to taste
1 (12-ounce) bag frozen chopped
  onions
1 (16-ounce) bag frozen
  cauliflower

1/4 cup olive oil, plus 2–3
  tablespoons more (for coating),
  divided
1 large egg, beaten
2 tablespoons bread crumbs

Boil and mash potatoes. Add butter or margarine, salt and pepper. In 12-inch frying pan, sauté the onions and cauliflower in 1/4 cup oil until they are soft enough to be mashed and added to the mashed potatoes. Add egg and bread crumbs; mix well.

Coat 2 aluminum cookie sheets with oil. Preheat oven to 400°. Using a tablespoon, spoon out mixture and flatten till patties are approximately 1/4 inch thick. Depending on the size, you should get 10–12 patties on each cookie sheet. Bake 20–25 minutes, until golden brown. Flip and bake another 15–20 minutes. Serve with applesauce, sour cream, or plain yogurt.

Doreen T. "Moosie" Gillardi (Hollywood, Florida)

There are over 20 QVC hosts, each working 3- to 4-hour shifts on air 4–5 days a week. They come from a variety of backgrounds, ranging from broadcast news to sales and restaurant management. Some have been with QVC since the beginning, others were discovered through the National Host Search held in cities throughout the country. Hosts are hired as "trainees" and spend six months in an intensive training program.

Potato Frittata

2 tablespoons oil
2 pounds boiled potatoes, peeled,
   sliced
1 large onion, chopped

5 eggs
2 tablespoons Parmesan cheese
Salt and pepper

In a large skillet, heat oil and add sliced potatoes and onion. Cook over medium heat until tender and brown. Keep turning.

Meanwhile, beat eggs in a bowl. Add cheese, salt and pepper. After potatoes are browned, add egg mixture over potatoes and lower heat. Cook gently, pushing in sides of egg mixture with a spatula. Let it set. Raise heat to brown underside. Invert frittata onto platter and slide back into skillet to brown the other side. Enjoy!

Elizabeth Rock (Baltimore, Maryland)

Nanny's Roasted Potato Balls

This recipe is everybody's favorite. The recipe originated from my Pennsylvania Dutch grandmother. I called her Nanny. She made this recipe every holiday. I felt very special when she allowed me to help in the preparation of this dish. Nanny has since passed on, but every holiday I feel she's right in the kitchen helping me prepare the holiday meal.

1½ cups fresh bread crumbs
½ medium onion, finely chopped
2 stalks celery, finely chopped
2 tablespoons chopped fresh
   parsley
½–1 cup milk (enough to
   moisten)

2 eggs, beaten
2½ cups mashed potatoes (plain)
Salt and pepper to taste
1 stick plus 4 tablespoons butter,
   melted, divided

Use a blender or food processor to make soft bread crumbs. Mix all of the above together except 4 tablespoons butter. Use an ice cream scoop to form mixture into balls. Place balls side-by-side in a buttered casserole dish. Drizzle the 4 tablespoons of melted butter over formed balls. Bake, uncovered, for 20 minutes, or until lightly browned in a pre-heated 350° oven. During last 2–3 minutes, run under broiler. Serves 4–6.

Laura DiFrancesco (Broomall, Pennsylvania)

Make-Ahead Mashed Potatoes

Once you try this recipe, you'll never make regular mashed potatoes again! Who couldn't use some extra time when preparing a special dinner? This recipe gives you a head start. Or . . . use it throughout the week.

5 pounds potatoes
1 (8-ounce) package cream cheese
1 cup sour cream
2 teaspoons onion powder

1 stick butter
Salt and white or black pepper to taste

Boil potatoes and then mash until smooth with some of the potato water (at least 1 cup). Add remaining ingredients while potatoes are still hot, and beat until fluffy. (I use a hand mixer—no lumps!) Serve immediately or cool, cover, and place in the refrigerator. Reheat in the microwave or oven.

Watching your weight? Try this with non-fat sour cream and cream cheese and butter substitute. This will keep for up to 2 weeks in the refrigerator. It also freezes well. Serves 15.

Annette Buckmaster (Sacramento, California)

Truly Scrumptious Potatoes

I have made this for holiday dinners and special occasions. My family and friends beg for this dish. My nephew will eat it cold the next morning.

5 medium-size potatoes
¼ pound butter (no substitute)
1 pound bacon, fried crisp, chopped
2 cups cubed (½ inch) Cheddar cheese

4–5 green onions, chopped
¾–1¼ cups sour cream
½ teaspoon salt
¼ teaspoon pepper

Peel and boil potatoes; drain. Mash with butter; add chopped bacon, cubed cheese, and chopped green onions. With mixer going, add sour cream until desired consistency. Add salt and pepper.

Merle Anderson (Seattle, Washington)

Jean and Theresa's
Praline Sweet Potatoes

My friends, Jean and Theresa, know how to make sweet potatoes extra delicious!

SWEET POTATOES:

3 cups mashed sweet potatoes
1 cup sugar
1/2 teaspoon salt
2 eggs, beaten

1/2 stick margarine, melted
1/2 cup evaporated milk
1/2 teaspoon vanilla

Combine all ingredients and pour in greased 8x8-inch (or similar) baking dish.

TOPPING:

1/3 cup flour
1/3 cup margarine, melted

1 cup brown sugar
1 cup finely chopped pecans

Combine ingredients and sprinkle on top of potatoes. Bake at 350° for 40 minutes.

Dave King, QVC Host (West Chester, Pennsylvania)

Proud daddy, Dave King, gives big hugs to handsome sons, Dylan and Devin. Prior to joining QVC, Dave was a successful actor, appearing in more than 100 commercials and several hit television series. He also has appeared in films such as *Single White Female, Guarding Tess,* and New York theater productions of *Jesus Christ Superstar* and *Dreamgirls.* Most recently, Dave played the role of Billy Cooper, Chief of Detectives on the NBC soap opera "Another World." Before acting, Dave was in sales and management, and before that he taught music and coached football.

Sweet Corn & Caramelized Onion Pudding

This is my most requested recipe. No celebration is complete without this delectable corn pudding. Wonderful with turkey at Thanksgiving, ham at Easter, and roast beef at Christmas. Its creamy custard-like richness and soufflé-like texture are highlighted with sweet corn, golden caramelized onions, and fragrant fresh herbs. It makes the perfect accompaniment to a wide variety of entrées.

½ cup (1 stick) unsalted butter
2 large sweet onions, thinly
   sliced
6 large eggs, room temperature
1 cup half-and-half
1 cup heavy whipping cream
¼ cup grated Parmesan cheese
¼ cup all-purpose flour
3 tablespoons sugar

2 teaspoons baking powder
1½ teaspoons salt
½ teaspoon white pepper
2½ cups fresh sweet corn kernels
   (or canned sweet corn), well
   drained
2 tablespoons slivered fresh basil
   or sage leaves

Grease 8 ramekins or custard cups (or 2-quart casserole dish) and set aside. In medium skillet, melt butter over medium-high heat. Cook onions until golden and caramelized, about 25 minutes, stirring frequently. Set aside.

Preheat oven to 350°. In large bowl, beat eggs thoroughly. Stir in half-and-half, cream and Parmesan. Gradually stir in combined flour, sugar, baking powder, salt and pepper. Fold in corn, basil (or sage), and caramelized onions. Divide mixture among prepared ramekins and place on baking sheet. Lightly sprinkle tops with additional Parmesan, if desired. Bake 15–20 minutes, until puffed and golden brown. Makes 8 servings.

Edwina Gadsby (Great Falls, Montana)

 On October 3, 2001, 90,000 pairs of shoes were sold through QVC's FFANY Shoes on Sale broadcast.

Corn Fritter Puffs

This is my grandson's favorite vegetable. When any are left over, he is often caught eating cold fritters for breakfast.

1 cup flour	2 eggs, well beaten
2 tablespoons sugar	1/2 cup milk
1/2 teaspoon salt	1 (11-ounce) can vac-pack corn,
2 teaspoons baking powder	drained

Sift flour, measure, and sift with sugar and salt. Add baking powder. Combine eggs and milk and add to dry ingredients. Mix until smooth. Add corn. Drop by teaspoons into hot, deep fat and fry until golden brown. You may have to turn them over during frying. Can be eaten plain or with syrup.

Eula Jean Udovich (Keyser, West Virginia)

Mississippi Squash Boats

1/2 pound pork sausage	1/4 teaspoon dill weed
6 fresh yellow squash	1/4 teaspoon freshly ground pepper
3 tablespoons water	1 tomato, chopped
1/4 cup chopped white onion	1/2 cup freshly ground Parmesan
2 tablespoons butter	cheese, divided
1/2 teaspoon onion salt	

Brown sausage, drain, and set aside.

Slice squash lengthwise. Microwave in a covered dish with 3 tablespoons water on HIGH for 6 minutes. Remove, cool, and drain. Scoop out squash pulp and set aside.

Sauté onion in butter until tender. Mix together onions, onion salt, dill weed, black pepper, squash pulp, sausage, chopped tomato, and 1/4 cup Parmesan cheese. Fill squash boats and sprinkle with remaining cheese. Place in covered dish and bake for 30 minutes in a preheated 300° oven. Serves 6.

Kay Candelora (Madison, Mississippi)

Zippy Squash Casserole

This is my favorite stand-by recipe for potlucks or company. Everybody loves it and asks for the recipe.

2 pounds frozen crookneck squash, cut in ½-inch slices

2 tablespoons dehydrated minced onion

2 (10-ounce) cans tomatoes with green chiles, well drained

2 cups grated Cheddar cheese

¾ cup (1½ sticks) butter, divided

Salt and pepper to taste

1½ cups round snack cracker crumbs

Preheat oven to 350°. Butter or spray a 2-quart baking dish. Cook squash and onion in salted water, enough to cover, for 7–8 minutes, until tender. Drain thoroughly. Add tomatoes and green chiles, cheese, ½ cup butter, salt and pepper. Stir to blend. Pour into prepared baking dish. Sprinkle crumbs evenly over mixture. Pour remaining ¼ cup melted butter over crumbs. Bake until bubbly, about 30 minutes. This dish freezes very well.

Linda Roberds (Dothan, Alabama)

Spaghetti Squash à la Jasper

1 (2-pound) spaghetti squash

4 cloves garlic, sliced

2 shallots, minced

1 tablespoon extra virgin olive oil

6–8 sun-dried tomatoes with oil, sliced

6–8 pitted, quartered Calamata olives

¼ cup crumbled feta cheese

Salt and pepper to taste

Fresh parsley, minced (optional garnish)

Prepare spaghetti squash either by steam, microwave, or baking method (halve, put cut-side-down on baking sheet, bake 1 hour at 350°). Cool and shred into spaghetti. Sauté sliced garlic and minced shallots in olive oil until tender, 2–3 minutes. Add spaghetti squash and remaining ingredients, adding more olive oil to taste. Season with salt and pepper. Serve at room temperature, topping with more crumbled feta and minced fresh parsley. Serves 2–4.

Alexandria Goff (Milford, New Hampshire)

Spaghetti Squash with Pepperoni and Spinach

2½ pounds spaghetti squash
1 medium onion, chopped
4 tablespoons olive oil, divided
2–3 garlic cloves, pressed
1 stick pepperoni, sliced and
　halved
¼ cup unsalted butter

Salt and pepper to taste
1 (6-ounce) bag pre-washed
　spinach
⅓ cup heavy cream
½ cup mayonnaise
⅓ cup grated Parmesan cheese

Slice spaghetti squash in half, lengthwise, and clean out seeds. Place cut-side-down on oiled baking sheet and bake 40–60 minutes in a 350° oven, until fork tender.

Scoop out flesh into bowl and separate into spaghetti-like strands; set aside. Discard the skin.

In a large chicken fryer, sauté the onion in olive oil over medium-high heat until tender, about 10 minutes. Add garlic and pepperoni and sauté another 5 minutes, stirring occasionally. Add the butter, salt and pepper. Stir until the butter has melted. Add the spinach and sauté until wilted. Add the spaghetti squash, cream, mayonnaise, and Parmesan cheese, stirring until combined and heated through.

Cynthia J. Miehle (McDonough, Georgia)

Besides the kitchen, dining room, living room, bedrooms, office, garage and sun-room sets that make up QVC's familiar home, there are several annexes where new sets are constructed all the time. QVC is a working studio, no doubt about that . . . they're always working to make it all work!

Creamy Zucchini Casserole

A delicious dish—this is a summertime favorite of ours. It's so good made with the fresh-picked zucchini from our garden.

6 cups peeled and cubed zucchini	**1 cup sour cream**
⅓ cup chopped onion	**1 small bag stuffing mix or croutons**
1 cup shredded carrots	**2–4 tablespoons butter, melted**
2 cans cream of chicken soup	

Cook zucchini and onion for 5 minutes in boiling water. Drain and set aside.

In a large bowl, combine carrots, soup, and sour cream. Stir in cooked zucchini and onion. Pour into a 9x13-inch casserole dish.

In a separate bowl, mix stuffing with the melted butter (use as much of each as desired) and sprinkle on top of casserole. Bake, uncovered, at 350° for 30 minutes.

Patty Walker (Cohoes, New York)

Zucchini Puffs

Kris, our grandson, was visiting one summer. Zucchini was very abundant. Kris did not like zucchini, but he liked garlic-flavored food. Not mentioning that these "little fritters" were made of zucchini, I called them "Puffs." Years later he still requests "Puffs" every time he comes to visit.

1 medium zucchini, finely chopped	**Dash of pepper**
1 egg, beaten	**½ teaspoon garlic powder**
⅓ cup biscuit mix	**½ teaspoon onion powder**
½ teaspoon salt	**3 tablespoons vegetable oil**

Mix all ingredients, except vegetable oil, and form into patties. Heat oil in skillet and drop mixture into pan by spoonfuls, frying till golden brown.

Joanne B. Bowman (Chambersburg, Pennsylvania)

Micro-Magic Zucchini Mix

3 (1–1½ inch thick) zucchini,
   sliced ¼ inch thick
2 medium onions, thinly sliced
2 tablespoons olive oil
1 teaspoon oregano
½ teaspoon marjoram

⅛ teaspoon garlic powder
½ teaspoon salt
1 (14½-ounce) can diced
   tomatoes, drained
Parmesan cheese

In a 2-quart casserole dish, covered, microwave all except diced tomatoes and cheese for 6–7 minutes on HIGH. Add tomatoes; mix and cook for 2–3 minutes. When done, sprinkle with Parmesan cheese.

Camilla C. Ryan (Baltimore, Maryland)

Grill Thrilled Vegetables

This was used for a Mother's Day cookout. I thought it would be a light way to serve vegetables. It was a big hit even with my husband, who saw it before it was cooked and turned up his nose, but couldn't get enough after it was done.

1 zucchini, sliced
1 summer squash, sliced
1 sweet onion, sliced
1 red pepper, sliced

½ cup olive oil
2 teaspoons lemon pepper
1 teaspoon kosher salt
2 teaspoons minced garlic

Mix sliced vegetables in large bowl. Stir in olive oil, lemon pepper, salt, and garlic. Grill on medium-high in vented grill rack for 7–10 minutes. Stir as needed. The vegetables will be lightly browned and still slightly crisp.

   Serve with grilled chicken breast and microwaved wild rice. This is a great summer dish with no kitchen clean-up! (Pictured on cover.)

Susan B. Taylor (Jacksonville, Florida)

 Approximately 100,000 products are available on QVC.com.

McAbee Goop

My grandmother invented this recipe—it reminds all of us of this truly amazing woman who lived her life to care for and love her family first. Makes a lot, but the more you reheat it, the better it gets! Also freezes well.

1 green pepper	**1½ cups seasoned bread crumbs,**
1 red or yellow pepper	**divided**
1 large onion	**½ cup Parmesan cheese**
6–8 small zucchini	**12 ounces shredded Cheddar**
2 tablespoons oil, margarine, or	**cheese**
butter, divided	**12 ounces shredded mozzarella**
2 cans pasta-ready 3-cheese	
tomatoes	

Coarsely chop peppers and onion. Peel zucchini and take out most of the seeds. Cut into roughly 1-inch square pieces. In 1 tablespoon of the oil, margarine, or butter, sauté peppers and onions until softened and onions are translucent. Set aside in large bowl.

Sauté zucchini in remaining butter until fork-tender. You may need to do this in 2 batches. Add to onions and peppers. Add tomatoes to bowl and mix well. Spray 9x13-inch pan with cooking spray. Spread ⅓ of vegetables on bottom of pan. Sprinkle ½ cup bread crumbs and Parmesan over top. For next layer, repeat with Cheddar instead of Parmesan. Repeat for final layer using mozzarella. Bake at 350° until cheese has melted.

Mary Lee McAbee Miller (Easton, Pennsylvania)

Spicy Spinach Crustless Quiche

This is so good, even the men will eat quiche!

12 eggs
1/2 cup flour
1 teaspoon baking powder
1 teaspoon salt
1 (10-ounce) package frozen
   spinach, thawed
1/2 cup butter, melted
1 (4-ounce) can chopped green
   chiles

1 (4-ounce) can jalapeño peppers,
   seeded, chopped, drained
1 pint small curd cottage cheese
1/2 pound shredded Cheddar
   cheese
1/2 pound shredded Monterey Jack
   cheese

Preheat oven to 400°. Beat eggs, flour, baking powder, and salt in large bowl. Squeeze spinach dry; add to egg mixture along with butter, chiles, jalapeños, and cheeses. Stir lightly until blended. Pour mixture into buttered 9x13-inch glass baking dish.

Bake at 400° for 15 minutes. Reduce heat to 350° and continue baking an additional 35–40 minutes to set. Cut into small squares to serve for hors d'oeuvres.

Alicia Taschner (Douglassville, Pennsylvania)

Always-a-Hit Spinach Squares

Always a hit at parties and with family and friends!

1/2 stick butter
3 eggs
1 cup flour
1 cup milk
1 teaspoon baking powder
1 (8-ounce) package mild Cheddar
   cheese

1 (8-ounce) package Monterey Jack
   cheese
2 packages frozen chopped
   spinach, cooked and drained
1 tablespoon dried onion
1 teaspoon seasoned salt

Preheat oven to 350°. Put butter in a 9x12-inch pan and melt in oven; remove. In a large bowl, beat eggs well. Add flour, milk, and baking powder; mix well. Chop cheeses in chunks; drain spinach, and add these to flour mixture. Mix well. Add dried onion. Spoon into baking pan, level off, and sprinkle with seasoned salt. Bake at 350° for 35 minutes. Remove and let cool; cut into squares. Freezes well. To defrost, heat at 350° for 10 minutes. Makes about 30 squares.

Paula Hiltz (Maynard, Massachusetts)

Seafood Spinach Madeline

*I came across this recipe in my momma's kitchen accidentally one day while look-
ing at some recipe cards. She served it often and now so do I! It is very popular at
holiday time. Try it; you will love it!*

4 boxes chopped frozen spinach
4 tablespoons chopped green
  onion
½ cup butter, melted
4 tablespoons flour
½ cup evaporated milk
2 teaspoons Worcestershire sauce

1 (8-ounce) package processed
  cheese, hot or mild
½ teaspoon garlic
½ teaspoon pepper
2 pounds peeled shrimp or
  crawfish tails

Cook spinach according to package directions, reserving 1 cup of
liquid. Set aside. Sauté onion in butter over low heat until tender.
Add flour, stir until smooth. Cook 1 minute, stirring constantly.
Gradually add reserved liquid and milk; cook over medium heat.
Stir constantly until mixture is thickened and bubbly. Add
Worcestershire sauce, cheese, garlic, and pepper, stirring until
cheese melts. Stir in spinach. Add shrimp or crawfish tails, blend
well, and cook until seafood is done.

Serve with melba toast or crackers. You can also use this recipe
without the seafood as a side dish with meats. Add a dash of hot
sauce for extra flavor. Recipe can be halved.

Betty Jo Ayers (Alexandria, Louisiana)

Artichoke & Spinach Frittata

For over 25 years this has been a big family hit. Delicious cut small for appetizers, or medium for a side dish at dinner, or large as a vegetarian meal with a salad. Yum!

**2 bunches green onions, chopped
  (tops also)**
3 cloves garlic, minced
2 tablespoons olive oil
**2 (9-ounce) packages frozen
  artichokes, thawed, chopped
  or 2 (10-ounce) cans**
**1 (10-ounce) package frozen
  chopped spinach, thawed,
  squeezed**

6 eggs, beaten well
**2 cups shredded cheese (Cheddar
  and/or Monterey Jack)**
2 tablespoons chopped parsley
1/4 teaspoon each salt and pepper
1 teaspoon Italian seasoning
**12 small square soda crackers,
  crumbled**
1/2 cup Parmesan cheese

In a 12-inch skillet, sauté onions and garlic in oil till soft. In a large bowl, put chopped artichokes and spinach; add remaining ingredients, except Parmesan cheese. Mix well. Pour into a well-greased 9x13-inch pan. Then spread Parmesan cheese on top. Bake in 350° oven for 40 minutes, or till sides pull away and it begins to brown and center begins to bubble.

Ginger Borg (Concord, California)

Fresh Garden Pizza

Veggie lovers are not the only ones who are going to LOVE this pizza!

1 prepackaged thin pizza crust
**2 cups shredded mozzarella
  cheese, divided**
**4 Roma or 2 large homegrown
  tomatoes, thinly sliced**

**1/4 cup fresh grated Parmesan or
  Romano cheese**
1/4 cup fresh snipped basil
2/3 cup mayonnaise
1 clove garlic, minced

Sprinkle half mozzarella cheese on crust. Place enough sliced tomatoes to cover all of crust. Combine remaining ingredients; spread over tomatoes. Bake at 375° for 20–25 minutes till golden brown and bubbly.

Kim Poole (Franklin, Tennessee)

Spinach Pancakes

My children hated spinach but loved fried foods. I concocted this recipe to see if they would eat spinach. They were so crazy about this dish, they took these pancakes cold to school in lunch boxes. They are grown now but still request these pancakes.

1 (24-ounce) can chopped spinach	½ cup finely grated Parmesan cheese
4–5 large eggs	Salt and pepper to taste
1 cup cracker crumbs, more if needed	½ cup cooking oil, more if needed

Drain spinach thoroughly, discard liquid. Mix all ingredients except oil. Texture should be thick. Heat oil in skillet. Drop mixture by heaping tablespoonfuls carefully into hot oil and flatten with fork. Fry on both sides; do not turn until each side is brown and crispy. Add more oil as needed to fry remainder of pancakes. Drain pancakes on paper towels. Serve hot.

Note: Zucchini can be substituted (approximately 6 small zucchini, grated).

Lola E. Mahler (Laguna Woods, California)

Product Display is responsible for creating an on-screen image of each product. Here Francisca Donato positions a pair of earrings for the camera. These "beauty shots" are recorded on a video server and used during the show. Product Display usually works a few hours ahead of the live show so that everything runs smoothly.

Colorful Stuffed Peppers

1 pound ground beef or chicken	2 cups cooked rice, hot
1/2 medium onion, chopped	1 cup bottled spaghetti sauce
10 mushrooms, chopped	(or more to taste)
Salt, pepper, herbs and	2 green peppers
seasonings to taste	2 yellow peppers
2 cups shredded Cheddar cheese,	2 orange peppers
divided	

Brown ground meat, onion, and mushrooms together. Season with salt, pepper and seasonings. Drain grease. Mix in 1 cup cheese, cooked rice (while still hot), and enough bottled spaghetti sauce to hold together (and to taste).

Cut peppers in half and clean out stem and seeds. Steam for 5–6 minutes, until softened a little. Fill each pepper half with mixture and top with remaining 1 cup cheese. Bake at 350° (or steam) for 15 minutes or more till hot throughout.

Mary Pin (Kent, Washington)

Zesty Stove-Top Peppers

This recipe has been passed down three generations. The secret "when the rice is done, the meat is done" is the general rule for the preparation. Our family likes salad and French bread served with these zesty peppers.

3 cans tomato soup	1/4 cup milk
2 1/2 cans water	1 medium-size onion, chopped
1 pound lean ground pork	1/2 cup uncooked long-grain rice
1/2 pound medium-lean ground	1/2 teaspoon garlic salt
beef	5–6 medium-size bell peppers
1 egg, beaten	

Pour tomato soup into a 4-quart stewpot or Dutch oven. Add water and stir thoroughly. Set aside.

Mix pork and beef until well mixed. Add beaten egg and milk. Mix well. Add chopped onion and uncooked rice. Add garlic salt.

Cut tops off bell peppers about 1 inch. Remove seeds and rinse inside of peppers. Stuff each pepper 3/4 full of meat mixture. Place peppers in soup mixture (do not let sauce cover peppers). Cook on low heat for 1 hour, 45 minutes.

Audrey E. Carter (Carlsbad, New Mexico)

Vegetable Caponata

This is a recipe my husband introduced to me. He is of Italian descent and has made it for years. It is great as a side dish or as an hors d'oeuvre on top of slices of crusty bread. It can also be used as a pasta topping.

1–2 tablespoons olive oil
2 cloves garlic, chopped
1 large onion, sliced
1 red pepper, cut into 1-inch squares
1 green pepper, cut into 1-inch squares

2 large eggplants, diced into 1-inch cubes (skin on)
2 tablespoons capers
1–2 tablespoons tomato paste
1 cup water, divided
Salt and pepper to taste
Red pepper flakes to taste

Heat olive oil in nonstick pan. Add garlic and sweat, don't brown. Add onion and when translucent, add peppers. Sauté until peppers soften. Add eggplants and cook/sauté for approximately 15 minutes, stirring regularly. Add capers and mix well. Add tomato paste and half of the water. Bring to boil. Cover and cook down for 30 minutes on low-medium heat. Taste for seasoning, then add salt, pepper, and pepper flakes to taste. After first 30 minutes, stir in remaining water and cover again. Cook until all water is absorbed, approximately 30 minutes more. Serve warm or at room temperature.

Bernadette Palumbo (Hackettstown, New Jersey)

Pat James DeMentri (opposite page) has done some unique things before coming to QVC. She once jumped out of a barn for a jeans commercial, and roller skated through the Lincoln Tunnel in New York City for a movie. Pat is an experienced, professional model and commercial actress in New York City and Japan. She has also been an on-air personality for television station WHSP in Wilmington, Delaware. Pat is a native of Catasauqua, Pennsylvania, and graduated from Temple University in Philadelphia.

Fresh Tomato Pie

My family has always enjoyed a garden filled with home-grown tomatoes. This year especially, my five-year-old and I have enjoyed our garden! This recipe makes great use of all of your garden tomatoes!

1 (9-inch) pie shell
3 medium tomatoes, thinly sliced
¼ cup chopped scallions
  (optional)
¾ cup chopped prosciutto, ham,
  or meat of choice
2 tablespoons chopped fresh basil

¼ teaspoon dried oregano
1 cup grated provolone or mix of
  favorite cheeses
¼ cup mayonnaise
⅛ teaspoon nutmeg

Preheat oven to 450°. Bake pie shell 5 minutes and remove. Arrange tomato slices in shell. Add scallions, meat, basil, oregano, and pepper to taste. Combine cheese, mayonnaise, and nutmeg. Spread on top of entire pie. Bake 35 minutes.

Pat James DeMentri, QVC Host (West Chester, Pennsylvania)

QVC Host, Pat James DeMentri with the "apple-of-her-eye," daughter Nicole Anna.

Country Skillet Meal

As a teenager in West Virginia, I often fixed this dish for Sunday dinner to give my mother—who had eleven children—a day out of the kitchen.

2 tablespoons bacon grease
1 large sweet onion, slivered
1 large bell pepper, slivered
1/4 teaspoon garlic powder (or 1 garlic clove, minced)
2 pounds small redskin potatoes, washed, not peeled, sliced 1/4 inch thick

1 link polish sausage, cubed
3 tablespoons water
1/2 teaspoon black pepper
8 ounces medium Cheddar cheese, shredded
Salt (optional)

Heat bacon grease in large skillet. Sauté onion and bell pepper with garlic. When onion and bell pepper are tender, move aside in skillet and add potatoes. Using medium-high heat, turn potatoes until browned; add sausage, water, and black pepper. Stir in onion and bell pepper. Cover, reduce heat, and simmer until potatoes are soft. Remove lid and cook out moisture. Spread cheese on top, replace lid, and turn off heat. Let stand until cheese has melted. Makes 8–10 servings.

Tim Fowler (Brandon, Mississippi)

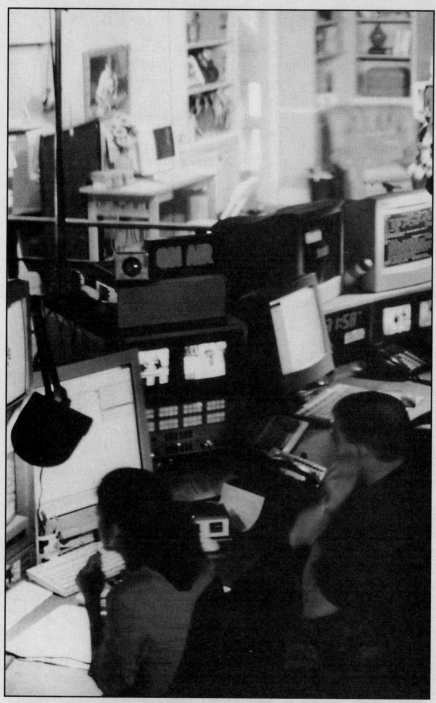

QVC's Line Producer is on top of the action, literally, on a balcony above a spiral staircase. He or she is in constant contact with the hosts and the Control Room, and is ultimately responsible for what goes on air, and how long it stays there, depending on how well it's selling and how much inventory is available.

Spicy Spring Vegetable Pasta

This is the recipe which I serve to my family as an alternative to a meat meal. My mother is a vegetarian and on a salt-reduced diet. I try to find spices to perk up her meals. This recipe has beautiful colors and is eye appealing. I hope you enjoy it as we have.

2 tablespoons olive oil
1 medium sweet onion, diced
2 garlic cloves, minced
1 medium yellow summer squash, sliced
1 medium green zucchini, sliced
1 each small red, yellow, and green pepper, diced

5 Roma tomatoes, sliced into wedges
½ teaspoon chili powder
¼ teaspoon salt-free seasoning
¼ teaspoon fresh ground black pepper
1 (16-ounce) box vermicelli pasta
4 tablespoons Parmesan cheese

In a large skillet or chicken fryer, heat oil over medium-high heat. Sauté onion and garlic for 3 minutes. Add sliced squash and zucchini and sauté for 3 minutes. Add diced peppers and tomato wedges. Stir in chili powder, salt-free seasoning, and pepper. Cover and simmer for 10–15 minutes, stirring occasionally.

Cook vermicelli according to package directions. Drain carefully. Toss vegetables with pasta and Parmesan cheese. Serves 8.

Karen Calhoun (Grayson, Kentucky)

Easy Linguine with Shrimp and Artichokes

Whenever I bring this to a potluck, everyone wants the recipe! Can also be made with chicken. My family loves this recipe.

1 (12-ounce) package linguine
½ pound medium shrimp, peeled and cleaned
2 tablespoons olive oil
2 tablespoons minced garlic

2 (6-ounce) jars marinated artichokes, diced (reserve liquid)
2 tablespoons chopped parsley
2 tablespoons capers (optional)

Cook linguine according to package directions; drain and set aside. Sauté shrimp in olive oil with minced garlic. Add liquid from artichokes. Toss in pasta to coat. Toss in chopped artichokes, parsley, and capers. Serves 6–8.

Annette Buckmaster (Sacramento, California)

Spicy Chicken Pasta Casserole

An incredibly good casserole! Big taste in every bite!

1 (2- to 3-pound) chicken	1 can tomato soup
Salt, pepper, and garlic powder to taste	1 can tomatoes with green chiles
2 bay leaves	½–1 pound fresh mushrooms, chopped
1 onion, chopped	1 (1-pound) block processed cheese, cubed
1 bell pepper, chopped	1 (12-ounce) package vermicelli
1 stick margarine or butter	

Boil chicken with spices and bay leaves in water to cover until fully cooked, reserving the stock. Remove chicken. Sauté onion and bell pepper in margarine; add tomato soup, tomatoes, mushrooms, and cheese. Cook vermicelli in chicken stock, adding water, if necessary. Add the cooked, drained pasta to the cheesy tomato sauce. Pull chicken off the bones and add to the vermicelli mixture. Pour into a casserole dish and bake at 350° until cheese bubbles, about 20–30 minutes. Serves 6–8.

Laurie Ransome (Baton Rouge, Louisiana)

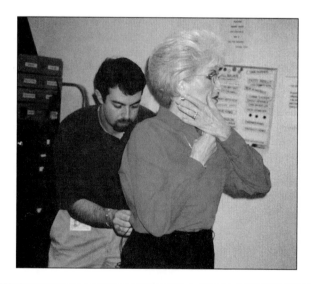

Basil Kershner is one of the efficient Studio Operations people who greet you upon arrival with information about when you will go on air, have your make-up done, etc. They also "mike" you just prior to air time. The "mike pack" tucks into the back of your belt, the tiny microphone itself clips on your collar, and an earpiece goes in your ear so you can hear the callers. "Mike check for Gwen on five." They hear me, I hear them, and it's off to the set!

Easy Chicken Florentine Pasta Casserole

We host a tailgate football party before and after every USAF Academy football game and I am always looking for easy and good dishes to prepare. This was so easy and a big hit.

2 (10-ounce) cans premium white chunk chicken, drained
1 pound penne pasta, cooked and drained
2 (26-ounce) jars or cans spaghetti sauce

1 (10-ounce) package frozen chopped spinach, thawed and drained
2 teaspoons dry Italian seasoning
2 cups grated mozzarella cheese

Preheat oven to 350°. Lightly spray a 9x13-inch deep baking dish with a nonstick spray. Mix all ingredients, except cheese, together. Mix well. Pour into baking dish and top with cheese. Bake 30–35 minutes. Serves 10–12.

Marilyn Maffet (Colorado Springs, Colorado)

Roni and Ham Casserole

1 onion, chopped
1 clove garlic, chopped
2 tablespoons oil
¼ cup chopped parsley
1 (16-ounce) can chopped tomatoes

½ pound macaroni, cooked, drained
1 can tomato soup
1 soup can milk
2 cups chopped ham
Dash of basil or oregano

Sauté onion and garlic in oil till soft. Add parsley and tomatoes; simmer 5 minutes. Put cooked macaroni in 3-quart casserole dish. Add soup, milk, ham, and herbs. Mix well. Bake, covered, at 350° for 25 minutes. Remove cover and continue baking for 15–20 minutes.

Dianne Stickney (Gilford, New Hampshire)

Roney Mazzetti

A crowd-pleaser that will feed a crowd. Great with garlic bread and salad!

2 pounds ground chuck
1 teaspoon garlic salt
2 stalks celery, diced
1 onion, chopped
1 (26-ounce) jar spaghetti sauce
1 small can tomato paste

1 (1-pound) package wide egg noodles
1 (2-pound) carton cottage cheese
1 (8-ounce) package cream cheese
1 (8-ounce) package shredded mozzarella cheese

Brown meat. Add garlic salt, celery, and onion. Add spaghetti sauce and tomato paste and simmer for ½ hour on low heat. Cook noodles for 6 minutes and drain.

Butter a 5-quart casserole dish. Add ⅓ meat sauce and half the egg noodles. Spread all of the cottage cheese on top. Cut cream cheese in slices and put on top of cottage cheese. Add ⅓ meat sauce and the remaining noodles on top. Pour the rest of the meat sauce over noodles and sprinkle with cheese. Bake ½ hour at 350°, till heated through. Scoop onto plates with large serving spoon.

Steffie H. Roney (Endicott, New York)

Old-Fashioned Macaroni & Cheese

1 (7-ounce) box elbow macaroni
¼ cup margarine or butter
¼ cup flour
½ teaspoon salt
Pinch of pepper

1 cup of 1% milk
1 (16-ounce) can diced tomatoes
8 ounces low-fat shredded Cheddar cheese
Paprika

Cook macaroni. Meanwhile in medium saucepan, melt butter. Stir in flour, salt and pepper and cook till bubbly. Gradually add milk and tomatoes; cook till thickened. Stir in cheese till melted. Drain macaroni, and stir into cheese sauce. Sprinkle with paprika. Serves 4–6.

Sandra Swadley (Quaker Hill, Connecticut)

Parcheesy Spaghetti Pie

½ pound spaghetti, broken in
  half
2 eggs
½ cup grated Parmesan or
  romano cheese
1–1½ pounds ground beef (or
  turkey)
½ cup chopped onion

Salt and pepper to taste
Chopped or powdered garlic to
  taste
1 (8-ounce) can tomato sauce
1 tablespoon butter or margarine
1 (8-ounce) carton sour cream
1 (8-ounce) package sliced
  mozzarella cheese

Cook spaghetti; drain. In separate bowl, mix eggs with grated cheese. Add cooked spaghetti to mixture.

Brown meat; drain fat. Season with chopped onion, salt, pepper, and garlic powder. Keep stirring until meat is well browned; add tomato sauce and let simmer 10–15 minutes.

Generously spread butter on circular baking dish. Add spaghetti mixture, pressing it down and making an indention in the center. Try not to let the spaghetti hang over the sides of dish. Let this cool for at least 5 minutes, then line the middle of the mixture with a thin coating of sour cream. (This will allow you to slice the pie without it crumbling into a million pieces.) Add meat to the center and spread it around the spaghetti. Add thin slices of mozzarella cheese on top. Bake in 350° oven for 25–30 minutes. Enjoy!

Helen D. Lomupo (Conesville, New York)

When your first name is Quality, you have to make sure you live up to it. That's why QVC has its own, in-house Quality Assurance Lab. Quality Assurance—QA for short—is QVC's team of over 140 people, whose mission is to make sure everything they sell meets the highest quality standards. Only about 15% of the products will pass through QA the first time; 34% fail completely and are not considered to be of sufficient quality to offer to QVC customers. The remaining 66%, after further development and testing, become quality products QVC is happy to sell.

Texas Mexican Spaghetti

About 20 to 25 years ago my mother, her four sisters and many of my cousins used to get together once a month at different houses for a potluck dinner and exchange of very small gifts, our way of staying a close family. We have many blessed memories. This was a favorite dish.

1½ pounds ground beef
1 onion, chopped
1 bell pepper, chopped
1 can tomato soup, undiluted
1 (5-ounce) jar green olives, drained, chopped
1 (15-ounce) can whole-kernel corn, drained

2 tablespoons margarine
12 ounces spaghetti, boiled and drained
12 ounces shredded mild Cheddar cheese (more, if you like)

Brown ground beef, onion, and pepper; drain. Add soup, olives, and corn. Sauté about 5 minutes. Meanwhile, melt margarine in a 9x13-inch dish. Put in drained spaghetti. Top with beef mixture then shredded cheese. Bake at 350° until cheese melts, about 10–15 minutes. Take out of oven and let cool about 10 minutes. Slice and enjoy!

Sonja Stringer (Ledbetter, Kentucky)

All-at-Once Spaghetti

I have passed this recipe on to my daughters and to many people who have crossed my path through life who love to cook. This recipe is easy and very good.

1 pound ground beef
1 medium onion, chopped
3 (8-ounce) cans tomato sauce
1½ cups water
¼ teaspoon garlic powder

¼ teaspoon pepper
1½ teaspoons salt
¼ teaspoon ground oregano
½ pound spaghetti, uncooked
1 cup shredded Cheddar cheese

Brown the ground beef and onion. Add the tomato sauce and water. Add the spices and stir. Bring to a boil and add the uncooked spaghetti, breaking it in half. Lower heat and simmer for 20 minutes. When done, add shredded cheese and place lid on top until cheese melts. Enjoy!

Marcy Kappner (Chula Vista, California)

Million Dollar Spaghetti

Serve this dish with a salad and garlic bread and it's a meal fit for a king. Everyone just loves this dish. I have to make two recipes of this for my family. They cannot get enough of it.

1 (7-ounce) package thin spaghetti	1/4 cup sour cream
1 1/2 pounds ground beef	8 ounces cottage cheese
2–3 tablespoons Italian seasoning, or to taste	1/2 cup chopped green onion
	1 tablespoon minced green pepper
1 (8-ounce) package cream cheese	2 tablespoons butter, melted
	2 (8-ounce) cans tomato sauce

Cook spaghetti according to package directions. Meanwhile, brown ground beef and add Italian seasoning.

Mix cream cheese, sour cream, cottage cheese, green onion, green pepper, and melted butter. Using a buttered 9x13-inch baking dish, put half of the spaghetti in the dish. Add all of the cream cheese mixture smoothly over the top. Add the rest of the spaghetti and top with ground beef. Pour tomato sauce over the top.

Chill for at least one hour, or overnight. Let stand at room temperature for 20 minutes, then bake at 350° for 45 minutes.

Susan A. Martin (La Crescenta, California)

Decidedly Italian Spaghetti Sauce

The sauce is simmered till rich red-brown . . . a great old-fashioned recipe.

1 large onion, chopped	1 (16-ounce) can tomato paste
1 large bell pepper, chopped	2 tablespoons chili powder
2 tablespoons vegetable oil	2 teaspoons garlic powder
1 1/2 pounds ground chuck	2 teaspoons Italian seasoning
Salt and pepper to taste	2 bay leaves
2 (28-ounce) cans tomatoes	1 pound hot Italian sausage links, sliced
3 (16-ounce) cans tomato sauce	

Sauté onion and bell pepper in vegetable oil. Add ground chuck; brown and drain well. Salt and pepper to taste. Add tomatoes, tomato sauce, and tomato paste. Add chili powder, garlic powder, Italian seasoning, and bay leaves. Mix well. Brown Italian sausage; drain and add to mixture. Simmer on low heat 2–3 hours. Serve over cooked spaghetti. Makes a lot. Leftover sauce freezes well.

Florence Coleman (Marcy, New York)

Southwestern Chicken Lasagna

4–6 skinless, boneless chicken
 breasts, cooked
3 (10-ounce) cans tomatoes with
 green chiles
1 (14-ounce) jar picante sauce
 or salsa
1 (1¼-ounce) package taco
 seasoning mix

1 (16-ounce) can black beans,
 rinsed and drained
1 (8-ounce) package lasagna
 noodles, uncooked
1 or 2 (4-ounce) cans chopped
 green chiles
1 (8-ounce) package shredded
 reduced-fat Monterey Jack cheese

Preheat oven to 350°. Cut chicken into 1-inch pieces; set aside. Mix tomatoes, picante, and taco seasoning. Add black beans. Spray a 9x13x2-inch casserole dish with nonstick cooking spray. Spread 1 cup of the tomato-bean sauce over the bottom. Top with 4–5 noodles, overlapping slightly, if necessary. Sprinkle with half the chicken, half the chiles, and 2 or more cups of the sauce. Top with half the shredded cheese. Repeat layers. Bake, uncovered, for 40 minutes, or until noodles are tender. Cool at least 20 minutes before serving. Serves 12.

Nancy O'Bryant (Ridgeland, Mississippi)

Luscious Lasagna

I've been working for several years on this recipe, combining different recipes and ideas. The secret, if there is one, would be browning the beef with all the spices so that the meat is flavorful, and simmering the sauce as long as possible to get the full flavor of the spices. On a cold winter day, I put the sauce together in the morning and let it simmer all day, making the house smell wonderful! By suppertime everyone is anxious and hungry!

2 pounds ground beef
1 clove garlic, minced
1 small onion, minced
3 tablespoons parsley, divided
  (dry or fresh)
3 tablespoons Italian seasoning,
  divided
1 teaspoon pepper
2 (14½-ounce) cans stewed
  tomatoes
1 (14½-ounce) can whole
  tomatoes

1 (12-ounce) can vegetable juice
2 packages dry zesty spaghetti
  sauce
2 eggs
24 ounces cottage cheese
¾ cup Parmesan cheese
1 package uncooked lasagna
  noodles (regular or no-cook)
16 ounces shredded Colby Jack
  cheese, divided

Combine and brown ground beef, garlic, onion, 1 tablespoon parsley, 1½ tablespoons Italian seasoning, and pepper. Drain well. Put all 3 cans of tomatoes in blender and blend. In a Dutch oven, combine meat mixture, tomatoes, vegetable juice, dry spaghetti sauce, and 1½ tablespoons Italian seasoning. Let simmer for at least 1 hour—the longer it cooks, the more flavorful it will become; I recommend 4 hours. Let it cool before serving and it will become thicker.

In a separate bowl, beat eggs, cottage cheese, 2 tablespoons parsley, and Parmesan cheese; mix well.

Spray a 9x13x2-inch lasagna pan with nonstick cooking spray. Start with a thin layer of the meat sauce, add 3 or 4 noodles lengthwise and one across the end (you'll have to break some off), another layer of meat sauce, ½ cottage cheese mixture, and ½ shredded cheese; repeat layers ending with meat sauce. Bake in 350° oven, uncovered, for about 60–70 minutes. Add remaining shredded cheese 10 minutes before the end. Let lasagna cool for 15–20 minutes before serving.

Kristi L. Sandal (Pierre, South Dakota)

Easy Spinach Lasagna

1 (26-ounce) jar spaghetti sauce	2–3 cloves garlic, minced
1 jar water	2 tablespoons olive oil
1 (12-ounce) package wide egg noodles	Salt and pepper to taste
1 package fresh spinach	1 pound ricotta
1 cup chopped onion	4 ounces shredded mozzarella

Pour spaghetti sauce into large nonstick pot. Fill sauce jar with water; add to sauce. Cover and bring to boil. Add noodles; stir and lower heat to simmer. Cover and cook until noodles are tender, about 10 minutes, stirring often.

Pinch off spinach stems and discard; rinse spinach, then dry. Sauté onion and garlic in oil until onion is translucent. Add spinach and salt and pepper to taste. Sauté until spinach is wilted. In large casserole dish, layer half the noodles, all the ricotta, then spinach, and rest of noodles; top with mozzarella. Bake, uncovered, at 350° for 30 minutes.

Joanne M. Rice (Deering, New Hampshire)

QVC provides convenience to their employees, too. Here Gail Maguire is ready to help customers who visit the QVC Convenience Store located on QVC's main level to buy various sundries in addition to a whole variety of services . . . drop off their dry cleaning, arrange to have their car washed, get their film developed . . . you name it, this place makes it convenient.

Carly's Real Pizza Pie

Carl loves pizza! He couldn't understand why it was called "Pizza Pie" because it didn't have a top on it. So, he made one like a pie—now the family calls it Carly's Pizza Pie.

1½ pounds hamburger
¼ cup chopped onion
½ tablespoon oregano
1 tablespoon garlic powder
Salt and pepper to taste
1 (14-ounce) jar pizza sauce,
   divided

2 loaves frozen bread dough,
   thawed, risen
1½ cups Cheddar cheese, divided
2 tablespoons Parmesan cheese
1 egg yolk

Fry hamburger breaking it apart; add onion, oregano, garlic powder, salt and pepper. Add ½ the pizza sauce. Cool and drain; roll out dough to fit pie pan. Coat dough with remaining pizza sauce. Sprinkle ½ Cheddar cheese on sauce. Put drained hamburger mixture on top of cheese. Add remaining Cheddar cheese on top of hamburger; sprinkle with Parmesan. Put second rolled dough on top; crimp edges together; poke holes in top of pie. Brush top of pie with beaten egg yolk. Bake at 350° for 30 minutes or until brown.

Joni Sliwoski (Honolulu, Hawaii)

Editors' Extra: For thin crust, use only one loaf of bread dough and divide when risen.

T-Roeux's Quick and Easy Jambalaya

Due to the simplicity of this recipe and its great Cajun flavor, it has become a family favorite of the Torregano's and Roe's, hence the name T-Roeux's.

1 stick butter or margarine,
 melted
1 (14½-ounce) can beef broth
1 (10-ounce) can diced tomatoes
 with green chiles
1 onion, chopped
1 celery stalk, chopped

1½ cups rice
1 tablespoon Cajun seasoning
 (may adjust to taste)
1 pound boiled crawfish tails
 (may substitute shrimp, or
 combine the two)

Put all ingredients in a rice cooker. Turn on. When done, bring to table! Mmmmm, Mmmmm, Good! Serve with French bread or garlic rolls.

Shannon Roe Torregano (Brandon, Mississippi)

Editors' Extra: This can also be done in a pot on the stovetop—just melt the butter first, add remaining ingredients, bring to a boil, stir, cover, and simmer on low till rice is cooked, about ½ hour. Yum!

Real Cajun Jambalaya

1 pound smoked sausage, sliced
4½ cups water, divided
1 pound boneless chicken
½ large bell pepper, chopped
1 large onion, chopped
½ cup chopped green onions
 (reserve stems)

4 cups cooked rice
½ teaspoon thyme
Cajun seasoning or red pepper to
 taste (optional)
Garnish with chopped green onion
 stems

Using a black iron pot, boil the sausage in 1½ cups water on high until all the water is cooked out. The sausage should be real brown and there should be a crust on the bottom of the pot. Put raw, boneless, chicken pieces in pot. Sauté and stir about 2 minutes. When chicken has turned brown, add pepper, onion, and green onions. Add 3 cups water and boil 10 minutes until chicken starts to fall apart. Add cooked rice and thyme; season to taste and stir well. Let sit for about 15 minutes. Serve in a bowl with onion stems as garnish.

Patsy Scates (Baton Rouge, Louisiana)

Brown Rice Casserole

This recipe is great as a side dish for beef.

1 stick butter or margarine
1 small onion, finely chopped
1 cup uncooked long grain white
  rice

2 cans beef consommé soup
¹⁄₃ cup shredded American cheese

In a saucepan, sauté butter and onion until translucent; set aside. In casserole dish, mix rice and soup. Stir in onion and butter mixture. Top with shredded cheese. Bake, covered, for 1–1¹⁄₄ hours at 350°. You may want to uncover the dish for the last 15 minutes of bake time. Serves 4–6. (Pictured on cover.)

David Venable, QVC Host (West Chester, Pennsylvania)

Prior to joining QVC, David was a television anchor/reporter for WOAY in Oak Hill, West Virginia and WTAJ in Altoona, Pennsylvania. David hosted the Children's Miracle Network Telethon for four years, and still remains involved with it as well as the Miss America Scholarship Pageant in Pennsylvania, where he has sung and emceed numerous pageants. He learned about QVC from his mom, a long-time QVC viewer and fan. In his free time, David enjoys exercise, public speaking, live theater, travel, and cooking. His love of food is contagious with his viewers. He has made his "Yum-Yum Face" famous on QVC.

When QVC had its Local Flavors Tour, there was a huge van that expanded out to become a first-class traveling kitchen. Here in San Antonio, David is getting a little pre-show taste of Margarita Pie before Gwen feeds it to him on air. (He made his "Yum-Yum Face" both times!)

Won't-Last-Long Sausage-Rice Casserole

This was a favorite recipe when I was growing up . . . still is!

1 pound pork sausage
1 cup chopped green pepper
1 cup chopped onion
1½ cups chopped celery
1 package chicken noodle soup
  mix

2½ cups boiling water
½ cup uncooked rice
¼ teaspoon salt
½ cup slivered almonds (optional)
1 tablespoon butter, melted

Brown sausage in large skillet. Pour off excess fat. Add chopped vegetables and sauté until tender. Cover; set aside.

Combine soup mix with boiling water in saucepan. Stir in rice, cover, and simmer 20 minutes. Add to sausage mixture, along with salt. Pour into greased baking dish. If using almonds, sprinkle on top. Drizzle with melted butter. Bake uncovered at 375° for 20 minutes. Serves 5–6.

Jan Siefert (Kankakee, Illinois)

Confetti Rice

My family is of Croatian descent and this one-dish meal was very popular when I was growing up. The original dish did not contain the varied vegetables, as there were a lot of picky eaters in our family. My mother used to sauté the raw rice in butter, then "baste" the rice with homemade chicken soup (fat and all!) until it was done. As you can see, we changed a few things along the way and came up with this. We all still enjoy this dish very much.

1 medium onion, diced
1 each, small green and red
  pepper, diced
1 small zucchini, diced
½ pound mushrooms, chopped
1 small yellow squash, diced
½ cup butter, divided
3 tablespoons oil
1 boneless chicken breast,
  sautéed and cubed

3–4 cups cooked rice (substitute
  chicken broth for water and
  follow directions on package)
⅓ cup frozen peas, thawed
Salt and pepper to taste
Garlic powder (optional)
Parmesan cheese (optional)

Sauté vegetables in ¼ cup butter and 3 tablespoons oil until crisp-tender or desired doneness. Add more butter or oil during this process, if needed. Remove vegetables from pan to bowl; set aside, and keep warm.

Add remaining ¼ cup butter to skillet and melt until medium brown in color. Add chicken and warm through. Add rice, peas, and vegetable mixture. Season with salt, pepper, and garlic powder to taste. Sprinkle with Parmesan cheese, if desired.

Great served with a salad of mixed greens with fresh grape tomatoes as garnish. We like a light vinegarette dressing with a light dusting of Roquefort cheese on top, with a side of crusty sourdough bread.

Janet Venditti (Pittsburgh, Pennsylvania)

Mike Serra shows Barbara Moseley that two samples of every item shown on QVC are stored in Product Central, a huge "Noah's Ark" of products. One item is used for on-air demonstration, while the other is recorded on a video server to be used as an on-screen image during the show. Product Central has the capacity to store 200,000 pieces of merchandise.

Marianne's Chicken Piccata

I rarely cook, but I do sometimes indulge in a few good home-cooked meals! Here is a recipe for one of the few dishes I make for myself at home that I really love.

⅛ cup all-purpose flour	1–2 tablespoons lemon juice
Dash of lemon pepper	(if using fresh lemon, reserve
Dash of salt	some slices for garnish)
1 boneless, skinless chicken	⅛ cup white cooking wine
breast, halved and pounded thin	⅛ cup chicken bouillon broth
2 tablespoons butter (or use	1 tablespoon capers (optional)
butter-flavored nonstick cooking	
spray)	

Combine flour, lemon pepper, and salt in a shallow bowl and lightly coat both sides of pounded chicken breast. Coat a skillet with melted butter (or spray generously with butter-flavored nonstick cooking spray), and sauté chicken over medium heat for about 3 minutes on each side, or until center of chicken is done. Remove chicken from skillet and cover to keep warm.

In small mixing bowl, combine lemon juice, wine, and broth and pour slowly into the same, still-warm skillet. Raise heat slightly (medium-high) and boil the sauce until it is reduced by about ⅓. If you like your sauce a little thicker, just add a sprinkle of all-purpose flour and stir immediately into mixture. Top chicken with sauce and garnish with fresh lemon slices and capers. Serves 1 very hungry QVC Host.

Marianne Manko, QVC Host (West Chester, Pennsylvania)

Prior to QVC, Marianne was in broadcasting in Florida and Ohio—on a morning show, as an airborne traffic reporter, a news reporter, then a TV weather reporter. Marianne has continued to study acting and comedy, and has been seen or heard in hundreds of commercials. While living in Orlando, she also picked up extra work in major motion pictures such as *Armageddon* and *Contact,* as well as in the HBO miniseries "From the Earth to the Moon." Marianne won the title of Mrs. Florida International, and still enjoys hosting various pageants. In her spare time Marianne enjoys working out, sightseeing, and snorkeling, but claims her golf game remains a work in progress. "When I'm on the course, I yell 'fore' before I even swing the club," she admits. "I figure . . . why risk it?"

Kim Parrish, Dan Wheeler, and Marianne Manko are always smiling for the camera. Here in QVC's Host Lounge they have a chance to unwind, relax, and get comfortable. It's also a good place to share ideas and information, and of course, a few laughs with each other.

Meet-Me-at-the-Border Chicken-Made-to-Order

8 skinless, boneless chicken
  breasts
2 quarts water
2 cups cooked rice
1 (16-ounce) jar thick and chunky
  salsa, hot or mild

1 (8-ounce) jar medium taco sauce,
  or to taste
Salt and pepper to taste
Pinch of crushed red pepper
  (optional)

In large pot, boil chicken in water until tender. Remove from broth and cut into cubes. Return chicken to pot of broth and add cooked rice. Add salsa and taco sauce. Season to taste. Serves 6–8. Also good for stuffing bell peppers.

Steven Dawkins (Brandon, Mississippi)

Crispy Southwest Chicken

After my husband and I had our fourth little girl, it seemed like the only kinds of food I wanted were spicy, Mexican-style dishes and lots of fresh salsa. When my family started grumbling about getting "Mexican food again?!," I began making up new recipes that still had a spicy flair to them, but would satisfy my whole family. I came up with this one as a variation to the Italian dish, Chicken Parmesan, and the whole family enjoys it. The salsa goes great here, and I can always add a few more peppers to my portion. Voilà! Everyone is happy.

FRESH TOMATO SALSA:

¾ cup chopped tomato
¼ cup chopped onion
2 tablespoons fresh lime juice

1 teaspoon salt
1–2 tablespoons minced jalapeño
 or green chile

Mix tomato, onion, lime juice, salt, and chile all together and allow to stand in order for flavors to mingle.

1 pound boneless, skinless
 chicken breasts
2 cups crushed butter crackers,
 divided
4 ounces cream cheese

½ teaspoon salt
1 teaspoon cumin
½ teaspoon cayenne pepper
1 cup picante sauce

Using a meat mallet, on a cutting board, flatten chicken breast pieces to ½-inch thickness or less. If chicken pieces are overly large, slice in half horizontally (butterfly), then flatten with mallet.

Spread 1 cup of crushed crackers onto a plate. Soften cream cheese to room temperature and mix thoroughly with salt, cumin, cayenne pepper, and picante sauce. Dip chicken pieces into cheese/sauce mixture, coating well. Then, piece by piece, place dipped chicken onto crushed crackers, turning over to coat both sides, and pressing crackers into cheese/sauce mixture.

When about ½ the chicken is coated, pour remaining crushed crackers onto the plate and finish coating remaining chicken. Place on a nonstick baking sheet/cookie sheet and bake at 400° for 20 minutes. Serve with Fresh Tomato Salsa which can be poured across the top of each piece at serving, or served on the side.

Leah Lyon (Ada, Oklahoma)

Chicken Talese

SAUCE:

1 tablespoon butter	**1 cup milk**
1 tablespoon flour	**1/2 cup grated Swiss cheese**
Pinch nutmeg	**1 tablespoon grated Parmesan**
Salt and pepper to taste	**cheese**

Melt butter in saucepan; stir in flour. Cook over low heat until smooth, stirring constantly. Add seasonings. Continue stirring while slowly adding milk. Slowly add cheeses, continuing to stir until smooth. Cook until Sauce begins to thicken, stirring occasionally. Remove from heat.

CHICKEN:

2 eggs	**1/2 pound fresh mushrooms, sliced**
4 skinless, boneless chicken	**8 ounces fresh spinach, torn into**
breasts	**bite-size pieces**
3/4 cup flour	**Paprika**
3 tablespoons oil	

Beat eggs lightly. Dip each piece of chicken in egg and then dredge in a light coating of flour. In a large skillet, sauté in oil on medium heat until both sides are brown and chicken is cooked through. Add mushrooms at the end of cooking and sauté until mushrooms are brown.

Arrange chicken and mushrooms on a bed of spinach and top with Sauce. Garnish with paprika. Serves 4.

Rebecca A. Rogers (Lexington, Kentucky)

QVC's phone numbers will be dialed over 148 million times this year. QVC has six phone centers worldwide for a total of more than 6,500 phone lines, and the ability to handle more than 108,000 calls per hour. At full capacity, 1,800 incoming calls can be handled simultaneously in one minute. Not all calls are taken by people: more than a third of all orders are taken by computerized Voice Response Units.

Easy Teriyaki Chicken

5–6 chicken breasts, cut in strips, or chicken tenders to serve 6
1 cup sugar
²/₃ cup soy sauce

Place chicken in skillet on medium-high heat. Mix sugar and soy sauce together and pour over chicken. Cook until chicken is done and sauce is caramelized. Water may be added sparingly if sauce thickens too much before chicken is done. Serve with rice.

Nola Hall (Ferndale, Washington)

Chicken Breasts in Cranberry Sauce

¹/₂ cup all-purpose flour
Salt to taste
4–5 boneless, skinless chicken breasts
2 tablespoons olive oil
1 (16-ounce) can whole cranberry sauce
1 tablespoon lemon juice
2 teaspoons cornstarch
1 chicken flavor bouillon cube
³/₄ teaspoon salt
1 cup water

On wax paper, combine flour and salt. Dip chicken breasts into mixture to coat. In nonstick 12-inch skillet over medium-high heat, cook chicken breasts in olive oil 3–4 minutes per side, until lightly browned. Remove to platter.

In same skillet, stir cranberry sauce, lemon juice, cornstarch, bouillon cube, ³/₄ teaspoon salt, and 1 cup water together. Cook, stirring constantly, until sauce boils and thickens slightly. Boil 1 minute.

Return chicken to sauce in skillet. Cook on medium heat for 20 minutes or until done. Place chicken on platter and top with cranberry sauce mixture.

Susan M. Kellogg (Novi, Michigan)

Chicken L'Orange

My husband works in Manhattan and most nights dinner is 8:00 p.m. This is a fast, healthy, and great tasting meal . . . one everyone enjoys.

½ cup flour	1 sweet onion, chopped
2 tablespoons salt-free blended seasoning	2 shallots, chopped
	½ cup white wine
Salt and pepper to taste (optional)	3 tablespoons honey
4 boneless chicken breasts	1 cup orange juice
3 tablespoons olive oil	1 can mandarin oranges, drained

Mix flour and seasoning on paper towel; salt and pepper, if desired. Coat chicken breasts with flour mixture. Cook chicken in olive oil 3 minutes on each side to brown. Remove from pan. Sauté onion and shallots till soft. Add chicken to pan with white wine; cook 5 minutes. Add honey and orange juice. Cook about 8 minutes, or till thickened. Add mandarin oranges and cook 2 more minutes. Serve over noodles or rice. Also nice served over wilted spinach with red onions and roasted peppers.

Esther Pericles Colton (Beacon, New York)

Peachie Chicken

4 boneless, skinless chicken breast halves	1 (15-ounce) can sliced peaches, reserve juice
¾ cup chopped onion	1 cup chicken broth
1 tablespoon flour	1 cup light sour cream
2 teaspoons paprika	Hot cooked egg noodles
¼ teaspoon salt	

In skillet coated with nonstick cooking spray, brown chicken on both sides. Remove. Spray again and add onion; sauté until soft. Add flour, paprika, and salt, stir until well blended. Gradually add peach juice and chicken broth, stirring until smooth and thickened. Remove from heat; stir in sour cream and peaches. Arrange chicken in 9x13-inch baking pan coated with nonstick cooking spray. Pour sauce over chicken. Bake uncovered at 350° for 1 hour or until chicken is tender. Place hot noodles in serving dish. Arrange chicken over noodles. Top with sauce. Yields 4 servings.

Teresa Fields (Marion, Indiana)

Orange Soda Chicken

The beauty of this recipe, besides it being easy and different, is that you can use as many chicken breasts as you need. It has a pretty glaze, too.

Boneless, skinless chicken breasts   **Orange soda**
Brown sugar   **Cornstarch mixed with water**

Slice halfway through each breast 4 or 5 times (season, if desired). Rub a little brown sugar on each piece and place in a 9x13-inch pan. Bake 20 minutes at 350°. Pour orange soda over chicken just to cover, then bake an additional 30 minutes.

Remove chicken and thicken sauce with cornstarch and water. Serve chicken with sauce on top.

Anita Martin (Clearlake, California)

Apple Chicken with Vegetables

No salt, no pepper, no sugar. Healthy never tasted so good!

$^1/_2$ cup chopped onion   1 tablespoon lemon juice
1 whole chicken breast, cut in   1 cup apple juice
  strips $^1/_2$ teaspoon basil
2 tablespoons olive oil   2 carrots, sliced diagonally
1 tablespoon Worcestershire   1 small zucchini, sliced diagonally
  sauce   8 medium broccoli flowers

Sauté onion and chicken in olive oil in large frying pan or wok. Mix Worcestershire sauce, lemon juice, apple juice, and basil together and pour over chicken. Add carrots and zucchini, cover, and simmer 20 minutes. Add broccoli and simmer another 10 minutes. Serve with rice. Serves 4.

Jennie A. Monroe (Torrington, Connecticut)

The emergency electric generators for Studio Park could supply enough electricity to power almost 3,000 typical residential homes.

Too-Easy Company Chicken

1 can cream of mushroom soup
1 (4-ounce) carton whipped
  cream cheese with chives
1/2 cup dry white wine

8 chicken breast fillets
1 teaspoon oregano
Salt and pepper to taste
Parsley (optional)

Mix soup, cream cheese, and wine together thoroughly. Arrange chicken breasts in greased 9x13-inch casserole dish. Pour mixture over all, turning to coat breasts well. Crush oregano between hands and sprinkle over the top. Salt and pepper to taste. Cover with aluminum foil. Heat in 350° oven for 1/2 hour, covered. Remove foil and cook another 1/2 hour. Baste and serve over cooked rice or noodles. Sprinkle with chopped parsley. Serves 8.

Sandra Wynn (Van Nuys, California)

Zak's Honey Lemon Chicken

My son, Zak, loves this dish and requests it often, especially on his birthday. It is quick, easy, and impressive. I like to serve this with Jasmine rice, a big salad, and crusty French bread. Enjoy!

1 1/2 pounds boneless, skinless
  chicken breasts, cut into strips
1/3 cup Italian bread crumbs
1/2 cup flour
1/4 cup finely ground almonds
1/4 teaspoon onion powder
1/4 teaspoon garlic powder

1/2 teaspoon tarragon
1/2 teaspoon parsley
Salt and pepper to taste
3–4 tablespoons butter
Juice of 1 lemon
3 tablespoons honey
1/4 cup white wine (or water)

Bread chicken strips with dry ingredients and spices by shaking in a plastic bag a few at a time. Brown in preheated 12-inch skillet in melted butter. Turn and brown evenly until golden. Squeeze the lemon juice over chicken breasts in pan. Next, drizzle honey over chicken. Sauté on medium heat approximately 10 minutes, or until chicken is tender. Turn heat up to medium-high. With chicken in pan, deglaze with white wine (or water). Swirl pan while wine is bubbling to coat chicken with honey lemon sauce. Serve immediately.

Lori White (Carbondale, Colorado)

Baked Chicken Supreme

We have been enjoying this recipe for 40 years.

6 boneless, skinless chicken breasts	**3 tablespoons margarine**
1/2 cup biscuit mix	**2 cans undiluted mushroom soup**
Salt and pepper to taste	**1 cup sherry**
	1 (16-ounce) carton sour cream

Roll chicken breasts in biscuit mix, season with salt and pepper, and then brown in skillet in margarine.

In separate bowl, combine soup, sherry, and sour cream. Place browned chicken breasts in casserole dish, and pour marinade over. Cover with foil and place in refrigerator overnight. Remove from refrigerator 2 hours before cooking time. Bake in 375° oven for 1 hour, uncovered. Serve with rice.

Mary Arrowsmith (Sun City West, Arizona)

Lemon Garlic Chicken

This dish will be tender on the inside, slightly crispy on top. Serve with rice or orzo and asparagus.

7 cloves garlic	**4 skinless, boneless chicken breasts**
1/4 cup light extra virgin olive oil	**1/4 teaspoon salt**
1 (16-ounce) can chicken broth, divided	**1/4 teaspoon pepper**
	1 lemon

Mince garlic cloves in garlic press. Sauté garlic in olive oil on low heat in a deep frying pan for about 5 minutes. Preheat oven to 325°. Add 8 ounces of the chicken broth to sautéed garlic and heat for 5 minutes. Lay chicken breasts in pan, raise heat to medium, and sear for 5–7 minutes on each side.

Once both sides of chicken are cooked well, lay all 4 pieces in a 2- to 3-inch deep baking dish. Pour remains of oil, garlic, and broth left in frying pan over top of chicken, allowing garlic to sit on top of chicken. Sprinkle with salt and pepper. Pour remaining chicken broth around chicken to cover about 1/2 to 3/4; do not fully cover. Cut lemon in half and squeeze juice from both halves on top of chicken. Lay 1 lemon half face-down in the baking dish with chicken. Bake at 325° for 35–40 minutes. Serves 4.

Margaux St. Ledger, QVC Host (West Chester, Pennsylvania)

Prior to joining QVC, Margaux St. Ledger (recipe on opposite page) was the assistant to the executive script consultant for "The Colbys" and was a freelance producer with KYW-TV in Philadelphia. Margaux has also appeared in commercials for products such as KFC, Sprite and Chevrolet, and had guest roles in "The Opposite of Sex," "Coach," "Men Behaving Badly," "The Bold and the Beautiful" and "Port Charles." In addition to her many roles on television, Margaux has also appeared in a number of theatre productions in the Los Angeles area, including "What is Art." Margaux's hobbies include crafts and floral design, painting, sailing, snow skiing, bike riding and power skating.

Cilantro Chicken

This is the most asked-for meal at our house. The combination of lime and cilantro is so flavorful.

8 ounces lime juice
2 garlic cloves, chopped
½ cup chopped fresh cilantro

4–6 boneless, skinless chicken
breasts

Combine first 3 ingredients. Place in a gallon-size zip-lock bag. Add chicken and chill for 1–2 hours. Grill. (Pictured on cover.)

Betty Lack (La Mesa, California)

Chicken and Artichoke Penne

Served with a green salad and warm French bread, it's the perfect meal for a romantic dinner.

1 (1-pound) package penne pasta
8 boneless, skinless chicken
   breasts, cut in chunks
1 stick butter
½ stalk celery, chopped
1 medium onion, chopped
1 clove garlic, chopped
2 (10-ounce) cans artichoke
   hearts (NOT marinated),
   drained, chopped

½ cup white wine
Celery salt and black pepper to
   taste
1 (10¾-ounce) can cream of
   mushroom soup
2 cups water
1 (8-ounce) package shredded
   mozzarella

Cook pasta; drain. Coat big skillet with cooking spray. Pan-fry chicken until cooked and golden brown. Set chicken aside. In same skillet, heat butter until melted; sauté celery, onion, and garlic until transparent. Add artichokes and wine. Cook on low heat for 20 minutes. Season with celery salt and pepper. Add chicken, soup, and water. Cook until bubbly. Turn off heat. Add mozzarella. Cover until cheese is melted. Toss chicken sauce with penne.

Kristen A. Graves (Brandon, Mississippi)

Kris's Sour Cream Chicken

1–1½ pounds chicken breasts
1 (16-ounce) carton sour cream
3 eggs
1 (8-ounce) bottle ranch dressing
Seasoned bread crumbs

Oil for frying
2 (12-ounce) jars chicken gravy
2 (12-ounce) jars mushroom gravy
Large package shredded
  mozzarella cheese

Thinly slice chicken and pound. Mix sour cream, eggs, and ranch dressing. Dredge chicken in sour cream mixture and bread crumbs. Pat bread crumbs firmly into chicken. (Do not discard remaining sour cream mixture; refrigerate it.) Fry chicken until brown. Drain on paper towels.

Preheat oven to 350°. Place chicken in baking pan, overlapping slightly. Mix remaining sour cream mixture, chicken gravy, mushroom gravy, and 1 jar of water with a whisk until thoroughly mixed. Pour over cutlets. Top with mozzarella cheese. Place in oven and bake until sauce is bubbly and cheese is melted and heated through, about 35 minutes.

Kristine L. Huchthausen (Centereach, New York)

Salsa Chicken and Noodles

I developed this recipe when I went on a popular and healthy diet program. It's very low-fat. The first time I served it, my husband wouldn't touch it because it was "diet." I waited a month, cooked it again, and didn't mention "diet." Now it is one of his favorites!

½ cup fat-free Italian dressing
4 boneless, skinless chicken
  breasts, cut into strips
1 large onion, sliced and broken
  apart

1 green pepper, sliced
1 (16-ounce) jar salsa
Cooked egg noodles to serve 4
  (yolk-free)

Cook chicken in Italian dressing until done (no pink), about 10 minutes. When just about done, mix in onion and green pepper and cook, covered, for about 3–6 minutes. Add salsa and heat thoroughly. Serve over cooked egg noodles.

Dianne L. Emmett (Altavista, Virginia)

Pleasureville Chicken

3–4 boneless, skinless chicken
  breasts
1 green pepper
1 red pepper
1 yellow pepper
1 medium onion
1 teaspoon each: thyme, tarragon,
  garlic

Salt and pepper to taste
1 (11-ounce) can mushrooms
  (optional)
1 (14-ounce) can chopped
  tomatoes
1 (8-ounce) can tomato sauce

Julienne (cut into thin strips) chicken and all vegetables except mushrooms. Season and sauté in saucepan until chicken is brown. Add mushrooms, tomatoes and sauce. Simmer for 15–20 minutes. Serve over rice.

Nancy McKane (Pleasureville, Kentucky)

Nan's Rolled Chicken

2 whole boneless, skinless
  chicken breasts
Salt and pepper
4 tablespoons Italian cheese,
  divided
2 slices ham, chopped

4 slices pepperoni, chopped
3 slices provolone cheese
¼ cup flour
1 egg
¾ cup Italian bread crumbs
¼ cup cooking oil

Cut boneless chicken breasts in half (will make 4) at the "V"; flatten with tenderizer. Sprinkle chicken with salt and 1 tablespoon Italian cheese. Layer with chopped ham, pepperoni, and Provolone cheese. Fold over and tie ends with string or use toothpicks. Roll chicken in flour seasoned with salt and pepper; then dip in egg seasoned with salt and pepper. Next roll in bread crumbs seasoned with 3 tablespoons Italian cheese.

Put enough oil in pan to cover bottom; fry on both sides until brown. Put into a baking dish that has been wiped with oil. Bake at 350° for 35–45 minutes.

Colleen A. Farnham (Hop Bottom, Pennsylvania)

Stuffed Chicken Breasts
with White Wine Sauce

This recipe is a bit of work, but is absolutely scrumptious and worth it.

STUFFING:

3 slices white bread, crusts
  removed and torn into pieces
¼ teaspoon paprika
¼ teaspoon pepper
¼ teaspoon poultry seasoning

½ teaspoon salt
1 tablespoon finely chopped onion
½ tablespoon hot water
3 tablespoons margarine

Mix together all above ingredients.

WHITE WINE SAUCE:

¼ cup diced onion
¼ pound fresh mushrooms,
  sliced
2 tablespoons margarine
1 can cream of mushroom soup

1 cup sour cream
¼ cup white wine (dry vermouth
  is best)
Salt and pepper to taste

Sauté onion and mushrooms in butter. Add soup and sour cream and mix well. Slowly add wine. Salt and pepper to taste. Simmer on low heat for 5 minutes. Serve warm over chicken.

1 stick margarine
1 tablespoon minced garlic
4 whole boneless chicken breasts
  (skin on)

Seasoned flour

Melt margarine in baking dish large enough to hold breasts. Add minced garlic to margarine. Wash, dry, and pound breasts (for easier rolling).

Add 1 tablespoon Stuffing to each breast. Roll tightly and skewer (with metal skewers) shut. Roll each breast in melted margarine and then in seasoned flour. Place in baking dish skin-side-down. Bake in preheated 325° oven for 1½ hours. Turn every 15–20 minutes. Skin should be golden and crisp. Place each on a bed of bibb lettuce on a platter, surrounded with spiced peach halves filled with mincemeat. Pour White Wine Sauce over breasts and serve. Place remaining Sauce in gravy bowl and serve alongside.

Chicken breasts and Sauce can be prepared in the morning and refrigerated. The Sauce must be reheated carefully to prevent curdling. Delicious!

Kay Plowman (Rapid City, South Dakota)

Tuscan Chicken with Garlic & Olives

6 boneless, skinless chicken
  breast halves
4 tablespoons flour
1/4 teaspoon salt
1/2 teaspoon pepper
2 tablespoons olive oil
1 cup coarsely chopped onion
3 garlic cloves, finely chopped
1 1/4 cups chicken stock
2 tablespoons sun-dried
  tomato paste
3/4 cup diced tomatoes

1 teaspoon balsamic vinegar
1/2 teaspoon freshly ground black
  pepper
1/2 teaspoon dried basil or
  2 tablespoons chopped fresh
  basil
1/2 teaspoon dried thyme
3/4 cup ripe pitted black olives
1 red pepper, cut in 1/2-x1/4-inch
  pieces
2 tablespoons chopped parsley
1/4 cup Parmesan cheese

Cut chicken breasts into 4 pieces. Combine flour, salt and pepper in a plastic bag and toss chicken pieces to coat well. Heat the olive oil in a large skillet and cook chicken until browned. Remove chicken from pan and drain on paper towel.

Add onion to the pan and cook over moderate heat until beginning to soften, then stir in chopped garlic and cook for an additional 2 minutes. Stir in chicken stock, tomato paste, tomatoes, balsamic vinegar, ground pepper, basil, and thyme. Bring to a simmer, add olives and reserved chicken strips, and stir well to combine.

Simmer, uncovered, for 15 minutes, or until chicken is cooked through and sauce is slightly thickened. Stir in the red pepper pieces and simmer an additional 5 minutes.

Sprinkle dish with chopped parsley and Parmesan cheese before serving. Serves 4–6.

Susan M. Runkle (Walton, Kentucky)

Chicken Mushroom Mozzarella

This is my most requested recipe. When family or friends come over, they like to suggest I make this. It can easily be increased to feed more people.

2 eggs
2 tablespoons water
1 cup dry Italian bread crumbs
1 (16-ounce) package boneless, skinless chicken breasts
2 tablespoons butter

1 (15-ounce) jar (or more) spaghetti sauce, divided
1 (8-ounce) package fresh mushrooms, sliced
1 (8-ounce) package shredded mozzarella cheese

Beat together eggs with water. Pour into plate. Place bread crumbs on a second plate. Dip chicken breast into egg mixture, then the bread crumbs, coating both sides. Press firmly. Melt butter in skillet over medium heat. Add breaded chicken and sauté until just brown (chicken will not be completely cooked). Spread ½ cup sauce on bottom of greased 9x13-inch pan. Arrange chicken over sauce, top with mushrooms, cheese, and remaining sauce. Bake at 400° for 30 minutes, or until chicken is done. Serve with mostaccioli pasta and French bread.

Wanda K. Schmitz (New Holstein, Wisconsin)

You-Invited-Who? and They're-Coming-When? Chicken

This is a very old recipe passed down and made often by many in our family. A wonderful main dish, it is elegant enough for company or quick and easy enough for an everyday meal!

1 cut-up chicken fryer, or as many breasts as needed
1 bunch green onions
1 cup shredded Cheddar cheese

1 can cream of chicken soup
1 can cream of celery soup
¼ cup sherry

Put chicken in 9x13-inch pan. Chop green onions with tops and spread over chicken. Spread 1 cup Cheddar cheese over onions. Heat soups with sherry and spread over chicken. Bake, uncovered, at 350° for 1 hour.

Lynda Paviolo (North Huntingdon, Pennsylvania)

Editors' Extra: This makes a delicious sauce that is superb over rice or pasta.

Layered Chicken Sopa

When my mom cooks us our birthday dinners, this dish is always requested. She pours a lot of love into her cooking and with this dish, we can really taste it. It's just plain yummy!

1 can cream of chicken soup
1 can cream of mushroom soup
1 cup chicken broth
1 onion, chopped
3 minced jalapeño peppers
1 chicken, stewed, and boned (or 4 skinless, boneless breasts)

1 teaspoon salt
1 dozen corn tortillas
2 cups grated cheese (Cheddar/ mozzarella blend)

Mix soups, broth, onion, jalapeños, and chicken. (Chicken should be torn or shredded.) Add salt and mix well. Put tortillas, chicken mixture, then cheese in layers in casserole dish, ending with cheese. Bake, uncovered, at 325° for 45 minutes.

Kristen Gladden (El Paso, Texas)

QVC Exeutive Chef Manager Mark Goodwin, Broadcasting Department Kitchen Manager Paula Bower, Host Jill Bauer, and BEST OF THE BEST editors Barbara Moseley and Gwen McKee pour over contest recipes in Gwen's kitchen. Everybody cooked, tested, and tasted. It's always fun having lots of people in the kitchen!

Ritzy Chicken

Ritzy Chicken is oven baked and has a golden brown color like fried chicken, but no fuss and no mess! Everyone likes this recipe!

1 (3–4 pound) fryer or chicken
   breasts
1½ cups round snack crackers,
   crushed
1½ teaspoons garlic salt
1 tablespoon shredded Romano
   cheese

½ cup oil
1 teaspoon dry basil
1 teaspoon parsley flakes
1 tablespoon butter or margarine,
   cut in small pieces
Paprika

Remove skin and cut chicken into serving pieces. Wash chicken and pat dry with paper towels. Put crackers in plastic bag and crush finely with rolling pin. Place crackers in dish and add garlic salt; mix well. Add shredded cheese and mix again.

In separate dish, add oil. Dip chicken in oil on both sides, and then in cracker mix, coating well. Place chicken in dry roasting pan. Sprinkle pieces with basil and parsley flakes. Dot with butter. Sprinkle paprika over top and cover chicken tightly with aluminum foil. Bake 1 hour at 375°. DO NOT uncover chicken or turn chicken while it's baking.

Viola E. Cirillo (Mohawk, New York)

Chicken & Pear Curry Spectacular

2 tablespoons butter or margarine
1 teaspoon curry powder
¼ cup chopped scallions
2 cups cooked chicken or turkey
1 firm, red or green bartlett pear,
   peeled, chopped

1 (10¾-ounce) can cream of
   mushroom soup with roasted
   garlic
1 soup can half-and-half
3 cups rice (white or brown),
   cooked

Melt butter in a 3-quart saucepan over medium-low heat. Add curry powder and sauté scallions for 5 minutes, or until tender. Stir in all remaining ingredients, except rice. Cook, stirring occasionally, until hot. Serve over hot rice. Makes 4 servings.

Betty Mitchem (Satsuma, Alabama)

Savory Eggplant and Chicken Curry

My family really enjoys this hearty and flavorful recipe that I created. Sometimes I serve it with a saffron rice, but always a crisp green salad and hot crusty French bread. Delicious!

1 tablespoon curry powder
1 teaspoon paprika
1½ teaspoons salt, divided
2½ pounds chicken pieces, skin removed
3 tablespoons olive oil
1 pound eggplants, peeled, quartered, and thinly sliced

1 onion, halved and thinly sliced
1 medium green bell pepper, sliced in thin strips
1 clove garlic, finely minced
1 cup tomato juice
1 teaspoon crushed red pepper (optional)

Mix curry powder, paprika, and 1 teaspoon salt. Roll chicken pieces in mixture. In a large skillet, heat olive oil; add chicken and brown. Remove chicken to platter.

In same pan, add eggplant, onion, green bell pepper, garlic, tomato juice, crushed red pepper, and ½ teaspoon salt. Mix well and place chicken over vegetable mixture. Cover and simmer until chicken is tender, about 35–45 minutes. Serves 4.

Mary Bayramian (Laguna Beach, California)

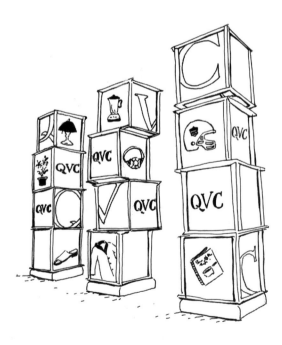

Alfredo Magdalena

1 stick butter
¼–1 cup diced green chiles
  (canned or frozen)
2 cups heavy cream
1 teaspoon chicken bouillon
  granules
1 tablespoon cornstarch, dissolved
  in ½ cup cold water

1 cup Parmesan cheese
3 cups cubed white chicken
  (pre-cooked or canned)
¼ teaspoon garlic powder
Salt and pepper to taste
1 package fettuccine pasta, cooked,
  drained

Melt butter in large saucepan. Sauté green chiles in butter (adjust amount of chiles to suite your taste). Add cream, bouillon, and cornstarch water to mixture. Cook over medium heat. As it thickens, add Parmesan, chicken, garlic powder, salt and pepper. Serve over hot pasta.

Glenda Sours (Magdalena, New Mexico)

Chicken Tortellini

1 (1-pound 4-ounce) bag frozen
  tortellini
1½ pounds boneless chicken
¼ cup olive oil
½ cup chopped onion
1 (7-ounce) can mushrooms,
  drained

1 (2½-ounce) can black olives,
  drained
1 (6-ounce) jar artichokes,
  drained
½ cup sun-dried tomatoes
1 (16-ounce) jar alfredo sauce
1 cup shredded mozzarella

Heat oven to 350°. Prepare tortellini as directed on package. Wash chicken and cube. Brown chicken in oil. Remove chicken; drain fat.

To same pan, add onions, mushrooms, and olives and cook for 5 minutes, stirring constantly, until onion is tender. Cut artichokes and sun-dried tomatoes into bite-size pieces. Combine all ingredients, except cheese, and pour into a 2-quart casserole dish. Sprinkle cheese on top. Bake, uncovered, for 30 minutes.

Sherry Mann (Windham, Ohio)

Chicken Pot Pie

2 cans cream of potato soup
1 (16-ounce) can of mixed
   vegetables, drained
2 cups cooked, sliced, white
   chicken or turkey

$\frac{1}{2}$ cup milk
$\frac{1}{2}$ teaspoon thyme
$\frac{1}{2}$ teaspoon pepper
2 (9-inch) pie crusts
1 egg, slightly beaten (optional)

Combine the soup, vegetables, chicken, milk, thyme, and pepper. Pour into pie crust. Cover with other pie crust. Crimp edges and seal. Slit the top crust and brush with egg, if desired. Bake at 375° for 40 minutes.

Ralph Rock (Baltimore, Maryland)

Easy Cheesy Chicken and Biscuits

We married after World War II and my husband went to college on the GI Bill. Money was tight, and my in-laws helped out often by coming to dinner on Sundays and bringing chickens they had raised. I developed this recipe to use the leftovers, and have changed it over the years to make it quicker and easier. It's a family favorite for 8 children, 13 grandchildren, and 2 great-grandchildren.

1 ($10\frac{3}{4}$-ounce) can condensed
   cream of chicken soup
$\frac{2}{3}$ cup evaporated milk
$\frac{1}{4}$ teaspoon salt
$\frac{1}{4}$ teaspoon pepper
2 cups shredded sharp Cheddar
   cheese
1 cup diced celery

$\frac{1}{2}$ cup diced green pepper
$\frac{1}{4}$ cup diced pimento
1 teaspoon poultry seasoning
3 cups diced cooked chicken or
   turkey
1 (8-count) can refrigerated
   biscuits

Preheat oven to 425°. Combine soup, milk, salt and pepper in a large nonstick saucepan. Heat, stirring constantly. Add cheese; stir until melted. Add remaining ingredients, except biscuits, and heat through, stirring well. Pour into a greased 2-quart casserole dish. Top with biscuits, and bake at 425° for 15 minutes, or until biscuits are lightly browned. Serves 4.

Mary Ann Saint (Plymouth, Michigan)

Poppyseed Chicken

8 boneless chicken breasts,
   cooked and shredded
1½ cups sour cream
2 tablespoons poppyseed
2 cans cream of chicken soup

½ cup chicken broth
1½ packages round snack
   crackers, crushed
1 stick butter or margarine

Mix first 5 ingredients in 9x13-inch baking dish. Spread the crushed crackers on top of mixture. Melt butter or margarine and drizzle over the cracker crumbs. Bake at 350° for about 50 minutes, or until browned on top.

Fran Reed (Kokomo, Indiana)

Fast Chicken à la King

As a working wife and mother, I have to have recipes that can be put together quickly at meal time. My husband and boys love this one.

2 tablespoons margarine
2 onions, chopped fine
4 celery stalks, chopped fine
1 green pepper, chopped fine
1 (8-ounce) can mushroom pieces,
   drained
1 (4-ounce) jar pimentos,
   drained

1 can cream of chicken soup,
   undiluted
1 can cream of celery soup,
   undiluted
1 can cream of mushroom soup,
   undiluted
3 boneless, skinless chicken
   breasts, cooked and cubed

Melt margarine in saucepan; sauté onions, celery, and green peppers till tender. Add mushrooms and pimentos for last minute of cooking. Drain well. In large saucepan, heat soups; add sautéed vegetables and cubed chicken. Simmer, uncovered, till heated thoroughly. Serve in French pastry puffs, or over hot biscuits or toast points. Serves 4.

June Frega (Woodstock, Georgia)

In January 2000, Q Records, a division of QVC, Inc., received a GRAMMY® Award Nomination for its first release. *Footloose—The Original Broadway Cast Recording* received a Best Musical Show Album of the Year nomination.

Terrific Overnight Chicken

CRUST:

1 (8-ounce) package seasoned
   stuffing mix

½ cup butter, melted
1 cup chicken broth

Mix together all ingredients and put half of the mixture on the bottom of a 9x13-inch casserole dish. Save the other half for the top.

2½ cups diced cooked chicken
1 teaspoon salt
½ cup chopped onion
½ cup chopped celery
½ cup mayonnaise

2 eggs
1½ cups milk
1 can cream of mushroom soup
1 cup shredded cheese

Mix chicken, salt, onion, celery, and mayonnaise together and spread over crust. Then cover with remaining crust mixture. Beat together eggs and milk. Pour on top, cover, and refrigerate overnight.

Spread mushroom soup over dish and bake at 350° for 1 hour. During the last 10 minutes of bake time, spread shredded cheese on top and leave in oven until melted.

Linda Lehman (Belvidere, Illinois)

*Literally a "scene behind the scenes," the views through the windows of the sets
are called Duratrans, and are made from photos taken in West Chester, Pennsylvania,
to make the sets as realistic as possible. The views are changed
with the changing of the seasons.*

Shrimp Remoulade

This sauce is good enough to eat by itself. I use it as a salad dressing, a vegetable dip, and alongside crab cakes.

1 cup finely chopped celery
1 cup finely chopped green onions
1 cup finely chopped parsley
3 tablespoons minced garlic
2 cups creole mustard
½ cup vegetable oil
½ cup red wine vinegar
2 teaspoons salt
2 tablespoons Worcestershire sauce
2 pounds boiled, peeled shrimp
Red leaf lettuce

Whisk together all ingredients, except shrimp and lettuce. Pour sauce over shrimp and lettuce.

Kristen A. Graves (Brandon, Mississippi)

Shrimp Lauren Ann

1 pound medium shrimp
2 sticks butter
1 medium onion, chopped
½ red, yellow, and green bell
    pepper, thinly sliced
Cayenne pepper
½–1 teaspoon salt
1 pound pepper cheese
1 (10-ounce) bag frozen stir-fry
    vegetables
Fettuccine or favorite pasta

Peel, devein, and clean shrimp. Melt butter in Dutch oven. Add onion and bell pepper and cook until onions are clear. Add shrimp and sprinkle cayenne pepper over them to taste and add salt. Stir shrimp until done (bright pink), about 3 minutes. Cube pepper cheese and add to pot. Reduce temperature to medium-low heat. Stir often, until melted. Add stir-fry vegetables and cook until vegetables are done to your liking. Serve over fettuccine. (Pictured on cover.)

Lauren Ann Morales (Nashville, Tennessee)

Editors' Extra: This is beautiful as well as delicious.

Cajun Shrimp Casserole

Tasty, spicy, superb!

1 onion, chopped
1 bell pepper, chopped
1 stick butter
Cajun seasoning or salt and
  pepper to taste
1 can creamy onion soup

1 can cream of mushroom soup
1 (10-ounce) can chopped
  tomatoes with green chiles
3 pounds peeled, uncooked
  shrimp
2 cups cooked rice

In large Dutch oven or deep fry pan, sauté onion and bell pepper in butter. Season to taste. Add soups, tomatoes, shrimp, and cooked rice; stir well. Empty entire mixture into a large casserole dish. Bake at 350° for 30–40 minutes.

Janet Odom (Baton Rouge, Louisiana)

Easy Shrimp Creole

My mother used to take all day making this family favorite. I just never found the time, but I did find a shortcut so we can still enjoy this delicious dish.

¹/₂ cup chopped onion
1 bell pepper
¹/₂ cup celery
1 pound shrimp

1 tablespoon butter
1 (26-ounce) jar spaghetti sauce
1 bay leaf
¹/₈ teaspoon pepper

Chop onion and cut bell pepper into thin, small strips. Thinly slice celery. Remove shell and devein shrimp. Put butter, onion, bell pepper, and celery in skillet. Cook until vegetables are tender and onion is opaque. Stir in spaghetti sauce, shrimp, bay leaf, and pepper. Cook until shrimp are curled. Remove bay leaf. Serve over rice. Makes 4 servings.

Jeanne Palos, QVC Employee (San Antonio, Texas)

At QVC's Studio Park, over 300 miles of cable link all the broadcasting equipment together.

Shrimp Rio Grande

Growing up on the Gulf Coast of Texas, shrimp was plentiful and abundant. Shrimp was our family's favorite meal. I've modified one of my mother's classic Sunday shrimp dinners to meet my family's taste. Whenever I serve this dish to company, I get incredible rave reviews.

4 ounces unsalted butter
24 raw jumbo shrimp, peeled
  and deveined
Flour
4 cloves garlic, diced
1 bunch green onions, thinly
  sliced
4 tomatoes, peeled and diced
2 shallots, diced

2 Anaheim chiles, roasted, peeled,
  seeded, and chopped
1 cup cream sherry
1 cup chardonnay
1 teaspoon each, salt and pepper
8 ounces cocktail sauce
8 ounces sliced mushrooms
2 cups fat-free half-and-half
Juice of 2 lemons

Melt butter in skillet; do not brown. Dredge shrimp in flour and place in skillet. Add garlic, green onions, tomatoes, shallots, and chiles; cook over low heat until garlic starts to brown. Add sherry and wine, salt and pepper. Cook until heated, stirring constantly. Stir in cocktail sauce and mushrooms; cook 2 minutes on low. When this starts to thicken, add half-and-half and lemon juice. Continue cooking until shrimp curl; this will indicate they are done. Serve with cooked, hot pasta and garlic bread.

Elaine Sweet (Dallas, Texas)

Imagine dozens of professional buyers, each specializing in a product category, each searching for the next great idea. Rachel Stevenson, QVC assistant buyer for food and cookbooks, is one such person.

Shrimp and Scallops QVC

Quick, Versatile, Cajun!

Pasta or tortellini for 2 servings (5 ounces)	Few grinds black pepper
1 medium onion, chopped	Pinch of salt
1–2 cloves garlic, minced	½ pound shrimp, shelled and deveined
1 tablespoon butter or olive oil	½ pound scallops
1–2 tablespoons chili powder	⅓ cup dry sherry mixed with 1 tablespoon cornstarch
1 tablespoon chopped parsley	¼ cup fat-free half-and-half
⅛–¼ teaspoon cayenne pepper	

Boil pasta; set aside. Sauté onion and garlic in oil in 10-inch skillet. Add chili powder, parsley, cayenne, black pepper, and salt. Add shrimp and scallops and cook 5–10 minutes (depending on size). Remove seafood and add sherry/cornstarch mixture. Simmer 3–5 minutes. Return seafood to pan and add half-and-half; stir to heat through. Serve over pasta and enjoy.

Variations: (1) Add 10 fresh spinach leaves. (2) Use all shrimp or all scallops. (3) Substitute grilled and sliced chicken breast or crab meat. (4) Serve over rice instead of pasta.

Debra Firth Eisel (Damascus, Maryland)

French Fried Shrimp

1 cup flour	1 cup ice water
½ teaspoon sugar	2 tablespoons vegetable oil
½ teaspoon salt	2 pounds shrimp (in shells)
1 egg, beaten	

Combine all ingredients except shrimp; beat until smooth. Shell shrimp, leaving last section and tail intact. Cut shrimp almost through at center back and remove black vein. Dry shrimp well, then dip into batter and fry in deep fryer (375°) till golden brown. Drain and serve with cocktail sauce.

Marsha Leistner (Bradford, Ohio)

Smothered Shrimp Gravy

The first time I made this, I made half again as much and my husband still wanted more! It is wonderful! A real winner served with plenty of hot grits.

2 tablespoons canola oil
1 tablespoon butter
1 cup chopped onions
3 tablespoons chopped green
  onions
1 teaspoon parsley flakes
2 tablespoons self-rising flour

1 cup water
½ teaspoon black pepper
1 teaspoon salt
½ teaspoon seafood seasoning
1¼ pounds shrimp, peeled,
  deveined
1 teaspoon lemon juice

Place oil, butter, and onions in a heavy skillet. Sauté over medium-high heat until onions are tender. Add green onions and parsley and sauté until onions are wilted. Sprinkle flour over onions and stir until smooth. Slowly stir in water and bring to a boil. Add pepper, salt, and seafood seasoning and reduce heat to low. Cover and simmer until onions are very tender and gravy is very thick (juice from shrimp will dilute gravy).

Remove lid and add shrimp. Toss to coat shrimp with gravy, replace cover, and simmer until shrimp are just curled and pink, about 4 minutes. Stir in lemon juice, taste, and adjust seasonings. Serve at once over hot grits or rice.

Debra W. McNair (Midway, Georgia)

The North Fork Commissary is one of two cafeterias serving QVC. The other one is located in the West Chester Operations Center. Combined, they serve 14,000 meals per week.

South Seas Shrimp

SOUTH SEAS SALSA:

¹/₃ chopped red bell pepper
2 tablespoons minced jalapeño
  peppers
²/₃ cup chopped pineapple

¹/₃ cup chopped red onion
¹/₂ teaspoon ground cumin
1 tablespoon fresh lime juice
1 tablespoon prepared chutney

In medium bowl, mix all ingredients. Set aside so flavors will blend.

18 slices turkey bacon, cut in
  half crosswise
1 pound large shrimp, peeled
  and deveined
¹/₄ cup pineapple juice

2 tablespoons prepared chutney
2 tablespoons low-sodium soy
  sauce
1 tablespoon brown sugar

Soak 8–10 wooden skewers in water. In a large skillet, cook bacon (on 1 side only) for 3 minutes; drain on paper towels. Spray barbecue grill or broiler rack pan with vegetable spray. Prepare grill or broiler to medium-high heat.

Wrap cooked side of bacon around each shrimp and thread onto skewers. Thread 4–5 shrimp onto each skewer. In a small bowl, whisk together the remaining ingredients. Grill or broil shrimp 4 minutes per side, brushing with pineapple juice mixture. To serve, carefully remove shrimp from skewers so bacon stays in place. Place onto 4 dinner plates along with South Seas Salsa. Yields 4 servings.

Margee Berry (White Salmon, Washington)

QVC's cafeteria entrance is in the atrium. Its huge seating area offers a cheerful place for a meal or a cup of coffee. It's a good meeting place, too, where planning may come easier in a casual atmosphere.

Ocean Bay Casserole

¼ cup minced onion
1 cup chopped mushrooms
  (fresh or canned)
2 tablespoons butter or margarine
½ pound cooked shrimp,
  chopped
1 pound crab meat (fresh or
  canned)
1 cup frozen peas (or vegetable
  of choice)

1 teaspoon cayenne pepper
1 can cream of chicken soup
1 (16-ounce) container sour cream
12 ounces wide egg noodles,
  cooked and drained
½ pound shredded mozzarella
  cheese
Seafood seasoning (optional)

Sauté onion and mushrooms in butter till onions are transparent. Add shrimp and crab meat, stirring to combine. Add peas, pepper, soup, and sour cream to mixture and combine thoroughly. Place cooked noodles in greased 9x11-inch casserole dish. Pour mixture over noodles and stir to blend. Sprinkle cheese over top and season with seafood seasoning, if desired. Bake at 350° for 40 minutes.

Carol A. Saylor (Monrovia, Maryland)

Outstanding Crab Soufflé

I love to cook and experiment with different recipes. This is a keeper!

½ green pepper, chopped
¼ cup mayonnaise
1 (6-ounce) can crab meat or
  shrimp
1 stalk celery, chopped
4 slices white bread

1 cup milk
3 eggs, beaten
½ cup cream of mushroom soup
½ cup shredded sharp Cheddar
  cheese
1 teaspoon chopped parsley

Mix first 4 ingredients to make sandwich filling. Spread between bread to make 2 sandwiches. Put the sandwiches next to each other in a loaf pan. Mix together milk and eggs and pour over sandwiches. Refrigerate overnight.

Remove from refrigerator 1 hour before baking. Bake in 325° oven for 15 minutes. Remove and top with the cream of mushroom soup, cheese, and parsley. Bake an additional 45 minutes.

Bev Moe (Mahnomen, Minnesota)

Asparagus Crab Quiche

12–15 asparagus spears, trimmed and cut into 2- to 3-inch pieces	¼ teaspoon salt
1 (10-inch) deep-dish pie shell, unbaked	⅛ teaspoon black pepper
	⅛ teaspoon cayenne pepper
1 tablespoon butter, melted	⅛ teaspoon dill weed
10–12 ounces king crab, cooked	3 cups shredded Colby cheese
2 teaspoons lemon juice	2 green onions, thinly sliced (including tops)
6 eggs, beaten	½ cup sliced mushrooms
¾ cup half-and-half	2 tablespoons chopped parsley

Steam asparagus until barely tender. Brush pie shell with melted butter. Prick sides and bottom with fork. Place asparagus in bottom of pie shell. Place crab meat on top of asparagus. Sprinkle lemon juice on top of crab.

In mixing bowl, beat eggs and half-and-half together. Add salt, pepper, cayenne, and dill weed. Mix. Stir in cheese, onion, and mushrooms. Pour this mixture into pie shell. Sprinkle parsley over center of quiche. Bake at 350° for 35–40 minutes or until golden brown and knife comes out clean. Let cool 20 minutes before cutting.

Bonnie K. Thomas (Anchorage, Alaska)

Editors' Extra: This can also be made in 2 (8-inch) pie shells rather than one large one.

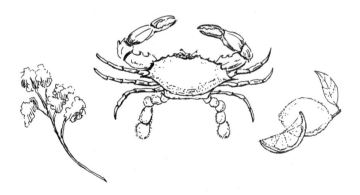

Crawfish Caroline

This recipe was a Gold Medal Winner in the 1988 Baton Rouge Culinary Classic. It features two Louisiana favorites, crawfish and eggplant.

2 medium eggplants	1 pound crawfish tails
1 cup milk	1 clove garlic, minced
2 eggs	½ cup white wine
½ cup Italian bread crumbs	1 tablespoon flour
½ cup flour	2 pints heavy cream
Vegetable or olive oil	½ cup green onions, chopped
1 medium yellow onion, chopped	Salt and pepper to taste
1 stick butter	

Peel eggplants and cut into ½-inch slices; soak in salt water for 2 hours. Rinse well.

Combine milk and eggs. In separate bowl, mix bread crumbs and ½ cup flour. Dip eggplant medallions in milk and egg mixture, then roll in bread crumbs and flour mixture. Pan fry in ⅛ inch of oil until golden brown. Set aside.

Simmer chopped onion in butter until clear. Add crawfish tails, garlic, and wine and bring to a boil. Stir in 1 tablespoon flour, making a light roux. Add heavy cream and bring to a boil. Reduce heat to a simmer and add green onions. Salt and pepper to taste.

Place 2 eggplant medallions onto a plate, spoon sauce over, and serve. Can be used as an appetizer or entreé. Serves 4.

Brett Ransome (Baton Rouge, Louisiana)

In a typical day, QVC is capable of handling over 300,000 incoming phone calls. The record for calls handled in a 24-hour period is more than 835,000.

St. Joseph Oyster Dressing

4 pints of fresh oysters in liquid
1 pound ground chuck
1 pound breakfast sausage (pork)
1 large onion, chopped
2 bunches of green onions,
chopped

5 garlic cloves, chopped
¹/₂ medium bell pepper, chopped
2 ribs of celery, chopped
Salt, black, and red pepper to taste
1 cup plain bread crumbs

Boil oysters in their own liquid, adding water if there is not enough liquid from the oysters. Boil till eye is tender. Skim off slag. Drain and chop oysters; save the liquid.

Fry beef, pork sausage, onion, green onions, garlic, bell pepper, celery, and seasonings in frying pan till meat is done and onions are tender. Add oysters and fry a little. Add some of the liquid from the oysters, if necessary. Pour into a pan sprayed with nonstick cooking spray and sprinkle bread crumbs over dressing. Bake in a 350° oven until bread crumbs are golden brown.

Amanda Mize (St. Joseph, Louisiana)

The Best Fried Clams

This recipe was my mother's, from Portland, Maine. It was a treat to vacation in my hometown and look forward to fried clams and boiled lobsters. I now claim her recipe, the best fried clams in the Northeast.

2 eggs, separated
¹/₂ cup milk
1 teaspoon olive oil
1 cup sifted flour

¹/₄ teaspoon salt
1 teaspoon lemon juice
1 pint small clams, drained

Beat egg yolks until thick and lemon colored. Add milk, olive oil, flour, salt, and lemon juice. Fold in stiffly beaten egg whites and clams; refrigerate at least 2 hours.

Drop by spoonfuls into deep fat heated to 375°. Fry until golden brown. Fry only a few at a time, as too many will cool the fat.

Nancy Martinson (Valparaiso, Indiana)

Key Largo Country-Style Fish

My cousin, Wanda Cheli, is the best cook in all the Keys of South Florida. She cooks with love. She taught me how to make this recipe for my family. The best day is to sit in front of the ocean, listen to the waves, and eat Key Largo Country-Style Fish.

2 rolls round snack crackers
2 pounds Tilapia (or other tender white fish)
Salt and pepper to taste

Seasoned salt or garlic salt to taste
Chopped parsley (optional)
1 cup half-and-half
1 stick butter, melted

Put 2 rolls of crackers in zip-lock bag. Crush with a rolling pin. Lightly oil 9x13-inch pan. Put ½ of crushed crackers in bottom of pan. Place fish on top of crackers. Season fish with salt, pepper, seasoned salt, and chopped parsley. Sprinkle remaining crackers over fish. Pour 1 cup of half-and-half over all. When cream has settled, pour melted butter over all. Let set 1 hour, or do the day before and refrigerate. Bake at 350° for 45 minutes.

Barbara Peluso (Cooper City, Florida)

Co-editors Gwen McKee and Barbara Moseley are busy in Gwen's kitchen giving the home-kitchen test to a contest recipe. Each selected recipe has to be easy to understand, and has to taste so good you'll want to make it again!

Chef Mark's Jazzy Snazzy Catfish

1½ pounds fresh catfish filets
4 teaspoons soy sauce
2 teaspoons lime juice
1 teaspoon no-salt seasoning
2 teaspoons spicy seafood
seasoning
2 tablespoons Italian bread crumbs
⅓ cup salsa

Spray baking dish with nonstick cooking spray; lay out fish filets so they do not touch. Top with soy sauce, lime juice, seasonings, bread crumbs, and salsa. Bake at 400°, uncovered, for 20–30 minutes, depending on thickness of filets. Serves 5–6.

Nutritional facts per 1 piece (150g) serving: Calories 222; Fat Calories 99; Saturated fat 2g (12%); Total fat 11g (17%); Cholesterol 87mg (29%); Sodium 429mg (18%); Total carbohydrate 3g (1%); Dietary fiber 0g (1%); Sugars 1g; Protein 27g.

Mark Goodwin, QVC Executive Chef Manager
(West Chester, Pennsylvania)

Easy Fried Catfish Filets

2 cups yellow cornmeal
2 tablespoons onion powder
2 tablespoons garlic powder
2 tablespoons black pepper
1 tablespoon cayenne pepper or
Cajun seasoning, or to taste
Salt to taste
12–16 ounces either: beer, milk,
water, or white wine
8 (3- to 4-ounce) catfish filets
Peanut oil

Mix cornmeal, onion powder, garlic powder, black pepper, cayenne pepper (or Cajun seasoning), and salt, if desired, into large zip-lock bag or small paper sack. Pour liquid into bowl and dip filets into liquid one at a time, completely covering filets. Remove from liquid and let drain, then place into seasoned cornmeal mix. Seal bag and shake filets until completely covered with mixture. Place on paper towel and repeat until all filets are coated.

Meanwhile, preheat peanut oil in deep fryer to 375°. Place fish in basket, or loose (do not crowd) in heated peanut oil and cook 5–10 minutes or until fish float to surface for 1–2 minutes. Remove from oil and drain well. Serve with tartar sauce, French fries, hushpuppies, and iced tea. Enjoy!

Timmerra Thomas (Memphis, Tennessee)

Halibut Primavera

1½ pounds halibut fillet
½ cup chopped broccoli
¼ cup chopped red bell pepper
¼ cup chopped zucchini
¼ cup shredded carrots
¼ cup chopped asparagus
  (optional)
¼ cup chopped green onion
4–6 ounces shredded mozzarella
  cheese

4–6 ounces shredded Monterey
  Jack cheese
3 ounces shredded mild Cheddar
  cheese
3 ounces shredded Parmesan
  cheese
Salt and pepper to taste

Preheat oven to 375°. Wash and pat dry halibut fillets. Place halibut on nonstick baking sheet. Sprinkle vegetables evenly over halibut fillet. Mix cheeses together. Sprinkle cheeses over halibut and vegetables. Season to taste. Place in oven and bake 30–40 minutes, until halibut flakes easily with a fork. Serves 6–8.

Jacki Equall (Des Moines, Washington)

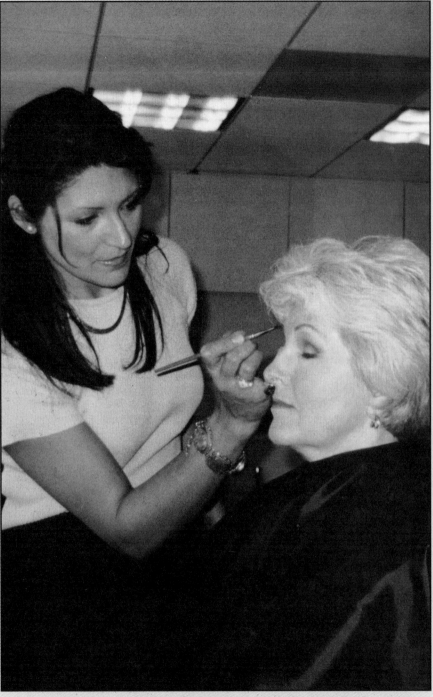

When guests go on air, QVC wants to help them put their best face forward.
Claudia Seylor is one of many talented make-up artists who, according to Gwen,
"Not only make you look pretty, they make you <u>feel</u> pretty."

Confetti Meatloaf

This is very colorful if you use two or more colors of peppers. Very flavorful.

1½ pounds ground beef
½ pound ground pork sausage
1 cup stuffing mix
2 eggs
½ cup milk
1 cup chopped peppers (red, orange, yellow and green)

1 medium onion, chopped
2 tablespoons fresh or dried parsley
1 cup ketchup
1½ teaspoons salt
1 teaspoon pepper

Mix all ingredients and form in long rectangular loaf; place in 9x13-inch pan. Bake for one hour at 350° or until meat is no longer pink.

Betty Lack (La Mesa, California)

Nacho Cheese Meatloaf

Since my husband was not a Mexican food eater but the rest of the family was, this idea was the best I had to tempt him. And it worked! Now this is the only way he'll eat meatloaf.

1½ pounds ground beef
1 egg, beaten
1 stack saltine crackers, crushed
½ cup diced onion
½ cup diced green pepper
1 cup ketchup

⅛ teaspoon black pepper
¼ teaspoon seasoned salt
¼ teaspoon garlic powder
1 large or small can nacho cheese soup, undiluted

Mix all ingredients except soup together thoroughly. Place mixture in loaf pan. Gently poke holes on top of meatloaf with tines of large fork to almost bottom. Pour undiluted soup over top of meatloaf and spread evenly. Bake 1–1½ hours at 350°. The soup makes it a hit. Great for cold sandwiches!

Carol Nugent (South Lyon, Michigan)

Marble-ous Meatloaf

The spinach creates a marbling effect. It's pretty and so easy, but the best thing about this recipe is that it gets my kids to eat their veggies!

2 pounds ground beef
1 package frozen spinach with
  cream sauce, thawed

1 envelope onion soup mix
1 egg

Preheat oven to 350°. Do not drain spinach. Mix the ground beef, spinach, onion soup, and egg in a large bowl. Be sure to mix well. Form the mixture into a loaf shape in the middle of a jellyroll pan. Bake for 60 minutes, or until done. Good served with a sauce on the side, if desired. (Pictured on cover.)

Julie A. Savu (Novi, Michigan)

Meatloaf Italiano

1 (8-ounce) can tomato sauce,
  divided
2 pounds ground chuck
1 pound sage-style sausage
2 eggs

1 cup Italian-style bread crumbs
1 small onion, finely chopped
2 cloves garlic, minced
2 tablespoons Italian seasoning
1/4 cup water

Set aside 1/3 can of tomato sauce. Place remaining ingredients in a large mixing bowl. Mix well by hand. Shape into a loaf. Pour remaining tomato sauce over top of loaf.

Bake, uncovered, 1 1/2 hours at 350° in a loaf pan or shallow baking dish. Let set about 10 minutes before slicing. Serves 6–8.

Victoria J. Valentino (Columbus, Ohio)

QVC is based in West Chester, Pennsylvania, with additional U.S. telecommunications centers in San Antonio, Texas, Port St. Lucie, Florida, and Chesapeake, Virginia. Its distribution centers are located in Lancaster and West Chester, Pennsylvania, Suffolk, Virginia, and Rocky Mount, North Carolina.

Cheeseburger Meatloaf

1½ pounds ground chuck
1½ cups dry breadcrumbs
½ cup chopped onion
½ cup pickles, chopped (sweet
  or sour, to your taste)

1 cup shredded cheese
2 eggs
¾ cup ketchup, divided
¾ cup mustard, divided
¼ cup mayonnaise

Preheat oven to 350°. Mix all ingredients, except for ¼ cup ketchup and ¼ cup mustard, in large mixing bowl. Pat into a loaf shape, and place on a greased roasting pan. If desired, mix ¼ cup each ketchup and mustard together and pour over top of meatloaf. Bake for 40–50 minutes, or until cooked through.

Variations: (1) Add ¼ cup crumbled cooked bacon to the ground beef. (2) Eliminate ketchup and mustard and use equal amount barbecue sauce instead. (3) Use drained pickle relish instead of pickles. (4) Use different cheeses, or a blend.

Sally Sibthorpe (Rochester Hills, Michigan)

Meatloaf Pies

My friends and family love this!

2 (9-inch) pie shells
1½ pounds ground sirloin
1 (14½-ounce) can diced
  tomatoes with green peppers
  and onions

1 cup bread crumbs
4 eggs
2 cups extra sharp cheese, divided
½ teaspoon salt
½ teaspoon pepper (optional)

Bake pie shells (pierce all over with fork) for 15 minutes at 400°. Mix all ingredients except 1 cup cheese and separate evenly into pie shells. Sprinkle reserved cheese over tops of pies. Bake at 350° for 1 hour.

Note: Turkey may be substituted for beef. These can be conveniently frozen.

Carol Russell (Walland, Tennessee)

Porcupine Meat Balls

1½ pounds ground beef
¾ cup uncooked minute rice
¾ cup water
½ cup chopped onion
½ teaspoon salt
1½ teaspoons celery salt
¼ teaspoon pepper

½ teaspoon garlic powder
1 (15-ounce) can plus
  1 (8-ounce) can tomato sauce
½ cup water
3 teaspoons Worcestershire sauce
½ cup burgundy wine

Preheat oven to 350°. Mix meat, rice, water, onion, salt, celery salt, pepper, and garlic powder. Make into balls. Place on ungreased 9x13-inch pan. Mix remaining ingredients and pour over meat. Cover with foil. Bake for 45 minutes; uncover, and bake 15 minutes longer.

Jean Scott (Walworth, New York)

More, Please!

A one-dish meal that's sure to please.

1½ pounds ground beef
3 large onions, sliced
½ teaspoon sugar
1 (12-ounce) package pasta shells,
  cooked
1 (4-ounce) jar chopped pimentos
1 (4¼-ounce) can sliced black
  olives, drained
1 (1-pound) can tomato sauce

1 can tomato soup
1 (1-pound) can creamed corn
1 tablespoon dry mustard
2 tablespoons Worcestershire sauce
1 clove garlic, minced
1 tablespoon paprika
Salt and pepper to taste
1 (8-ounce) package shredded
  Cheddar cheese

Brown meat. Sauté onions with sugar. Mix all ingredients together. (One teaspoon of powdered coffee may be added to mixture.) Bake in a greased 9x13-inch pan at 350° for 40 minutes.

Nancy E. McLeod (San Diego, California)

Elizabeth's Favorite Beef Stroganoff

2 tablespoons butter	1 can cream of mushroom soup
1/2 cup chopped onion	1 cup milk
1 teaspoon chopped garlic	1 cup sour cream
1 pound hamburger	Salt and pepper to taste

Melt butter in a stockpot. Sauté chopped onion and garlic; brown hamburger with onion and garlic. Mix soup and milk and add to hamburger mixture. Let simmer for 5–10 minutes. Add sour cream and simmer 5 minutes longer. Salt and pepper to taste. Serve over egg noodles or mashed potatoes.

Mary Beth Roe, QVC Host (West Chester, Pennsylvania)

The epitome of the working mother, Mary Beth Roe is well-known to viewers for her dedication to her family, husband Mark, her three sons, Eric, Cory and Ryan, and her new little princess, Elizabeth. Mary Beth has acted in a CBS mini-series, made over 30 television commercials, been a news anchor, and has done newspaper, radio and television reporting. She was Miss Teen Minnesota, and was later crowned Mrs. Minnesota.

Sloppy Joe Eddys

1½ pounds ground beef
1 onion, finely chopped
1 green pepper, finely chopped
½ cup chopped celery
2 tablespoons brown sugar
2 tablespoons prepared mustard
1 tablespoon Worcestershire
  sauce

1 (8-ounce) can tomato sauce
1 (11-ounce) can sliced
  mushrooms, drained, save juice
Mushroom juice with water to
  equal 1 cup
½ cup ketchup
Salt and pepper to taste

Brown beef, onion, pepper, and celery in large saucepan or Dutch oven. Add remaining ingredients. Cook over low heat, uncovered, for 1 hour. Stir often. Delicious served on toasted hamburger rolls. Serves 8.

Jeanne Eddy (Camden, New York)

Sloppy Joe Turnovers

1 pound ground beef or venison
¼ cup chopped onion
½ teaspoon salt
¼ teaspoon garlic powder
½ cup ketchup
¼ cup sour cream
1 (10-count) can good-quality
  biscuits

1 (8-ounce) package shredded
  mozzarella, Cheddar, or taco
  blend cheese
½ cup chopped green or red
  peppers

Heat oven to 375°. In large skillet, brown beef and onion; drain. Add next 4 ingredients and mix well.

Separate the biscuits. Press each one into a square (about 4x4 inches). Place about ¼ cup meat mixture on center of each square. Sprinkle with cheese and peppers. Fold over corner of square to form a triangle. Seal edges with a fork. Put 3 slits on top and bake on ungreased cookie sheet at 375° for 15–20 minutes. Yields 10 biscuits.

Rita Lohr (Middletown, New York)

Tamale Casserole

This recipe was developed when I didn't have anything else in my cabinets that would go together to make a meal. My family liked all the ingredients separately, so I just layered them together and topped it off with what I had available. It was a hit!

2 cans beef tamales
1 medium onion, chopped
2 cans chili, with or without
   beans

1 cup shredded Cheddar cheese
1 bag of corn chips (1–2 cups)

Remove paper from tamales. Cut tamales into 1-inch pieces and place in a casserole dish. Sprinkle onion over tamales and spread chili on top. Cover with foil.

   Cook in a 350° oven for 45 minutes. Remove foil and sprinkle with cheese. Cover again with foil and keep hot till cheese melts. When ready to serve, crush corn chips and sprinkle on top.

Nancy R. Burford (Senatobia, Mississippi)

Growing Boys Taco Casserole

When I first made this recipe, I had two growing boys who had unusually large appetites. I was a working mom so I had to have quick and good meals. Since they liked Mexican food, I started creating quick Mexican meals. My husband can eat his weight in this casserole.

2 pounds lean ground beef
3 teaspoons chili powder
3 teaspoons garlic powder
1 (14½-ounce) can corn, drained
1 (8-ounce) container sour cream

1 (16-ounce) jar medium hot salsa
1 large bag plain tortilla chips,
   crushed, divided
5 cups shredded Colby Jack cheese,
   or 4-cheese Mexican mix, divided

Preheat oven to 350°. Brown ground beef. Add chili powder and garlic powder. In a large bowl, mix together ground beef, corn, sour cream, and salsa. Coat bottom of 9x13-inch pan with ½ of meat mixture. Crush ½ tortilla chips on top, and then add a layer of cheese. Continue layering, ending with cheese on top. Bake for approximately 20 minutes, or until heated through.

Anna M. Hixon (Rutledge, Tennessee)

Easy Mexican Hot Dish

Very easy and delicious, with a little bite.

1 pound hamburger
1 medium onion, chopped
6–8 (7-inch) tortillas
1 can mild enchilada sauce

1 (4-ounce) can chopped green
  chiles
1 can cream of celery soup
2 cups shredded Cheddar cheese

Brown hamburger and onion in skillet; drain. Grease bottom of round casserole dish. Tear tortillas in fourths. Dip each piece in enchilada sauce and cover bottom and sides of casserole. Put some hamburger mixture on top of tortillas, then enchilada sauce, chiles, and soup. Dip more tortillas and layer again till everything is gone. Bake at 325° for 1 hour, uncovered. Sprinkle cheese on top the last 20 minutes of baking time.

Emily Cafourek (Austin, Minnesota)

Chili Tortilla Bake

1 pound ground chuck
2 (8-ounce) cans tomato sauce
1 (14½-ounce) can black beans,
  drained and rinsed
1 (8¾-ounce) can whole corn,
  undrained, or 1½ cups frozen
  corn
1 (4½-ounce) can green chiles,
  undrained
2 tablespoons chili powder

2 tablespoons dried minced onions,
  or 1 medium onion, chopped
1 teaspoon ground cumin
1 teaspoon garlic salt or powder
½ teaspoon oregano
6 flour tortillas, divided
2 cups shredded Cheddar cheese,
  divided, or 1 cup Monterey Jack
  and 1 cup Cheddar cheese,
  divided

Preheat oven to 350°. In a large skillet, brown ground chuck over medium heat. Drain and add tomato sauce, beans, corn, and green chiles. Stir in next 5 ingredients; bring to a boil. Then reduce heat and simmer, uncovered, for 15 minutes.

In a 2-quart baking dish coated with nonstick cooking spray, place 3 of the tortillas to cover bottom, overlapping, if necessary. Layer with half of chili mixture and half of cheese. Repeat layers again and bake for 30 minutes.

Serve with salsa, sour cream, guacamole dip, jalapeño peppers, or black olives on the side. Serves 8.

Brenda Harrison (Chattanooga, Tennessee)

Quick and Easy Enchiladas

2 (10-ounce) cans enchilada
  sauce, divided
1 pound lean hamburger
1 medium onion, chopped
¾ cup salsa
1 package (8) flour or corn
  tortillas

1 cup shredded Monterey Jack
  cheese
1 cup mild shredded Cheddar
  cheese
1 small can sliced black olives,
  drained (optional)

Preheat oven to 375°. Pour ½–¾ can of enchilada sauce into 9x13x2-inch baking pan. Brown hamburger in skillet, adding chopped onion. Add salsa and cook until hot. Spoon hamburger mixture onto tortillas. Roll tortillas up and place on top of enchilada sauce in pan. Pour remaining enchilada sauce evenly over rolled tortillas. Sprinkle shredded cheeses evenly over top of rolled tortillas. Sprinkle sliced olives over top of cheese, if desired. Bake at 375° for 30 minutes or until bubbling. Serves 6.

Jacki Equall (Des Moines, Washington)

Crescent Crust Taco Pie

1 pound hamburger
1 package taco seasoning mix
1 package crescent rolls

1 cup crushed corn chips, divided
1 (8-ounce) carton sour cream
6 slices American cheese

Brown hamburger in skillet till done; drain. Add taco seasoning to the cooked hamburger and mix together according to package directions. Spray a 9-inch pie pan with vegetable oil and place crescent rolls in pan; pat together. Brown in a 375° oven for 15 minutes. Put half of the crushed corn chips on crescent roll crust. Spread with hamburger mixture and top with sour cream; add slices of cheese on top. Sprinkle the other half of corn chips on top. Bake at 375° for 20 minutes. Cut in wedges. Serves 6–8.

Brenda Grimes (Union City, Indiana)

Margarita Fajitas

Don't be tempted to drink the marinade. (It smells like a margarita!)

2¹/₂–3 pounds skirt steak
¹/₃ cup lime juice
¹/₂ cup tequila
¹/₄ cup vegetable oil
2 tablespoons chopped cilantro
1 teaspoon crushed red pepper flakes

1 teaspoon cumin
1 teaspoon oregano
1 teaspoon finely chopped garlic
1–2 onions, sliced
1 large green pepper, cut in strips
1 large red pepper, cut in strips

Slightly score steaks and put in zip-lock bag. Mix lime juice, tequila, vegetable oil, cilantro, red pepper flakes, cumin, oregano, and garlic together and pour over steaks. Marinate 6–8 hours, or preferably overnight.

Grill meat 6–10 minutes on each side, depending on thickness.

In a 4-quart chef pan, or similar, sauté onions and peppers until crisp tender. Add thinly sliced steaks and mix together. Serve with warm flour tortillas, pico de gallo or salsa, guacamole, refried beans, and sour cream.

Charlotte Duffield (Scottsdale, Arizona)

Having just come from "Noah's Ark" (Product Central), these perky animals wait in the wings for their turn to be on camera.

Peppery Pineapple Stir-Fry

I've been making this dish for about 17 years. My family and I are lovers of Chinese-style foods, but did not like having to spend the money required for a family of four to enjoy. This meal is wonderfully delicious, satisfyingly filling, and covers most of our daily desired requirements of meat, fruit, vegetables, and grain (if you use rice). It's colorful, too!

2 pounds stew beef chunks
1 (16-ounce) can pineapple chunks
   in light syrup, drained
1 (10-ounce) bag frozen broccoli,
   thawed
2 tablespoons olive oil
½ cup water
¼ cup soy sauce

4 teaspoons cornstarch
2 teaspoons ginger
1 tablespoon crushed red pepper,
   or to taste
2 teaspoons sugar
White rice or egg noodles, cooked
   as directed

Before cooking, cut beef, pineapple, and broccoli to desired bite size. In large skillet or wok, brown beef in oil over low to medium heat until thoroughly cooked (medium-well to well done). Drain meat and return to pan with heat off. Add pineapple and broccoli to meat. In separate bowl, combine water, soy sauce, cornstarch, ginger, red pepper, and sugar; mix thoroughly.

Return meat to medium-low heat. Add liquid mixture to meat, and mix all ingredients well. Continue mixing until liquid thickens to a sauce coating meat, fruit, and vegetables. Serve over rice or noodles of your choice.

Vicki L. Marlette (Lancaster, California)

Editors' Extra: I saved the pineapple juice and used some to stretch the sauce.

 On an average day in 2000, QVC shipped approximately 180,000 boxes in the United States and 33,000 in the United Kingdom and Germany.

Italian Pot Roast Dinner

I have cooked this pot roast for family and friends many times. Everyone enjoys it. I like it because I can do it ahead and enjoy my guests when they arrive.

1 (3- to 4-pound) rump roast
3 cloves garlic, sliced, divided
2 tablespoons olive oil
Italian seasoning, rosemary, salt and pepper to taste
1 (28-ounce) can stewed tomatoes
1 onion, sliced

1 (8-ounce) can sliced mushrooms (or 2 cups fresh)
1/2–3/4 cup red wine
6 carrots, sliced
1 (12-ounce) package egg noodles
2 tablespoons butter (for sauce)
2 cloves garlic, chopped (for sauce)

Make small cuts in rump roast to put a few slices of garlic in roast. Rub olive oil on roast; coat with Italian seasoning, rosemary, salt and pepper. Brown roast on stove top or in oven at 450°. After it is browned, turn oven to 350°.

In a small bowl, put tomatoes, onion, garlic, more seasonings (if needed), mushrooms, and wine. Pour over roast; cover and cook for 2½–3 hours, or until tender.

Cook carrots separately or put around roast the last ½ hour. Cook egg noodles when roast is done; drain. Heat butter and chopped garlic in saucepan. Serve sliced roast, carrots, and sauce over noodles.

Ginger Borg (Concord, California)

Beef Pot Roast with Onions

3 large onions, sliced
2 teaspoons roasted garlic
2 teaspoons ground nutmeg, divided

2 teaspoons salt, divided
1 teaspoon pepper, divided
1 (6-pound) beef roast
2 cups dark beer or beef broth

Preheat oven to 350°. Lay onion slices on bottom of Dutch oven; top with garlic and half each nutmeg, salt, and pepper. Place roast on top; sprinkle with remaining seasonings and pour beer or broth around. Cover pan with foil and place lid on. Roast 35 minutes. Reduce temperature to 300°; cook 1 hour longer. Reduce heat to 250°; cook 2 hours longer. Remove meat from pan; let stand 15 minutes before slicing. Skim fat from liquid and spoon over meat. Makes 8–10 servings.

Marilou Robinson (Portland, Oregon)

Creamy Beef Bourguignon Steak

2 pounds top round steak
Flour to coat steak
Oil
1 can cream of mushroom soup
1 can cream of onion soup
1 envelope brown gravy mix

1 small can mushroom pieces, drained
$\frac{1}{3}$ cup diced yellow onion
$\frac{1}{2}$ cup red wine
Salt and pepper to taste

Trim fat and bone from round steak and then cut into serving-size pieces. Pound flour into steaks with meat mallet. Brown both sides of steak in oil. Combine soups, gravy mix, mushrooms, onion, wine, salt and pepper. Pour this mixture over meat and simmer for $1\frac{1}{2}$ hours, or until tender. Serve over rice.

Charlene M. Olson (Minot, North Dakota)

Beef Birds

2 pounds beef round steak
Mustard of choice for spreading
Salt and pepper to taste
1 small onion, thinly sliced

3–4 medium carrots, peeled and
   sliced in hand-length strips
Flour

Take round steak and cut in long strips about the width and length of your hand. (Round steak can be pounded to about ¾-inch thickness.) Spread these pieces with a thin layer of mustard, then salt and pepper to taste. Next, layer the onion slices, then a finger of carrot. (The carrot should be placed on the round steak in a horizontal position to look like wings.) Roll up the round steak mixture and hold together with a toothpick.

Lightly flour and brown "birds" on stove top in a nonstick Dutch oven or deep fry pan. After browning, add a small amount of water, cover, and simmer for 50–60 minutes, or until tender. The juice can be poured over the birds or used to make a delicious gravy.

After the birds are done simmering, I usually remove them to a platter, prepare the gravy, then place them back in the gravy to simmer for 10 minutes prior to serving. These are good served with dumplings or mashed potatoes.

Optional: A piece of bacon may be wrapped around each bird prior to initial browning. If bacon is used, each bacon slice should be limply cooked prior to securing around the round steak with the toothpick.

Kathryn A. Nava (Milwaukee, Wisconsin)

This huge video wall (8.5 x 5 x 6.5 feet), often used on the fitness set, is similar to a big screen TV. It enables the control room to enhance products by feeding pictures and videos into the wall.

Beef Filets with Creamy Creole Sauce

This quick and easy recipe is very special around my house for two reasons. It tastes wonderful, and the family thinks I really "put myself out" on this one. I guess, if it gets chosen to go in this cookbook, I'll be exposed! It's so simple, a child could do it. I hope you like it.

2 tablespoons unsalted butter or margarine

2 (6- to 8-ounce) beef filets or rib eyes

Over medium heat, in a 10-inch skillet, heat the 2 tablespoons butter until melted and sizzling. Add steaks, reduce heat to medium-low and cook 10–12 minutes per side, or until internal temperature reaches 145–155 °. While the steaks cook, make the Sauce.

SAUCE:

1 teaspoon unsalted butter or margarine
1 tablespoon creole mustard
1/2 cup half-and-half
2 teaspoons freeze-dried chives

1/2 teaspoon whole celery seed
1 teaspoon garlic powder, or 1 garlic clove, minced
1 teaspoon Worcestershire sauce
Salt and black pepper to taste

Over medium heat, in a small saucepan, heat butter, mustard, half-and-half, chives, and celery seed. Reduce heat to medium-low and simmer until the sauce thickens; add garlic and Worcestershire sauce. Season the steaks with salt and pepper to taste. Serve steaks, topped with warm Sauce.

Betty Mitchem (Satsuma, Alabama)

Best Ever Oven-Baked Barbecue Ribs

Five minutes to prepare! Come home to an impressive meal.

1 family pack baby back ribs
1 (18-ounce) bottle hickory smoke barbecue sauce

1 (14-ounce) jar spaghetti sauce
1–1 1/2 cups brown sugar

Line a deep roasting pan with foil. Put ribs in foil. Pour remaining ingredients over ribs (no need to mix). Bake, uncovered, at 250° for 6 hours, or at 225° for 8–10 hours.

Heather Creel (Franklin, Tennessee)

Drive-In Beef Barbecue

As a child, my father would take us to the local drive-in restaurant. Waitresses on roller skates served us and attached a metal tray to the car door. We always ordered beef or pork barbecue sandwiches . . . so tasty . . . just like these.

**2 pounds left-over round steak,
chuck roast, or pork roast,
cut into pieces or shredded**
1 cup ketchup
¼ cup chopped onion
¼ cup water

2 tablespoons brown sugar
2 teaspoons prepared mustard
2 tablespoons lemon juice
1 tablespoon vinegar
1 cup diced celery

Combine all ingredients in a nonstick pan and simmer for ½ hour. Serve on hamburger buns with cole slaw. Serves 4–6.

Joanne Ridley-Pacicca (Syracuse, New York)

Melt-in-Your-Mouth Barbecue

1 cup beef broth or gravy
⅔ cup ketchup
1 teaspoon prepared mustard
2 tablespoons brown sugar
1 teaspoon Worcestershire sauce
1 clove garlic, minced
1 small onion, minced
1½ tablespoons vinegar

**¼ teaspoon liquid smoke
seasoning**
Juice of 1 lemon
¼ teaspoon pepper sauce
Salt and pepper to taste
**2–3 cups cooked beef or pork
roast, thinly sliced**

Mix all ingredients except meat. Place meat in a 2-quart oven-safe pan and pour sauce over meat. Cover and bake at 350° for 1 hour, or until sauce is thick.

Shirley Harper (Sheridan, Wyoming)

 On average, 40,000 people make their first purchase from QVC or QVC.com each week.

Sausage Potato Casserole

This recipe is so popular that everyone wants a copy of it. My mother-in-law fixed it one year for an Easter family camping trip and I've lost count of the number of times I've fixed it for potlucks. Great dish to put together the night before and bake the following morning.

FILLING:

1 pound browned pork sausage
1 (32-ounce) package frozen
  hashbrowns
½ cup butter, melted
1 teaspoon salt

¼ teaspoon pepper
½ cup chopped yellow onion
1 can cream of mushroom soup
2 cups (16 ounces) sour cream
2 cups shredded Cheddar cheese

TOPPING:

½ cup shredded Cheddar cheese
2 cups crushed round snack
  crackers

¼ cup butter, melted

Preheat oven to 350°. Mix together all filling ingredients in very large mixing bowl. Spread mixture into a greased 9x13-inch casserole dish. Top with ½ cup shredded cheese. Mix crushed crackers and melted butter together. Spread over cheese and bake for 45–50 minutes.

Sandy Robinson (Vancouver, Washington)

Lemon 'n Pepper Pork Chops

I love making up recipes. This recipe came to me one night out of the blue. My husband loves lemon pepper, so I decided I would make the pork chops have a great lemon taste. He declared them the best pork chops he has ever eaten.

4 tablespoons lemon juice
½ teaspoon salt
½ teaspoon pepper
½ teaspoon lemon pepper

1 cup flour
5–6 thin sliced pork chops
Cooking oil for frying

Mix lemon juice, salt, pepper, and lemon pepper. Brush liquid mixture onto both sides of each pork chop. Roll each pork chop in flour. Fry in skillet in oil until tender.

Shonda Stephens (Lubbock, Texas)

Pork Chops Baked with Sour Cream

4 (½-inch-thick) pork loin chops
Seasoned flour
4 whole cloves
½ cup water
½ bay leaf
2 tablespoons vinegar

1 tablespoon sugar
¾ cup sour cream
¼ teaspoon savory
Pinch of thyme
2 slices mild cheese, halved
   (optional)

Dredge chops with seasoned flour and insert 1 clove in each chop. Brown them lightly on both sides and place in baking dish. Combine water, bay leaf, vinegar, sugar, sour cream, savory, and thyme; heat and pour over pork chops. Cover the dish and bake in a 350° oven for about 1 hour, or until done. You may add mild cheese and return to oven; bake uncovered until cheese is melted.

Viola E. Cirillo (Mohawk, New York)

Grandma Riggs' Heavenly Ham

This is the ONLY ham recipe that everyone in our family uses. My Grandma Riggs created this recipe shortly after she was a young bride. The smell of this ham cooking is sooo heavenly that words cannot do it justice, and the taste is even more delectable. Anyone who enjoys ham is sure to fall in love with this dish.

1 ham half with bone	2 liters ginger ale, divided
½ teaspoon dry mustard	1 cup brown sugar, divided
½ cup flour	Whole cloves

Boil ham for 15 minutes in a pot of water. In a small bowl, mix dry mustard, flour, a splash of ginger ale, and enough water to make a thick paste. Remove ham from pot of water; place in roasting pan. Pat ham with brown sugar, enough to cover entire ham well; then pat with mustard paste mixture. Pat ham once again with brown sugar to cover well. Now push whole cloves into ham, as many as desired, but at least one every inch or two. Pour an inch or so of ginger ale around the bottom of the ham (do not pour over ham). Bake at 350°, covered, for 3 hours, adding more ginger ale and basting every 30–40 minutes.

Kathleen Arbuthnot (Morgantown, West Virginia)

Cakes

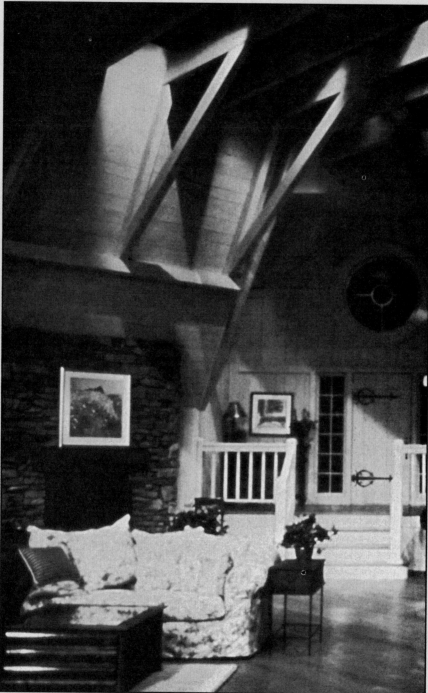

The QVC Home includes a living room (shown), dining room, kitchen, home office,
two bedrooms, a garage and a sunroom along with one working fireplace.
Put together, it covers 8,000 square feet and is in the style of a converted farmhouse
including beams from a century-old Pennsylvania barn.

Fluffy Top Candy Bar Cake

This recipe is a hit wherever I take it. I am always asked for the recipe; it is such a moist and light cake with fluffy marshmallow-like icing. This is pretty to break the cake and layer with icing in trifle bowl.

1 box German chocolate cake mix with pudding in mix	3 eggs
1 small box instant chocolate pudding	1½ cups milk
	¾ cup oil

Mix all ingredients and pour into 2 greased and floured 8-inch layer pans. Bake at 350° for 25–30 minutes. Let cool 10 minutes in pans, then remove and cool completely.

ICING:

1 (8-ounce) package cream cheese, softened	2 milk chocolate candy bars, chopped
1 cup powdered sugar	½ cup finely chopped pecans (optional)
1 cup sugar	
1 (12-ounce) carton whipped topping, thawed	

Mix cream cheese and sugars; fold in whipped topping. Stir in chopped chocolate bars and pecans. This recipe makes plenty of icing, so feel free to pile it on between the layers.

Sue Harris (Salisbury, North Carolina)

Chocolate Chip Mocha Cake

I have never made this cake for a party, function, or co-worker without someone asking for the recipe.

1 box devil's food cake mix (non-pudding)	4 eggs, beaten
1 small box instant vanilla pudding	¾ cup vegetable oil
1 pint sour cream	⅓ cup coffee liqueur
	1 (6-ounce) package chocolate chips

Grease and lightly flour Bundt pan. Combine all ingredients, mixing well until blended. Pour into Bundt pan. Bake at 350° for 1 hour, or until a toothpick comes out clean. (The baking process dissipates what little alcohol is in coffee liqueur, leaving a rich flavor and lots of moistness.)

Delores Dye (Riverside, California)

Chocolate Graham Éclair Cake

CRUST AND FILLING:

1 tablespoon butter
1 (1-pound) package graham
crackers
2 small packages instant French
vanilla pudding

3½ cups milk
1 (8-ounce) container whipped
topping

Butter a 9x13x2-inch pan. In a single layer, line bottom of pan with whole crackers (do not crumble). Beat pudding mixture with milk for 2 minutes; fold in whipped topping. Pour ½ of mixture over crackers, then place another layer of crackers on top. Pour remaining pudding over the top, ending with 1 more layer of crackers. Refrigerate for 2 hours, then frost.

FROSTING:

2 heaping tablespoons cocoa
1½ cups powdered sugar
3 tablespoons softened butter

3 tablespoons milk
3 tablespoons white corn syrup
1 teaspoon vanilla

Beat all ingredients till smooth, and spread over top layer of crackers. Refrigerate overnight. Serve in squares. Makes 14–16 servings.

Marietta Shigekawa (Santa Ana, California)

Studio Park's garage setting gives viewers the feeling that they are right at home using products that they would use in their own garage.

Queen Anne's Lace Cake

1 box Swiss chocolate or devil's
  food cake mix
1 small box instant vanilla
  pudding

1 cup vegetable oil
3 eggs
1¼ cups milk

Sift cake and pudding mixes together. In another bowl beat oil, eggs, and milk. Add to dry mixture and beat well. Pour into 3 greased 9-inch cake pans. Bake at 325° 15–20 minutes.

ICING:

1 (8-ounce) package cream
  cheese, softened
1 cup powdered sugar
1 cup granulated sugar
1 cup finely chopped nuts

5 plain milk chocolate bars,
  shaved (or a 7-ounce bar)
1 (12-ounce) container whipped
  topping

Beat together cream cheese and sugars until very creamy. Fold nuts and chocolate bar pieces into cream cheese mixture. Fold in whipped topping. Ice layers and top of cake. (Pictured on cover.)

Vivian C. Ferguson (Gaston, North Carolina)

Cherry Chocolate Chilled Cake

1 (3-ounce) package cherry gelatin
¾ cup boiling water
½ cup cold water

1 box devil's food cake mix
1 container vanilla frosting
1 can cherry pie filling

Preheat oven to 350°. Dissolve gelatin in boiling water and then add cold water. Set aside at room temperature. Mix and bake cake per box directions in a greased, floured 9x13x2-inch pan. Cool cake for 20 minutes.

Using a meat fork, poke many holes throughout the cake. Pour the gelatin mixture slowly over the holes. Refrigerate cake until thoroughly chilled. After 2 hours, spread the frosting over the cake. Top with cherry pie filling and serve chilled. Keep refrigerated.

Jan Marie Albert (Carson City, Nevada)

Chocoholic Cookie Cake

This extra chocolate-y cookie cake was created for a birthday party for a family member. This cake is very quick to make, but tastes like it was made from scratch.

1 (18¼-ounce) package devil's food cake mix
1 (6-serving) package chocolate instant pudding
¼ cup chocolate syrup
1 cup vegetable oil

4 eggs, beaten
½ cup warm water
1 package double-stuffed chocolate sandwich cookies, crushed
2 cups semisweet chocolate chips

Preheat oven to 350°. In a large bowl, mix together the cake and pudding mixes, chocolate syrup, oil, eggs, and water. Stir in the chocolate cookie pieces and pour batter into a well-greased 12-cup Bundt pan. Bake for 50–55 minutes, or until top is springy to the touch and a wooden toothpick inserted comes out clean. Cool cake thoroughly in pan, at least 1½ hours; invert and remove from pan. Melt chocolate chips in microwave or saucepan, stirring often. Drizzle melted chocolate chips over top of cake and let cool again. Makes 12 servings.

Rhiana L. Graves (San Jose, California)

Richly Divine Cappuccino Wedges

1 cup butter
1½ cups brown sugar
1 egg
1 teaspoon vanilla
⅓ cup instant coffee crystals

1¾ cups flour
1¾ teaspoons baking powder
½ teaspoon salt
8 ounces milk chocolate chips

Preheat oven to 350°. Melt butter. Mix in with sugar, then egg. Add vanilla and instant coffee crystals. Sift together flour, baking powder, and salt. Mix into butter mixture. Stir in chocolate chips. Spoon into greased, 9-inch round cake pan. Bake 25–30 minutes. Remove from oven, cool slightly, and cut into slender pie-shaped wedges. Serve with ice cream or whipped cream, if desired.

Liz Sack, QVC Employee (West Chester, Pennsylvania)

Beet-the-Devil Devil's Food Cake

Whenever we have a family get-together, a birthday, or just because, this is the cake we make. It's the moistest chocolate cake I've ever made. It's the only recipe I have of my grandmother's and it's the only one I need. Don't tell anyone it has beets in it until after they've taken the first bite!

1¾ cups flour
¼ teaspoon salt
1½ teaspoons soda
1½ cups sugar
4 tablespoons cocoa

3 eggs
1 cup vegetable oil
1 (16-ounce) can beets, drained
  (1½ cups), mashed
½ teaspoon vanilla

FROSTING:
3 ounces cream cheese, softened
¼ cup margarine, softened
1 teaspoon vanilla

2⅓ cups powdered sugar
2 tablespoons milk

Preheat oven to 350°. Grease and flour a 9x13-inch cake pan. Sift together flour, salt, and soda. Add sugar, cocoa, eggs, oil, beets, and vanilla. Beat together at medium speed for less than 4 minutes. DO NOT OVER BEAT! If it looks mixed in 2 minutes, STOP. The less time spent beating, the better.

Pour into prepared pan and bake at 350° for 30–35 minutes. Blend Frosting ingredients together and frost when cooled.

Kathy Palamara (Greenwood Village, Colorado)

Yogurt Raisin Cake

This recipe has a very recent family history as a result of my experimenting in the kitchen. It was an instant hit with my family. I think you will like this cake, too.

1 stick butter, softened	2 cups minus 1 tablespoon flour
1 cup sugar	2 teaspoons baking powder
2 eggs	1 teaspoon baking soda
1 (6-ounce) carton low-fat	Pinch of salt
fruit yogurt	1/2 cup milk, divided
1 (6-ounce) carton low-fat	1 cup raisins, coated with
vanilla yogurt	1 tablespoon flour
1 teaspoon vanilla	

Butter and flour a 5x9-inch loaf pan. Preheat oven to 350°. Cream butter and sugar by hand or with electric mixer. Add eggs, one at a time. Mix well until mixture is fluffy. Add yogurts and vanilla.

In a small bowl, place flour, baking powder, baking soda, and salt. Add alternately with milk to creamed mixture. Add in raisins and mix well. Place batter in prepared pan and bake for 50–65 minutes at 350°. Let cool 10–15 minutes, then turn out onto wire rack. Dust with powdered sugar when thoroughly cooled, if desired.

Laura Simmons (Staten Island, New York)

Strawberry Cake

CAKE:

1 box white cake mix
3 tablespoons flour
1 (3-ounce) package strawberry
  gelatin
⅓ cup vegetable oil

4 eggs
½ cup cold water
½ small package frozen
  strawberries (reserve juice)

Combine cake mix, flour, and gelatin. Add oil and the beat in the eggs. Combine water and strawberries (reserve 4 tablespoons juice from strawberries for Icing). Add the water and strawberry mixture to flour mixture and mix well. Grease and flour 2 (8-inch) round cake pans. Divide batter between the 2 cake pans. Bake according to directions on cake mix box. This can also be made in 9x13-inch pan.

ICING:

4 tablespoons reserved strawberry
  juice

4 tablespoons butter, melted
2 cups powdered sugar

Combine juice and melted butter. Mix into sugar until it is of spreading consistency. This is more like a glaze when ready.

Jill Bauer, QVC Host (West Chester, Pennsylvania)

Jill really is a good cook. She helped test and evaluate contest recipes here in Gwen's kitchen in Mississippi.

Cherry Pineapple Delight Cake

A mouth-watering tasty treat.

1 (18¼-ounce) package yellow
  cake mix
1 (11-ounce) can mandarin
  oranges, drained
½ (20-ounce) can unsweetened
  crushed pineapple, drained
1 (3.4-ounce) package vanilla
  instant pudding mix

1 (12-ounce) carton frozen
  whipped topping, thawed
½ cup shredded coconut
1 (10-ounce) jar maraschino
  cherries; reserve 2–3 tablespoons
  juice
1 small can pineapple rings

Prepare cake batter according to package directions. Beat in oranges until blended. Pour into 2 greased and floured 9-inch-round baking pans. Bake at 350° for 25–30 minutes or until a toothpick inserted in center comes out clean. Cool for 10 minutes before removing from pans to wire racks to cool completely. Combine pineapple and dry pudding mix; fold in whipped topping, coconut, and cherry juice. Spread between layers and over top and sides of cake. Top cake with pineapple rings and cherries. Store in refrigerator. Yields 12 servings.

Carol Reynolds, Nanticoke, Pennsylvania

Rose's Jewish Apple Cake

My friend Pat's mother, Rose, gave me this recipe years ago; I always called the cake "Rose's Jewish Apple Cake." This cake is very easy to make and people actually beg you to make it. It never disappoints.

3 cups flour
2 cups sugar
1 cup oil
4 eggs
3 teaspoons baking powder

½ cup orange juice
5 large Golden Delicious apples
5 tablespoons sugar
2 teaspoons cinnamon

Measure first 6 ingredients in large mixing bowl and mix well. Batter will be on thick side, but should be pourable.

Peel apples and slice very thin; mix in a bowl with sugar and cinnamon. Pour ½ the batter in a greased tube pan. Put ½ the apple mixture on top. Pour remaining batter on top of apples and then top off with remaining apple mixture. Bake in 350° oven for 1½ hours. Take cake out of oven after 1½ hours, even if top of cake still looks slightly moist.

Linda Paravisini (Philadelphia, Pennsylvania)

Apple Pie Cake

This cake recipe is my claim to fame. No matter if I double or triple the recipe, it always runs out. A great do-ahead dessert.

1½ cups oil
3 eggs
2 cups sugar
1 cup chopped pecans

1 teaspoon vanilla
1 teaspoon cinnamon
3 cups self-rising flour
1 can apple pie filling

Grease and flour a 9x13-inch baking dish. Mix oil, eggs, sugar, pecans, and vanilla. Stir in cinnamon and flour; mix well. Add and stir in pie filling; pour into baking dish. Bake at 300° for about 1 hour, or until golden brown. Cut cake in squares while still hot and pour warm Icing over.

ICING:
1½ cups sugar
1 cup margarine

1 can condensed milk
1 teaspoon vanilla

Combine sugar, margarine, condensed milk, and vanilla in small saucepan. Cook on medium heat just until sugar and margarine are dissolved—careful not to burn. Pour over hot cake squares. Chill.

Becky McDaniel (Clanton, Alabama)

Cool and Creamy Orange Cake

You simply won't believe how good this is!

1 orange cake mix
1 small package orange gelatin
1 cup boiling water
½ cup cold water
1 small package instant vanilla
  pudding

1 cup milk
1 teaspoon vanilla extract
1 teaspoon orange extract
1 (8-ounce) carton whipped
  topping

Mix orange cake mix according to directions. Pour in a 9x13-inch cake pan and bake according to directions. After removing cake from oven, poke holes in cake 1 inch apart with fork. Set aside until cool.

Mix gelatin with boiling water till dissolved; add cold water. Pour immediately over cooled cake. Mix pudding and milk till thick; fold in extracts and whipped topping. Beat until thoroughly mixed. Spread evenly over cake. Refrigerate.

Brian Sigman (Lancaster, Pennsylvania)

Kiss-of-Orange Cake

TOPPING:

¹/₃ cup sugar   ¹/₂ cup chopped walnuts
1 teaspoon cinnamon

Combine ingredients; set aside.

1 (6-ounce) can frozen orange   ¹/₂ cup shortening
   juice, thawed, divided   ¹/₂ cup milk
2 cups flour   2 eggs
1 cup sugar   1 cup raisins
1 teaspoon baking soda   ¹/₃ cup chopped walnuts
1 teaspoon salt   (optional)

Grease and flour bottom of 9x13-inch pan. Combine half of the orange juice concentrate with remaining ingredients in large mixer bowl. Blend at lowest speed of mixer for one minute; then beat 3 minutes at medium speed. Pour into pan. Bake at 350° for 40–45 minutes. Drizzle remaining orange juice concentrate over warm cake; sprinkle with topping.

Delores Dye (Riverside, California)

Quick Orange Dream Cake

1 box orange cake mix   1 (16-ounce) carton sour cream
1 (16-ounce) carton whipped   1 box powdered sugar
   topping, defrosted

Mix cake as directed on box. Put into 2 greased and floured 8-inch round cake pans. Bake at 350° for 30–40 minutes. Cool in pans on cake rack for 15 minutes. Remove from pans and cool completely on rack.

Take a thread or knife and cut each layer in half (so you now have 4 round layers). Mix whipped topping and sour cream together. Slowly add powdered sugar; mix well. Put 1 layer on cake plate. Frost, then place next layer on top, making sure it is level. Repeat until all 4 layers are assembled. Frost sides, then top. Refrigerate.

R. Elaine Garrett (Corbin, Kentucky)

Luscious Lemonade Cake

This is a wonderful variation on a recipe my grandmother gave me when I was first married. It is a huge hit at family gatherings and church potlucks.

1 package lemon cake mix
1 envelope unsweetened
   lemonade-flavored drink mix
3 eggs
1 cup water
⅓ cup vegetable oil
2 (3-ounce) packages lemon
   gelatin, divided

1 cup boiling water
1 cup cold water
1 cup cold milk
½ teaspoon lemon extract
1 (¾-ounce) package instant
   lemon pudding mix
1 (8-ounce) carton frozen whipped
   topping, thawed

In a mixing bowl, combine cake mix and drink mix, eggs, water, and oil. Beat on medium speed for 2 minutes. Pour into an ungreased 9x13x2-inch baking pan. Bake at 350° for 25–30 minutes, or until a toothpick inserted near the center comes out clean. Using a chopstick, poke holes in cake. Cool in pan set on a wire rack for 30 minutes.

Meanwhile, in a bowl, dissolve one package of gelatin in boiling water. Stir in cold water. Pour over cake. Cover and refrigerate for 2 hours.

In a mixing bowl, combine milk, lemon extract, pudding mix and remaining gelatin; beat on low for 2 minutes. Let stand for 5 minutes; fold in whipped topping. Frost cake. Refrigerate leftovers. Makes 12–15 servings.

Nanci C. Keatley (Salem, Oregon)

QVC's first broadcast was on November 24, 1986, at 7:30 p.m., and lasted four hours, with sales totaling $7,400. A Windsor Shower Companion AM/FM radio was the first product sold on the air at QVC.

Sunshine State Key Lime Cake

I entered this in our local bake contest and won!

8 egg yolks	1 tablespoon baking powder
³/₄ cup butter, softened	¹/₄ teaspoon salt
1¹/₄ cups sugar	³/₄ cup whole milk
2¹/₂ cups cake flour or plain	1 teaspoon fresh key lime juice
flour (take out 2 tablespoons	1 teaspoon grated key lime rind
for each cup cake flour used)	1 teaspoon vanilla extract

Beat egg yolks at high speed with an electric mixer 4 minutes or until thick and pale. Set aside.

In a separate bowl, beat butter at medium speed until creamy; gradually add sugar, beating well. Add egg yolks, beating well.

Combine flour, baking powder, and salt. Add to butter mixture alternately with milk, beginning and ending with flour mixture. Mix after each addition. Stir in lime juice, rind, and vanilla.

Spoon batter into 2 greased and floured 8-inch cake pans. Bake at 350° for about 30–35 minutes or until wooden pick inserted in center comes out clean. Cool in pans for about 5 minutes. Remove from pans and cool completely on wire racks. Split each layer of cake so you will have 4 layers. Frost with Key Lime Frosting.

For decoration, take 3 key limes and roll in egg whites, then granulated sugar. Let dry and place in center of cake. You can make frosting leaves around the limes.

KEY LIME FROSTING:

1 cup butter, softened	2 pounds powdered sugar
2 teaspoons grated key lime rind	1–2 tablespoons half-and-half,
¹/₃ cup key lime juice	if needed

Beat butter at medium speed with electric mixer until creamy; stir in key lime rind and juice. Mixture will look curdled (this is okay). Gradually add sugar and beat at high speed for about 4 minutes. Gradually add the half-and-half, if needed.

Ruth Wetmore (Madison, Florida)

Marshmallow Rhubarb Cake

Rhubarb goes to the bottom and marshmallows come to the top; no frosting needed.

3 cups chopped rhubarb
3/4 cup sugar
1/2 cup water
1 (3-ounce) box strawberry
  gelatin

1 (10 1/2-ounce) bag
  mini-marshmallows
1 box yellow cake mix, mixed per
  package directions

Cook rhubarb, sugar, and water together about 6 minutes, till rhubarb is soft. Remove from heat and add dry gelatin; stir to dissolve. Place marshmallows in bottom of greased 9x13-inch pan. Pour prepared cake mix batter over marshmallows and add rhubarb mixture on top of cake batter. Bake at 350° for about 35 minutes, or until brown on top.

Esther Brower (Hillsdale, Michigan)

Fuzzy Navel Cake

1 box yellow cake mix (without
  pudding)
1/2 cup vegetable oil
2 (3 1/2-ounce) packages vanilla
  pudding

4 eggs
3/4 cup peach schnapps liqueur
1/2 cup orange juice
1/2 teaspoon orange extract

Grease and flour Bundt pan. In large bowl, combine all ingredients. Mix to moisten. Beat 2 minutes. Pour into pan. Bake 45–50 minutes at 350°. Poke holes and pour Topping over while hot.

TOPPING:
4 tablespoons peach schnapps
  liqueur

1 cup powdered sugar
2 tablespoons orange juice

Mix well. Allow cake to cool 2 hours. Place serving tray on top of cake pan and invert.

Julie Ciacelli (LaSalle, Michigan)

Pineapple Carrot Cake

I remember my Mom always making a carrot cake where she had to grate the carrots. It always took a long time and was messy. I like this recipe because it is so quick and simple.

2 cups all-purpose flour
2 cups sugar
2 teaspoons baking soda
2 teaspoons ground cinnamon
1 teaspoon salt
1½ cups vegetable oil

4 eggs
2 (6-ounce) jars carrot baby food
1 (8-ounce) can crushed pineapple, drained
½ cup chopped walnuts

In a mixing bowl, combine the dry ingredients. Add the oil, eggs, and baby food; mix on low speed until well blended. Stir in pineapple and nuts. Pour into 2 greased and floured 9-inch round baking pans. Bake at 350° for 35–40 minutes. Cool for 10 minutes before removing from pans.

FROSTING:
1 (8-ounce) package cream cheese, softened
½ cup butter or margarine, softened

1 teaspoon vanilla extract
3¾ cups powdered sugar
Chopped walnuts

Beat cream cheese and butter until smooth. Beat in vanilla and sugar until it is of spreading consistency. Spread between layers and over sides and top of cake. Garnish with walnuts.

Laura Dickens (Gaston, North Carolina)

QVC is one of the largest purveyors of gold jewelry in the world, but the entire jewelry category accounts for only 32% of air time. Still, millions of dollars in necklaces, bracelets, earrings, keychains, charms, and rings are sold on QVC. But all that glitters is not gold: QVC is also second-to-none when it comes to selling sterling silver jewelry.

Pineapple Plantation Cake
with Rum Glaze

My husband calls this "PDG Cake"—Pretty Darn Good!

1 (18¼-ounce) package
  pineapple cake mix
1 (3.4-ounce) package coconut
  cream instant pudding
4 eggs
1 (8-ounce) can crushed pineapple,
  drained (reserve juice)

¾ cup combined reserved
  pineapple juice and water
¾ cup oil
1½ teaspoons coconut flavoring
½ teaspoon vanilla
½ cup chopped pecans

Blend all ingredients (including reserved pineapple juice) except pineapple and nuts. Beat until smooth, about 2 minutes. Add pineapple and nuts. Stir until well blended. Pour into greased tube (or Bundt) pan. Bake at 350° for 1 hour, or until done. Let cool in pan for about 10 minutes. Remove from pan. Let cool.

RUM GLAZE:
2 cups powdered sugar, sifted
½ teaspoon rum or rum
  flavoring

Enough milk to make glaze of
  spreading consistency

Blend ingredients well. You may also substitute lemon extract or 1 tablespoon lemon juice for rum.

Nancy L. Weaver (Annapolis, Maryland)

Praline Spice Cake

This is my most requested dessert at luncheons or potluck dinners. When baked in a disposable cake pan, it makes a wonderful gift.

1 box spice cake mix	**30 caramel candies (or 1 cup bulk**
2 cups sugar	**caramel for candy making)**
½ cup half-and-half	**2 cups pecan halves**
1 stick butter	**1 teaspoon vanilla**

Bake spice cake according to directions on box in a greased 9x13-inch pan. (Add a little cinnamon, nutmeg, and allspice, if desired.) Cook the sugar, half-and-half, and butter to soft ball stage. Add caramels until melted, then add pecans and vanilla. Poke holes in cake with large fork. Pour praline topping on cake. Serve as soon as praline topping sets.

Kate Love (Houma, Louisiana)

Good-as-Gold Carrot Cake

2 cups flour	**1½ cups oil**
2 teaspoons baking soda	**2 cups raw shredded carrots**
2 teaspoons baking powder	**1 (8½-ounce) can crushed**
1½ teaspoons salt	**pineapple, drained**
2 teaspoons cinnamon	**½ cup chopped nuts**
4 eggs	**3½ ounces coconut flakes**
2 cups sugar	

Sift together flour, baking soda, baking powder, salt, and cinnamon. Cream eggs and sugar; add oil. Mix into dry ingredients. Add carrots, pineapple, nuts and coconut. Blend thoroughly. Pour into 3 (9-inch) greased round cake pans. Bake at 350° for 35–40 minutes. Cool 25 minutes. Fill layers with Cream Cheese Frosting; then frost top and sides.

CREAM CHEESE FROSTING:

½ cup butter, softened	**1 pound powdered sugar**
1 teaspoon vanilla	**1 (8½-ounce) can crushed**
1 (8-ounce) package cream	**pineapple, well drained**
cheese, softened	**(optional)**

Cream ingredients well (double recipe if you like lots of frosting). Decorate with nuts and shredded carrots on top.

Sharon A. Beirola (Tiverton, Rhode Island)

Lazy Daisy Cake

This is a family favorite. In the 1960s our little church wanted to do a banquet. We had a social hall but no kitchen. My friend and I cooked all the food on my little gas range. We baked ten of these cakes for 120 people. The gas stove had the broiler below so we popped them out of the oven and then under the broiler while the next one was in the oven. We had a real assembly line going. The cakes were delicious!

2 large eggs	**1 teaspoon baking powder**
1 cup sugar	**1/2 teaspoon salt**
1 teaspoon vanilla	**1/2 cup milk**
1 cup flour	**1/3 stick butter**

Beat eggs until very light. Gradually beat in sugar and vanilla. Add flour sifted with baking powder and salt. Heat milk with butter until almost boiling, then add all at once to flour mixture, and mix, beating all the time. Bake 25 minutes at 350° in a greased 9x13-inch pan.

TOPPING:

2/3 stick butter	**1 cup chopped walnuts**
3/4 cup packed brown sugar	**1/2 cup coconut**
2 tablespoons evaporated milk	

While cake is baking, put topping ingredients in small pan over medium heat until butter is melted and sugar is dissolved. Spread on cake as soon as it is finished baking. Put under broiler until bubbly and light brown. Watch it carefully.

Laura Wall (Monument, Colorado)

Every item QVC inspects is subjected to the "drop test." Samples are packaged as if they are being sent to a customer and then the package is dropped eleven times on different sides and corners. This helps the shippers to know how the item must be packaged in order for it to arrive safely.

Now *This* Is a Coconut Cake

A make-ahead marvel, it gets better by the day.

1 box white cake mix	1 (15-ounce) can cream of
¾ cup oil	coconut
1 (8-ounce) carton sour cream	1 teaspoon vanilla
3 eggs	½ teaspoon coconut flavoring

Combine above ingredients until just blended; don't over mix. Bake in a 350° oven in 2 greased and floured 9x9-inch pans for about 20-25 minutes, or until a toothpick comes out clean. Cool completely, cover cakes with plastic wrap, and put in refrigerator overnight.

FLUFFY FROSTING:

½ (8-ounce) package cream cheese, softened	¼ teaspoon almond flavoring
½ cup powdered sugar	3½ cups whipped topping, room temperature
2 tablespoons milk	2 cups flake coconut

With mixer, combine cream cheese, powdered sugar, milk, and almond flavoring. Using a rubber spatula, fold in whipped topping and coconut till well blended; don't over blend. If Frosting is too thick, add 1 more tablespoon of milk. This cake stores well in the refrigerator in a covered container (up to 5 days).

Linda Adkins *(Charlotte, North Carolina)*

Pat's Heavenly Angel Cake

My mother has made this cake for church events, picnics, and family gatherings. It is always a hit, with absolutely no crumbs left behind. It is very easy to prepare. During overnight hours, the flavors blend into a light, moist and delicious cake!

1 angel food cake mix
1 (20-ounce) can crushed
   pineapple, undrained

1 small package instant vanilla
   pudding mix
1 (16-ounce) tub whipped topping

Prepare angel food cake as per package directions (or use store-bought). Cool. Slice cake into 3 horizontal sections. In a large bowl, combine pineapple with juice and vanilla pudding mix. Stir until well mixed. Gently fold in the whipped topping until well mixed. Spread mixture between layers and on top of cake. Cover and place cake in refrigerator. Allow to sit overnight. Slice, serve, and enjoy!

Dian Trammell-Bentley (Jefferson City, Missouri)

Sugar-Free Cream Puff Cake

Absolutely delicious! You'll never know it's sugar-free.

1 cup water
½ cup margarine
1 cup flour
4 eggs
2 small boxes sugar-free instant
   vanilla pudding

2½ cups milk
1 (8-ounce) package cream cheese,
   softened
1 (16-ounce) container heavy
   cream
3 teaspoons sugar substitute

Preheat oven to 400°. Boil water and margarine in a saucepan. Remove from heat. Stir in flour and eggs, one at a time, until all 4 are incorporated. Spread mixture into a greased 9x13-inch pan and bake 25–30 minutes, or until brown. Let cool.

Combine pudding mix and milk. Blend in cream cheese with electric mixer until smooth. Spread over cooled cake.

Beat the heavy cream till the consistency of whipped cream (forms stiff peaks). Then beat in sugar substitute. Spread whipped cream evenly over all. Refrigerate approximately 2 hours before serving. Enjoy!

Ginger Butler (Sewell, New Jersey)

Candied Yam Casse-Roll Cake

CAKE:

3 eggs
1 cup sugar
²/₃ cup yams, mashed until
  smooth
³/₄ cup all-purpose flour
1 teaspoon baking powder

1¹/₂ teaspoons ground cinnamon
¹/₂ teaspoon ginger
¹/₂ teaspoon ground cloves
¹/₂ teaspoon nutmeg
¹/₂ teaspoon salt
Powdered sugar

In a large bowl, combine eggs and sugar; blend. Add yams to sugar; mix thoroughly. In another bowl, blend flour, baking powder, cinnamon, ginger, cloves, nutmeg, and salt. Add to egg mixture; mix well. Spray a 10x15-inch jellyroll pan with cooking spray; line with wax paper, leaving 2 extra inches on the short sides for lifting. Lightly spray wax paper. Spread batter in pan evenly, filling in corners. Bake on middle rack in preheated 375° oven for 15 minutes.

When cake is done, lift cake by paper and place on rack; cool 10 minutes. Sprinkle a smooth cloth (a little larger than cake) with powdered sugar. Place cake on towel, remove paper, and roll cake in towel by short side. Lay cake seam-side-down and cool another 10 minutes.

FILLING:

1 (8-ounce) bar cream cheese,
  softened
4 tablespoons butter or margarine,
  softened

1 cup powdered sugar
1 teaspoon coconut extract
¹/₄ cup shredded coconut
¹/₄–¹/₂ cup chopped pecans

Beat together cream cheese and butter till creamy. Add powdered sugar and extract. Beat till smooth. Fold in coconut and pecans; set aside.

Unroll cake; spread Filling evenly over cake. Reroll cake, without the towel, by the short side. Wrap the cake with plastic wrap and place seam-side-down in the refrigerator for at least 2 hours. This cake can be made the day before serving (flavor enhances). Keep refrigerated.

Sonya Bynum (Florahome, Florida)

Caramel Apple Cupcakes

4 cups diced fresh apples
2 cups sugar
½ cup oil
1 cup chopped nuts (optional)
2 eggs, well beaten
2 teaspoons vanilla

2 cups flour
2 teaspoons baking soda
2 teaspoons cinnamon or apple pie
    spice
1 teaspoon salt

In large bowl, mix the apples and sugar. Then add the oil, nuts, eggs, and vanilla. Mix well. Next, add the flour, baking soda, cinnamon, and salt. Mix until well blended.

Fill cupcake pans with liners. Fill liners ⅔ full. Bake at 350° for 20–25 minutes, until springy to the touch. Cool. Frost with Caramel Frosting.

CARAMEL FROSTING:
1 cup brown sugar
⅓ cup cream
¼ cup butter

1 teaspoon vanilla
2½–3 cups powdered sugar

Bring brown sugar, cream, and butter to a full boil. Add vanilla. Pour mixture into mixing bowl with powdered sugar and beat until cool and thickened.

Julanne Myers (Blachly, Oregon)

In addition to the kitchen set and a full-scale professional-grade Prep Kitchen, the QVC Show Kitchen pulls double-duty. Sometimes used for on-air presentations, it is also available, as seen on the next page, as an additional work station during busy cook-day events.

Virginia's Confederate Pound Cake

This is a family recipe that my grandmother, Virginia M. Walton, who I called Nannie, learned from her mother and father. Her father was a Confederate soldier in the Civil War. Nannie was one of four surviving Daughters of the Confederacy in the state of Virginia, until her death in February of 2001. She was well known for her pound cake with her family and friends and members of our small country church. She always made sure that I had one or two extras in the freezer to have when I just wanted a slice as a treat. A few years ago, I sat with her and we wrote down the recipe items and process, which was one that she always did from memory . . . the typical grandmother method! I am so pleased, and she would be, too, to share her pound cake recipe.

3 sticks butter (or margarine),
  softened
3 cups sugar
¼ teaspoon salt

3 cups flour
1 cup milk
5 eggs
1 tablespoon vanilla

Cream butter, sugar, and salt until creamy. Add a little flour and milk at a time until mixed well. Add eggs one at a time; mix well when adding each. Add vanilla and beat on slow mixer speed. Put in a greased tube pan and put in cold oven. Turn oven heat to 300° and cook for 2 hours. Do not open door until 2 hours are up. Take out of oven and let set for 5 minutes before removing from pan.

Eddie R. Sears (Alexandria, Virginia)

Food stylists utilize the large cook top island in the show kitchen to cook and style dishes for product demonstrations.

Candy Bar Chocolate Pound Cake

My mother would make this a lot when I was growing up. It is so good and so moist; everybody who eats some wants the recipe.

2 cups sugar
2 sticks butter, softened
4 eggs
1 large (7-ounce) chocolate bar, melted
1 large (16-ounce) can chocolate syrup
2 teaspoons vanilla
1 cup buttermilk
1/2 teaspoon soda
2 1/2 cups all-purpose flour

Cream sugar and butter; add eggs one at a time. Add melted chocolate bar, syrup, and vanilla. Add the buttermilk with soda added to it alternately with the flour, a little at a time. Bake in greased tube pan at 325° for 1 hour 15 minutes. Let cool 15 minutes before cutting.

Yvonne Anderson (Greensboro, North Carolina)

Peanut Butter Pound Cake

This cake is very easy to make and it's delicious.

1 box yellow cake mix (without pudding)
1 (4-ounce) package instant vanilla pudding
4 eggs
1/4 cup oil
1 cup water
1 cup peanut butter, or to taste
Chopped peanuts (optional)

Combine all ingredients in a large bowl and mix for 3 minutes. Batter will be thick. Pour into a greased and floured Bundt pan. Bake at 350° for 40–45 minutes, or until toothpick comes out clean. Cool for 15 minutes and remove from pan and finish cooling on a rack, then frost. This cake may also be baked in a 9x13-inch pan.

FROSTING:

You can make your own buttercream frosting and add peanut butter to taste, or you can cheat and purchase a vanilla frosting in the can and add about 3–4 tablespoons of peanut butter. It's just as good, and best of all, less work. Sprinkle chopped peanuts on top, if desired.

Gladys Jones (Fort Pierce, Florida)

Chipsy Turtle Cheesecake

CRUST:

1¼ cups graham cracker crumbs
¼ cup cocoa

¼ cup sugar
¼ cup melted butter

Heat oven to 350°. In small bowl, stir together graham cracker crumbs, cocoa, sugar, and melted butter. Press evenly into the bottom of a 9-inch springform pan.

CHEESECAKE FILLING:

3 (8-ounce) packages cream
   cheese, softened
1½ cups sugar
4 eggs
2 teaspoons vanilla extract

1⅔ cups mini-semisweet
   chocolate chips
⅓ cup caramel ice cream
   topping
½ cup chopped pecans

In large mixing bowl, beat cream cheese and sugar until smooth. Add eggs and vanilla. Beat until just combined. Stir in mini chips with a spoon. Pour over graham cracker crust. Bake 50–55 minutes until slightly puffed and center is set, except for a 4-inch circle in center. Remove from oven. Cool 30 minutes. With knife, loosen cheesecake from side of pan. Cool completely before removing side of pan. Place on cake plate.

   Drizzle caramel topping on top of cooled cheesecake with spoon until it starts to run down the sides. Next, make Chocolate Drizzle and drizzle on top of caramel with spoon. Sprinkle on chopped pecans. Refrigerate and enjoy!

CHOCOLATE DRIZZLE:

½ cup mini-semisweet chocolate
   chips

1 tablespoon shortening (do not
   use butter, margarine, or oil)

In small bowl, place mini chocolate chips and shortening. Microwave at HIGH 30–45 seconds, or until chocolate is melted and mixture is smooth when stirred. (If not completely melted, keep microwaving for 10–15 second intervals.)

Jean M. Busalacchi (Muskego, Wisconsin)

Irish Cream Malted Milkball Cheesecake

The flavors and textures of this prize-winning cheesecake leave your tastebuds speechless.

25 chocolate cream-filled cookies
  (for crust)
4 (8-ounce) packages cream
  cheese
1 cup sugar

3 eggs
1 teaspoon vanilla
$\frac{1}{3}$ cup Irish cream liqueur
1 cup malted milkballs

Preheat oven to 400°. In a food processor fitted with a steel blade, finely grind the cookies. Pour into a $9\frac{1}{2}$-inch cheesecake pan and press the crumbs around the bottom and up the sides. Bake in oven for 4 minutes. Remove and let cool.

Place cream cheese in processor bowl with sugar, and blend until creamy smooth. Start by pulsing (quick on and off) and then on continuous. Add eggs, vanilla, and Irish cream. Blend until smooth again. Add malted milkballs and pulse about 5–7 times. (This breaks up the malted milkballs just enough and distributes them throughout the cake without turning them into crumbs, so that you get the crunchiness.) Pour into baked crust. Put into 400° oven for 12 minutes. Turn heat down to 300° for 45–60 minutes, or until set. Remove from oven and run a knife between the crust and pan. Let cool and refrigerate.

Remove 20 minutes before serving. Slice and serve. For a little different texture (more like ice cream), freeze and serve frozen. Either way, this is a wonderful ending to any meal.

F. David Farnsworth (Dover, New Hampshire)

QVC ranks right behind NBC as the second largest television network in the United States in terms of revenue.

Delightfully Light No-Bake Cheesecake

1 (8-ounce) package cream
  cheese, softened
¾ cup sugar
1 teaspoon vanilla
1 (8-ounce) carton whipped
  topping (or ½ pint heavy
  cream, whipped)

1 graham cracker crust
1 can pie filling (blueberry,
  cherry, pineapple, strawberry,
  lemon, or chocolate)

Beat cream cheese, sugar, and vanilla together till smooth. Fold whipped topping into cream cheese mixture. Pour into graham cracker crust and push cream cheese mixture to sides to make well in center. Add pie filling of your choice. (Pictured on cover.)

Karen Tosten (Yorktown, Virginia)

Mom's Favorite Cheesecake

I am allergic to eggs, so my mother developed and collected recipes that I could eat and the whole family enjoyed. This cheesecake is different and requested often by my children and grandchildren. Try it!

¾ cup whole milk
1 (8-ounce) package cream
  cheese, softened
¼ cup sugar

1 teaspoon vanilla
4–5 drops fresh lemon juice
1 (9-inch) graham cracker crust

TOPPING:
1 (8-ounce) carton sour cream
¼ cup sugar

1 teaspoon vanilla
3–4 drops fresh lemon juice

Combine first 5 ingredients till creamy. (If using hand mixer, use low speed.) Pour into crust. Bake at 300° for 25 minutes. Cool a few minutes. Combine topping ingredients and carefully spread over pie. Bake 10 minutes more at 300°. Sprinkle a few graham cracker crumbs on top, if available. Chill several hours before cutting.

Marilyn G. Addison (Paradise, California)

Hot Fudge Cheesecake

Oh my, is this good!

CRUST:
2 cups crushed saltine crackers   ⅔ cup butter, melted
1 cup finely chopped walnuts   ⅓ cup sugar

Combine above ingredients; stir well. Firmly press onto bottom and 2½ inches up sides of a lightly greased 9-inch springform pan. Bake at 350° for 8 minutes. Remove to a wire rack; let cool. Reduce oven temperature to 300°.

FILLING:
12 (1-ounce) squares semisweet   1½ cups sugar
  chocolate   6 large eggs
1½ cups butter
2 (8-ounce) packages cream
  cheese, softened

In a heavy saucepan, combine chocolate squares and butter. Cook over medium-low heat until mixture is melted and smooth, stirring frequently. Remove from heat and let cool. Beat cream cheese at medium speed of an electric mixer until creamy. Add sugar and beat well. Add eggs, one at a time, beating after each addition. Stir in cooled chocolate mixture. Pour into prepared crust. Bake at 300° for 1½ hours, or until almost set. Turn oven off. Let cheesecake cool in oven 1 hour. Remove to a wire rack; let cool to room temperature. Remove sides of pan. Serve cheesecake at room temperature with Hot Fudge Sauce, or chill till ready to serve.

HOT FUDGE SAUCE:
1 (12-ounce) package semisweet   1 tablespoon butter
  chocolate morsels   1 teaspoon vanilla extract
1 cup half-and-half

In a heavy saucepan, combine chocolate morsels and half-and-half. Cook over medium heat till chocolate melts and mixture is smooth, stirring frequently. Remove from heat; stir in butter and vanilla. Serve warm.

Denise Ann Cook (Bonney Lake, Washington)

Simply the Best Chocolate Amaretto Mousse Cheesecakes

This is my easy-to-make adaptation of a chocolate cheesecake. By using a bag of chocolate chips and store-bought chocolate crusts, prep time is greatly reduced. The best part is that this recipe makes 2 cheesecakes—to serve for a big party, or reserve one for weeks later. Every time I make this, my guests beg for the recipe. I got so tired or rewriting it for everyone, that I had one of my student assistants at the college type it into my computer so I could e-mail it or print it out on request.

1 (12-ounce) package semisweet chocolate morsels
3 (8-ounce) packages cream cheese, softened
¾ cup sugar
3 large eggs
½ cup amaretto (optional)
1 (8-ounce) carton sour cream
2 tablespoons heavy cream
2 teaspoons vanilla extract
2 prepared chocolate graham cracker crusts
Whipped cream for garnish (optional)
Chocolate curls for garnish (optional)

Place chocolate morsels in pan; melt over low heat, stirring constantly, or microwave on HIGH for 2 minutes and stir. Beat cream cheese with electric mixer until light and fluffy; gradually add sugar, mixing well. Add eggs one at a time, beating well after each addition. Stir in the melted chocolate and beat until blended.

In separate bowl, stir together the amaretto, sour cream, heavy cream, and vanilla; beat into the chocolate mixture. Pour into 2 prepared crusts. Bake in preheated 350° oven for about 35 minutes. (Center may be soft but will firm when chilled.) Let cool to room temperature on a wire rack; refrigerate overnight. (Second cheesecake may be tightly wrapped and frozen for up to 1 month.) Garnish with whipped cream and/or whatever else you desire (I use chocolate curls). Serves 8–10 people.

Karen J. Rosell (Huntingdon, Pennsylvania)

 QVC's main studio is 20,000 square feet—one of the largest live television studios in the world.

Arizona Sunset Cheesecake

My older daughter lives near Phoenix, and she is an avid fruit and cheesecake fan. When I was visiting her, we sat outside one evening, and the sunset was a gorgeous blend of red, yellow, and orange. The next day, she asked me to fix a dessert for dinner, and I took my regular cheesecake recipe and created a three-layer blend of strawberries, peaches, and pineapple (which is what she had in the fridge) and made it look rather like the sunset we had seen the evening before. It was beautiful, and it tasted wonderful. When sliced, it really looks like a sunset in the desert.

2 cups shortbread cookie crumbs
½ cup butter, melted
4 (8-ounce) packages cream
  cheese
1½ cups sugar
4 eggs
2 tablespoons lemon juice
2 teaspoons strawberry extract
1 cup chopped strawberries,
  drained dry

3 drops red food coloring
2 teaspoons almond extract
1 cup chopped peaches, drained
  dry
3 drops orange food coloring
2 teaspoons pineapple extract
1 cup crushed pineapple, drained
3 drops yellow food coloring

Preheat oven to 350°. Mix together cookie crumbs and melted butter. Pat into bottom of a buttered 9-inch springform pan. Bake crust at 350° for 20–25 minutes, or until golden brown. Allow crust to cool completely.

Using an electric mixer, beat cream cheese until light and smooth. Add sugar and continue to beat on medium speed. Add eggs one at a time. Blend in lemon juice. Divide mixture into three parts. To the first part, add strawberry extract, strawberries (dried with paper towel), and red food coloring. Pour mixture into prepared crust. To the second part, add almond extract, peaches (dried with paper towel), and orange coloring. Very gently, spoon this mixture over the strawberry one. Add pineapple extract, pineapple (dried with paper towel), and yellow food coloring to the third part. Spoon this over the peach mixture.

Place in a 350° oven for 60–75 minutes, or until cake is set and top is golden brown. Remove cake from oven and place on a wire rack. Allow cake to cool slightly, then place in refrigerator for 6 hours or overnight.

Garnish with whipped cream and fresh fruit, if desired. Add more food coloring to each mixture to obtain brighter colors.

Sally Sibthorpe (Rochester Hills, Michigan)

Banana Split Cheesecake

A great alternative to the old ice cream banana split, this recipe was created out of necessity—we wanted to have a banana split, but we had no ice cream! So I whipped this up and we enjoyed it so much that it is now a regular part of our celebrations.

PUDDING:

1 (4-serving) package instant banana pudding and pie filling

2 cups cold half-and-half

Prepare pudding according to package directions, substituting half-and-half for the milk. Cover with plastic wrap and refrigerate until ready to use.

CRUST:

1 1/2 cups chocolate wafer crumbs

1/2 cup butter, softened
1/2 cup finely minced pecans

Mix chocolate wafer crumbs and butter. Press firmly into 9- or 10-inch springform pan. Sprinkle minced pecans evenly over crust. Chill until ready to use.

CREAM CHEESE FILLING:

2 (8-ounce) packages cream cheese, softened
1/2 cup sugar
3 eggs, slightly beaten
2 tablespoons vanilla

1 tablespoon banana extract
1/4 cup half-and-half
2 1/2 bananas (firm)
4 cups whipped topping

In food processor or mixer, blend cream cheese and slowly add sugar. Then add eggs, one at a time. Add vanilla and banana extract along with the 1/4 cup half-and-half. Thinly slice bananas and layer on top of crust. Pour cheesecake mixture on top of bananas, spreading evenly. Bake at 325° for 50–60 minutes, or until center has only a slight wiggle. Allow to cool 30 minutes. Run a knife around rim, then remove sides from pan and place on large plate. Spread Pudding over cheesecake. Finish by spreading whipped topping over entire pie. Allow to chill in refrigerator at least 1 hour before serving.

GARNISH:

12–15 maraschino cherries

1/2–1 cup favorite chocolate sauce

Slice and present on chilled, glass dessert plate drizzled with chocolate sauce. Sprinkle a few chopped pecans on top each slice and top with a cherry.

Sandra Vanthoff (San Diego, California)

French Vanilla and Fudge Ice Cream Cake

This is our family's favorite birthday cake—a layer cake that needs to be frozen after each layer to make it come out correctly.

½ gallon good quality French vanilla ice cream, slightly softened
1 jar hot fudge sauce
1 small package chocolate sandwich cookies

1 jar caramel sauce
1 (8-ounce) container whipped topping

In a 9x13-inch pan, spread a layer of French vanilla ice cream. Freeze at least 2 hours. Next spread softened hot fudge sauce evenly over ice cream layer; freeze 2 hours or overnight.

Place chocolate sandwich cookies in food processor to make crumbs (reserving ¼ cup for garnish). Spread evenly over hot fudge layer; freeze. Pour caramel evenly over crumbs; freeze. Spread with whipped topping and garnish with crumbs.

Sandy Barnett (Castle Rock, Colorado)

When QVC is on the road, "show food" is often prepared in local kitchens. Food stylist Bobbi Cappelli and editor Barbara Moseley are a dynamic behind-the-scenes duo making all the food look yummy before Gwen goes "In the Kitchen With Bob."

Grandma's Sheet Cake Brownies

My grandma always made these when we came to visit, mainly because there was always enough for seconds. I have made them for my family and friends for 25 years now, and they are still one of the better brownie recipes—simple, without expensive ingredients.

2 cups sugar	4 tablespoons cocoa
2 cups flour	½ cup sour cream
½ teaspoon salt	2 eggs
2 sticks margarine	1 teaspoon soda
1 cup water	

In a large bowl, combine sugar, flour, and salt; set aside. In a saucepan, bring margarine, water, and cocoa to a boil. Take from heat and immediately pour over dry ingredients, stirring to mix. Then add sour cream, eggs, and soda. Mix well (until uniform in color). Pour into greased and floured 11½x15½-inch pan. Bake at 375° for 25–30 minutes. Frost cake while warm. Have ingredients ready, but do not make frosting until cake comes out of the oven.

FROSTING:

6 tablespoons milk	1 cup chopped nuts
½ cup margarine	1 teaspoon vanilla
4 tablespoons cocoa	1 box powdered sugar

Boil milk, margarine, and cocoa until bubbly. Remove from heat and add nuts, vanilla, and sugar. Mix until smooth; spread on warm cake. Let Frosting set before serving.

Cheryl L. McRae (West Valley, Utah)

QVC utilizes 32 cameras—22 of which are robotic. The cameras are operated from the control room—the heart of the live show—where all audio and video elements come together to make the final on-air "product" before it's sent to millions of viewers. Everyone who works in the Control Room is capable of doing any job in the room, if necessary, so the live show is never interrupted.

Black and White Brownies

When asked to bring dessert bars to a function, this recipe is always well received.

1 cup margarine, softened	**½ teaspoon salt**
2 cups sugar	**1 teaspoon vanilla**
4 eggs, beaten (or egg substitute)	**2 squares unsweetened baker's chocolate, melted**
2 cups flour	

Cream margarine, sugar, and eggs. Add flour, salt, and vanilla; mix well. Divide the batter in half (2 separate bowls) and add 2 squares of melted chocolate to half the batter, stirring well. Spread the chocolate portion on a medium-size greased cookie sheet with sides. Add the white batter over the chocolate. (I use a table knife to spread each portion very thin.) Bake in a preheated 350° oven for 25 minutes. Meanwhile, prepare the Frosting.

FROSTING:

1 cup sugar	**¼ cup milk**
1 square unsweetened baker's chocolate	**Pinch of salt**

Combine all ingredients and bring to a boil; boil for 1 minute. Let stand for 5 minutes and beat 20 strokes. Pour Frosting over brownies as soon as the brownies come from the oven. (I put crushed walnuts on top while still warm.) Cool and cut into small squares. Makes 25–30 small brownies.

Nancy Martinson (Valparaiso, Indiana)

Apple Brownies

²/₃ cup butter, softened
2 cups brown sugar
2 eggs
1 teaspoon vanilla
2 cups flour

2 teaspoons baking powder
¼ teaspoon salt
3–4 apples, peeled and chopped
   (Granny Smiths work well)
Powdered sugar

Cream butter and sugar. Add eggs and vanilla; mix well. Add flour, baking powder, and salt; stir well. Stir in apples. Bake in a 9x13-inch pan that has been sprayed with nonstick spray. Bake at 350° for 30 minutes. These are light brown when done. When cooled, sprinkle with powdered sugar.

Jill Bauer, QVC Host (West Chester, Pennsylvania)

Rich Caramel Brownies

1 box German chocolate cake mix
³/₄ cup butter, melted
²/₃ cup evaporated milk, divided

½–1 cup chopped nuts (optional)
1 bag caramels
1–2 cups chocolate chips

Mix together cake mix, melted butter, ⅓ cup evaporated milk, and nuts. In another pan on low heat, melt caramels and another ⅓ cup evaporated milk. In a 9x13-inch pan, put half (or a little more) of mix in pan. Spread with hand. Bake at 350° for 6 minutes. When done, spread chocolate chips to cover top. Then spread caramel mixture evenly over top. When finished, drop remaining cake mixture by spoonfuls on top of everything. Bake at 350° for another 15 minutes.

Lisa R. Hoersten (Delphos, Ohio)

 QVC shipped its 500 millionth package in the United States on October 29, 2001.

Black Forest Brownie Pizza

1 (19.8-ounce) package brownie
  mix, batter prepared according
  to package directions
½ cup powdered sugar
⅓ cup cocoa
1 (8-ounce) package cream cheese,
  softened

1 teaspoon vanilla
1 (8-ounce) container frozen
  whipped topping
1 (20-ounce) can cherry pie
  filling

Preheat the oven to 350°. Coat a 12-inch pizza pan with cooking spray. Spread the prepared brownie batter evenly over the bottom of the pan. Bake for 20–25 minutes, or until a wooden toothpick inserted in the center comes out clean; let cool.

Sift powdered sugar and cocoa. In a large bowl, mix cream cheese, powdered sugar mixture, and vanilla. Add whipped topping to the cream cheese mixture. Beat until smooth. Spread the mixture over the brownie pizza, and then spoon the cherry pie filling evenly over that. Chill.

Jennifer Dahms (Boise, Idaho)

Texas Muddy

I came up with this recipe after trying a Mississippi Mud Cake. The cake part was always too cakey, even if I did underbake it. I love this version using the brownie mix.

1 (family-size) package brownie
  mix
1 (7-ounce) jar marshmallow
  creme

1 can milk chocolate frosting
½ cup finely chopped nuts

Mix and bake brownie mix according to package directions; bake in a 9x13-inch pan. Cool 3 minutes. Drop marshmallow creme by spoonfuls onto brownies. Carefully spread smooth to cover top. Cool completely (I put mine in the refrigerator).

Drop the chocolate frosting by spoonfuls and swirl through the marshmallow creme. Sprinkle with pecans; cover and refrigerate before serving.

Annette Barling (New Boston, Texas)

Chocolate Peanut Butter Bars

PEANUT BUTTER BARS:

½ cup butter
½ cup sugar
½ cup brown sugar
1 egg
½ cup peanut butter

½ teaspoon baking soda
½ teaspoon salt
½ teaspoon vanilla
1 cup flour
1 cup oatmeal (or quick oats)

Cream together butter, sugars, egg, and peanut butter. Add baking soda, salt, vanilla, flour, and oatmeal. Bake in a well-greased 9x13-inch pan at 350° for 22–27 minutes, or until the bars test done with toothpick test. Prepare Cookie Dough while bars are baking.

COOKIE DOUGH:

1 package brownie mix (8x8 pan size)
½ cup flour

¼ cup water
¼ cup melted butter or oil

In a bowl, mix together brownie mix, flour, water, and melted butter. Spread over Peanut Butter Bars as soon as they come out of oven. (Dough will be a little hard to spread.) Chill in refrigerator while preparing topping.

TOPPING:

1 (12-ounce) package peanut butter chips

1 tablespoon vegetable oil

Melt peanut butter chips with oil in a double boiler. Spread over Cookie Dough. Refrigerate until set.

Beverly Raleigh (Tulsa, Oklahoma)

Chocolate Chip Bars

2 eggs	1 teaspoon vanilla
1½ cups packed brown sugar	1½ cups self-rising flour
⅔ cup vegetable oil	1 cup semisweet chocolate pieces

Beat eggs until thick and foamy. Gradually add brown sugar and continue beating until very well blended. Add oil and vanilla; mix well. Add flour. Fold in chocolate pieces. Spread in a greased 11x15-inch pan. Bake in a moderate oven, 350° for 18–25 minutes. Cool. Cut into 1x3-inch bars. Yields 30 bars.

Leona Tennison (Brandon, Mississippi)

Gooey Decadence Bars

These bars are so rich and different. Once I served them to a large group of doctors. When I asked if they liked them, one of the doctors said they were so good he wanted to roll himself in them! They are absolutely yummy!

CRUST:

1 large egg	1 cup butter, melted
1 package plain devil's food cake mix	1 teaspoon almond extract

Preheat oven to 350°. Grease 9x13-inch glass casserole dish. Mix egg, cake mix, melted butter, and almond extract. Batter will be thick. Spread evenly over bottom of pan so batter touches all sides.

TOPPING:

2 large eggs	1 package semisweet chocolate chips
2½ cups mini-marshmallows	

Beat the eggs till frothy. Add in marshmallows and mix to coat. Spread this mixture evenly over crust. Sprinkle chips evenly over marshmallows. Bake until cake has set, approximately 30 minutes. Remove and let cool completely, at least 1 hour. Cut into bars. Store in covered container for up to 5 days.

Von Marie Strieker (Longview, Texas)

Key Lime Pistachio Shortbread Bars

Growing up, I lived with my grandma in her Victorian home, which was always filled with wonderful aromas and a cornucopia of good comfort-type food including baked goods. This cookie recipe is a special family baking tradition because it brings back nostalgic reminiscences of childhood days gone by.

PISTACHIO SHORTBREAD CRUST:

1 cup flour
1 cup toasted, finely ground
  pistachio nuts

½ cup powdered sugar
1 cup butter, chilled and sliced in
  small pieces

Lightly grease and flour bottom and sides of 9x13-inch casserole dish. Preheat oven to 350°.

In a food processor, process flour, ground nuts, powdered sugar, and butter, briefly, just until butter pieces are pea-sized or smaller, and mix is yellow and resembles a coarse cornmeal texture. Pour into greased casserole dish and firmly press crust in place so it all holds together. Bake crust at 350° for 20 minutes.

FILLING:

4 eggs, slightly beaten
1 cup granulated sugar
1 cup light brown sugar
½ cup key lime juice
1 teaspoon baking powder
2 tablespoons flour

1 tablespoon grated lime peel
½ cup shredded coconut,
  unsweetened
Powdered sugar for sprinkling atop
  bars (about ⅓ cup)

While crust is baking, process eggs in food processor, allowing them to break up, and then gradually add sugars, lime juice, baking powder, flour, grated lime peel, and coconut. Pour lime filling over hot shortbread crust as soon as it comes out of oven. Return to oven for 25 additional minutes. Let cookies set 5–10 minutes prior to sprinkling powdered sugar over them. Cut into bars. Makes about 24 cookies.

Veronica Bercaives (San Ramon, California)

"Oh!" Baby Food Bars

This long-time family favorite recipe will be one you can't stop eating. It's very moist and great to eat on the run.

2 cups sugar
1¼ cups vegetable oil
3 eggs, beaten
2 cups flour
1 teaspoon salt
1 teaspoon baking soda

2 teaspoons cinnamon
1 (4-ounce) baby food jar carrots
1 (4-ounce) baby food jar peaches
1 (4-ounce) baby food jar apricots
½ cup chopped nuts (optional)

Preheat oven to 350°. Mix sugar, oil, and eggs. Add flour, salt, baking soda, and cinnamon. Next add all baby food. Add nuts if desired. Mix well. Pour into 13x17-inch greased and floured cookie sheet with sides. Bake 25 minutes or until done.

ICING:

1 stick butter, softened
1 (8-ounce) package cream cheese, softened

1 pound powdered sugar
1 teaspoon vanilla

Cream butter and cream cheese. Gradually add powdered sugar. Add vanilla. Spread on cake while still warm.

Deborah C. Fullerton (Northport, Alabama)

QVC's kitchen set invites viewers in for friendly chatter, always introducing products that make cooking and baking easier and more efficient.

Pineapple Squares

My mother, grandmother, and I always pitch in to make this for friends and family events. We've been making these for over 25 years and nobody ever gets tired of them.

CRUST:

5 cups flour	**1 teaspoon salt**
2 cups shortening	**½ cup milk, or less**

Mix all ingredients. Divide dough into 2 equal parts, then roll out. Place one dough in a jellyroll pan for bottom crust. Then set other aside for top.

FILLING:

2 (20-ounce) cans crushed pineapple, drained (or 2 cans apple or cherry pie filling)	**1 cup sugar**
	2 eggs, beaten
	4 teaspoons cornstarch

Mix all ingredients together and pour over bottom crust. Place second dough on top. Bake in oven at 350° for 35–40 minutes, or until golden brown. Frost when cool.

FROSTING:

1 (8-ounce) package cream cheese	**1 teaspoon vanilla**
2–2½ cups powdered sugar	**Crushed nuts (optional)**
4 teaspoons milk	

Mix with mixer and spread on top crust. Crushed nuts may also be placed on top. Enjoy!

Patty Gibbons (Niagara Falls, New York)

Sets are often constructed especially for the seasons, like this cozy Christmas parlor with paper flames dancing in the fireplace.

Pecan Toffee Squares

These are so easy to make and taste so good . . . always have wonderful comments whenever I take them somewhere.

2 cups flour
1/2 cup powdered sugar
1 cup butter, cut up
1 (14-ounce) can sweetened
  condensed milk

1 large egg
1 teaspoon vanilla
1 (8-ounce) package brickle chips
1 cup chopped pecans

Combine flour and powdered sugar in medium bowl. Cut in butter with pastry blender till crumbly. Press mixture evenly into greased 9x13-inch pan and bake at 350° for 15 minutes. Combine condensed milk with remaining ingredients. Pour over prepared crust. Return to oven and bake for an additional 25 minutes, until golden. Cool and cut into squares. Yields 4 dozen.

Mary Kay Ryan (Jefferson City, Missouri)

Editors' Extra: Good subbing toffee bits for brickle chips, too.

It-Wouldn't-Be-Christmas Cookies

2 (4-ounce) bars German
  chocolate
1 tablespoon butter
2 eggs
3/4 cup sugar
1/4 cup flour

1/8 teaspoon salt
1/4 teaspoon baking powder
1/4 teaspoon cinnamon
Dash (or 2) nutmeg
1/2 teaspoon vanilla
3/4 cup pecan pieces

Melt chocolate and butter together; cool. Beat eggs until foamy. Add sugar 2 tablespoons at a time, until thickened, about 5 minutes. Blend in chocolate mixture. Add flour, salt, baking powder, cinnamon, and nutmeg, blending well. Stir in vanilla and nuts. Drop by tablespoons onto greased cookie sheets. Bake at 350° for 8–10 minutes, until cookies feel set. Cookies will appear cracked. This recipe doubles easily.

Helene M. Hamilton (Hickory, North Carolina)

Candy Bar Cookie

This is a delicious cookie that I have made for my family for 30 years or so. It is a must with my Christmas baking.

¾ cup powdered sugar	**1 teaspoon vanilla**
¾ cup butter, softened	**2 cups flour, sifted**
2 tablespoons evaporated milk	**¼ teaspoon salt**

In a large bowl, combine sugar, butter, milk, and vanilla. Stir in sifted flour and salt. Chill dough slightly for easier handling. Heat oven to 325°. Roll out ½ of dough to 12- to 18-inch rectangle. Cut into 2-inch circles. Place on ungreased cookie sheet. Repeat with remaining dough. Bake for 12–15 mintues.

FILLING:

28 caramels	**¼ cup butter**
¼ cup evaporated milk	**½ cup chopped pecans**
¾ cup powdered sugar	

In medium saucepan, heat caramels and milk, stirring until smooth. Remove from heat and stir in rest of ingredients. Spread a teaspoonful on each cookie.

FROSTING:

½ cup chocolate chips	**1 tablespoon butter**
2 tablespoons evaporated milk	**½ teaspoon vanilla**
¼ cup powdered sugar	

In a small saucepan, melt chocolate chips and milk on low heat until melted, stirring until smooth. Remove from heat and add rest of ingredients. Spread small amount on caramel layer of each cookie.

Barbara Bullard (Coffeyville, Kansas)

 In 2000, more than 79 million packages were shipped to customers around the world as a result of some 132 million phone calls, leading to more than $3.5 billion in sales.

Chocolicious Peanut Butter Cup Cookies

1 cup butter or margarine, softened	1 teaspoon vanilla
¼ cup sugar	2 eggs
¾ cup packed brown sugar	2¼ cups all-purpose flour
1 (4-serving) package instant chocolate pudding	1 teaspoon baking soda
	Mini-peanut butter cups, unwrapped (about 50)

Preheat oven to 375°. Combine butter, sugars, pudding mix, and vanilla in a large mixing bowl; beat until smooth and creamy. Beat in eggs. Gradually add flour and baking soda. (Batter will be stiff.)

Drop by rounded teaspoonfuls onto ungreased baking sheet, about 2 inches apart. Bake at 375° for 8–10 minutes. While cookies are baking, remove all wrappers from peanut butter cups. Immediately after removing cookies from oven, place a peanut butter cup in center, pressing down slightly. Let cool on pan for 2 minutes. Remove to rack and let cool completely. The candy will harden in an hour or more. Yields 4 dozen.

Heidi Reichenberger (Newton, Massachusetts)

Crunchy Cookies

1 cup margarine, softened	1 cup chopped pecans
1 cup sugar	1 cup shredded coconut
1 cup packed brown sugar	2 cups crisp rice cereal
2 eggs	½ teaspoon baking powder
½ teaspoon vanilla	1 teaspoon soda
2 cups flour	Pinch of salt
2 cups instant oatmeal	

Cream margarine and sugars. Add eggs and beat well. Add vanilla, then flour. Mix well. Blend in the rest of the ingredients. Drop by small teaspoons on greased cookie sheet. Press each mound of dough with a flat surface dipped in sugar (the bottom of a cup or saucer works well). Bake in a 350° oven for 12–15 minutes, or until lightly browned.

Norma Bracher (Boonville, Indiana)

Dude's Raisin Oatmeal Cookies

I love to bake cookies, so I created this cookie recipe for a friend who loves oatmeal cookies, using all the ingredients my friend likes. These are big-dude delicious!

3 cups oatmeal	1 cup sugar
2½ cups flour	1 cup light brown sugar
1 teaspoon salt	2 jumbo eggs
1 teaspoon baking soda	2 tablespoons cream de cocoa
1 teaspoon cream of tartar	2 cups raisins (soaked in ¾ cup
2 teaspoons cinnamon	water, then microwaved for
1 cup chopped hazelnuts	1 minute)
1 cup unsalted butter, softened	

Preheat oven to 350°. In a separate bowl, mix all of the dry ingredients together, including the nuts; set aside. With your electric mixer on slow speed, cream butter and sugars until well blended. Mix together eggs and cream de cocoa, then add to butter mixture; beat until very fluffy. Squeeze out liquid from raisins, then add. Mix in the dry ingredients.

Line cookie sheets with baking parchment paper. Measure about ¼ cup of cookie mixture, roll into balls, and place on cookie sheets 2 inches apart. Flatten each with 4 of your fingers (dip fingers in bowl of water to keep from sticking). Bake at 350° for 12 minutes, or until cookie is set. Cool cookies on wire racks. Yields 4 dozen.

J. Lalee Backus (Buffalo, New York)

Malt Cowboy Cookies

We have eleven children who always took these to school in their sack lunches. They said my cookies could be traded for anything, because everyone loved them. Now my son who works for the county says if he wants to take off, the boss says, ". . . only if you bring the crew some of your mom's delicious cookies!"

1 cup butter or margarine, softened	$\frac{1}{2}$ teaspoon baking powder
1 cup sugar	1 teaspoon salt
1 cup brown sugar	$\frac{1}{2}$ cup malted milk powder
2 eggs	$4\frac{1}{4}$ cups flour
1 teaspoon vanilla	2 cups quick cooking oatmeal
1 teaspoon baking soda	2 cups milk chocolate chips

Beat together butter, sugars, eggs, and vanilla. Stir in baking soda, baking powder, salt, malted milk powder, and flour (makes a stiff dough). Stir in oats and chips. Flatten teaspoonsful onto ungreased cookie sheet and bake at 350° for 9–11 minutes, or until golden.

Joan Hicks (Etna, California)

Kitchen Sink Cookies

1 cup butter or margarine, softened	$\frac{1}{2}$ teaspoon salt
$\frac{1}{2}$ cup brown sugar	$2\frac{1}{2}$ cups oatmeal
1 cup sugar	1 cup crisp rice cereal
2 eggs	6 ounces chocolate chips
1 teaspoon vanilla	6 ounces peanut butter chips
$1\frac{1}{3}$ cups all-purpose flour	$\frac{1}{3}$ cup sesame seeds
1 teaspoon baking soda	$\frac{3}{4}$ cup raisins (optional)
	$\frac{1}{2}$ cup finely ground nuts

Mix first 8 ingredients together. Add remaining ingredients. Mix well. Place 2 inches apart on ungreased cookie sheet. Bake 350° for 10–12 minutes, or until golden brown.

Add your favorite nuts, finely ground (we like pecans). These are also good with coconut; omit the raisins then.

Nancy Optekar-Dickman (Yakima, Washington)

Cherry-Macadamia Cookies

1/2 cup butter, softened	3 ounces maraschino cherries,
2/3 cup sugar	drained, chopped (about 1/3 cup)
1 egg	3 1/2 ounces macadamia nuts,
1 teaspoon vanilla	chopped (about 1 cup)
1 cup all-purpose flour	1 cup white chocolate chips (do
1/2 teaspoon baking soda	not substitute)

Preheat oven to 325°. Cream butter and sugar. Add egg and vanilla. Sift flour and baking soda and combine to mix. Now fold in cherries, nuts, and chips. Drop by melon ball scooper (or rounded teaspoon) onto ungreased cookie sheet. Bake 8–10 minutes, just until edges are light brown.

Terrie W. Tyree (Chadbourn, North Carolina)

Editors' Extra: I always let cookies set on cookie sheet about 2 minutes before removing to racks or brown paper or parchment paper—makes them a little crispier!

Orange Christmas Cookies

Easy and delicious any time of year.

1/2 cup butter-flavored shortening,	Grated rind of 3 oranges
margarine, or butter	1 3/4 cups flour
1 cup sugar	1/2 teaspoon salt
1 egg, beaten	1 teaspoon baking powder

Thoroughly cream shortening and sugar. To this mixture, add egg and grated orange rind, beating well. Add flour sifted with salt and baking powder; beat until smooth. Divide dough into 2–3 portions; wrap each in waxed paper and chill overnight until firm.

Roll each portion out thin and cut with cookie cutters; decorate to suit. Bake in a slow oven at 325° for 8–10 minutes. Do not burn. Makes about 80 pieces. For more orange flavor, use more orange rind.

Doris V. N. Dodd (Alexandria, Virginia)

Blueberry Surprise Pecan Sandies

I wanted to do something different with blueberries, and I came up with this recipe. Because it works well with frozen blueberries, you can make it all year around. I have been making this cookie for about 25 years.

1 cup butter
¹/₂ cup sugar
1 teaspoon vanilla
¹/₂ cup crushed pecans
¹/₂ cup crushed potato chips
2 cups flour
1–2 heaping tablespoons hot fudge topping, refrigerated

24–30 blueberries, frozen in 1 layer
¹/₄ cup rainbow-colored sugar crystals (or granulated sugar mixed with a few drops of food coloring)

Cream butter, sugar, and vanilla. Crush pecans and potato chips (I use a small hammer and plastic bag) and add to mixture. Add flour and mix well. Put cold fudge topping in a saucer. Take 1 tablespoon of dough and roll it into a ball. With your finger, make a hole in the ball. Dip a blueberry in fudge, then put it in cookie dough ball. Roll again to cover blueberry evenly. Put balls on ungreased cookie sheets.

Put sugar crystals in a small bowl. Take a glass, dip it lightly in water, then in sugar crystals. Put sugared glass bottom on each cookie and flatten the cookie lightly, covering the top with sugar. (Don't flatten it too hard, as you don't want to expose the blueberry.) Bake at 350° for 15–18 minutes, or until light brown. Cool on racks. Makes 24–30 cookies.

Patricia Wierzbicki (Baldwinsville, New York)

In December 2000, QVC handled 65,000 web e-mails and 69,000 live chats.

Listenin' to the Crickets
Lemonade Cookies

As a child, before I would return to school in September, I would spend time with my grandparents in their home in Vermont. My grandfather would take me for long walks in the woods and teach me about all the different wildflowers and what mushrooms were good or bad. When returning to the house, my grandmother would be all prepared to make my favorites—Lemonade Cookies! We would make a double batch because they would always disappear. Later in the evening after supper, we would sit out on the porch and enjoy these cookies with tea or milk while we listened to the crickets.

1 cup butter, softened	1 teaspoon baking soda
1 cup sugar	1 (6-ounce) can lemonade
2 eggs	concentrate
3 cups flour	Sugar for sprinkling

Cream butter and sugar. Add eggs, one at a time, beating after each. Combine the flour and baking soda and add to the creamed mixture alternately with 1/3 cup lemonade concentrate. (Chill for 1/2 hour for easier handling, if desired.) Drop by rounded teaspoons on an ungreased cookie sheet. Bake at 350° for 11 minutes. Remove to a rack and brush immediately with the remaining concentrate, then sprinkle with sugar, and let them cool. Makes 6 dozen.

Debbi Dymek (Worcester, Massachusetts)

This is but a corner of a huge warehouse-size room where props and sets are continuously being constructed.

Beverly's Fruit Cookies

2 cups dried fruit bits
²/₃ cup water
1 cup butter
1¾ cups sugar
2 eggs
1 teaspoon vanilla

1 teaspoon orange extract
3½ cups all-purpose flour
1 teaspoon baking powder
1 teaspoon baking soda
1 teaspoon salt
1 cup chopped pecans

Combine fruit and water in 1-quart saucepan and boil 1 minute; remove from heat and cool (do not drain). Cream butter; gradually add sugar. Add eggs, vanilla, and orange extract. Combine dry ingredients and gradually add to creamed mixture and blend thoroughly. Stir in nuts and fruit. Drop by teaspoon onto greased cookie sheet. Bake at 350° for 12–14 minutes.

Beverly Salgado (Ocala, Florida)

Frosted Orange Chippers

Some of the best cookies ever! Soft . . . fantastic!

¾ cup butter or margarine, softened
1 (3-ounce) package cream cheese, softened
1 cup sugar
2 eggs

1 teaspoon vanilla
1 tablespoon grated orange rind
2 cups flour
1 teaspoon salt
6 ounces chocolate chips, or more

Cream butter, cream cheese, and sugar till light and fluffy. Beat in eggs one at a time. Stir in vanilla, orange rind, flour, and salt; beat well. Stir in chocolate chips. Drop by teaspoonfuls on ungreased cookie sheet and bake at 350° for 8–10 minutes. (Do not over bake, just cook until slightly brown around the edges.) Cool on cooling rack, then frost.

FROSTING:
2 cups powdered sugar
2 tablespoons butter, softened

1 teaspoon grated orange rind
3 tablespoons orange juice

Beat together and frost cookies.

Lynne Fort and Janelle Matchett (Klamath Falls, Oregon)

Frosted Roll-Out Sugar Cookies

The cream of tartar and nutmeg really make this cookie good!

1 cup sugar	1 teaspoon baking soda
1 cup shortening	1 teaspoon cream of tartar
1 teaspoon vanilla	1/4 teaspoon salt
2 eggs	1/4 teaspoon nutmeg
3 cups flour	

Cream together sugar, shortening, vanilla, and eggs. Beat until light and creamy. Mix together flour, baking soda, cream of tartar, salt, and nutmeg. Stir into creamy mixture. Take 1/2 of mixture at a time and place on floured counter. Roll out and use cookie cutter to make shapes. Place on greased cookie sheet and bake at 350° for 12–15 minutes. (For softer cookies, take out of oven when lightly brown around the cookie edges.) Make Icing and spread on cookies after cookies have cooled. Makes 36 or more, depending on thickness. No refrigeration needed for the cookie dough. Just mix and roll out.

ICING:

4 cups sifted powdered sugar	6 tablespoons milk
2 tablespoons butter, melted	Few drops food coloring (optional)
2 teaspoons vanilla	

Beat together all ingredients. Add food coloring, if desired. (Pictured on cover.)

Kris Casper (Paris, Texas)

Chocolate Snickerdoodles

The first time I made these for my family, it was because I was ¹/₂ cup short of flour to make snickerdoodles, so I substituted cocoa. We loved them!

¹/₂ cup butter, softened	2 teaspoons cream of tartar
¹/₂ cup shortening	1 teaspoon baking soda
1¹/₂ cups sugar	¹/₄ teaspoon salt
2 eggs	2 tablespoons sugar plus
2¹/₄ cups flour	2 teaspoons cinnamon (or to
¹/₂ cup cocoa	taste)

Preheat oven to 350°. Cream butter, shortening, and sugar; add eggs and cream again. Blend dry ingredients together, except 2 tablespoons sugar and 2 teaspoons cinnamon. Add dry ingredients to creamed mixture. Mix well.

Shape dough in balls and roll in reserved sugar and cinnamon mixture. Bake on ungreased cookie sheet 10–12 minutes. Let set on sheet for a few minutes before removing to cooling rack.

Julanne Myers (Blachly, Oregon)

Crescent Moon Cookies

An old secret recipe from my grandmother's friend 50 years ago. Unbelievably, heavenly good!

1 pound butter, softened	12 ounces finely ground almonds
1 cup sugar, less 2 tablespoons	or walnuts
(reserved)	1 egg, beaten lightly
4 cups flour	2 teaspoons vanilla

Preheat oven to 325°. Cream butter and sugar. Add flour, nuts, egg, and vanilla. Roll into crescent moon shapes, about 1¹/₂ inches high, and space on cookie sheet (unfloured, or use parchment paper) about 2 inches apart. Bake for 15–20 minutes; do not get too dark on edges. While cookies are still hot, roll each in sugar to coat. Makes about 100 crescents.

Gabriel Verbeke (Barnegat, New Jersey)

Coconut Raisin Nut Apple Spice Oatmeal Cookies

A low-fat cookie you'll make again and again.

½ cup old fashioned oats
1½ cups quick cooking oats
½ cup coconut flakes
½ cup raisins
½ cup chopped pecans
5 tablespoons butter, softened
½ cup chopped dried apples

½ cup chopped dried apricots
1 teaspoon baking powder
½ teaspoon apple pie spice
1 egg
½ teaspoon vanilla
¼ teaspoon salt

Preheat oven to 350°. Lightly grease a nonstick cookie sheet with oil. In a large mixing bowl, gently combine both oats, coconut flakes, raisins, chopped pecans, softened butter, dried apples, dried apricots, baking powder, apple pie spice, egg, vanilla, and salt. Place teaspoons of the prepared dough 2 inches apart on greased cookie sheet. Bake 8–10 minutes, or until light brown. Cool completely and then remove. Place in a cookie jar or airtight plastic container. Makes 2 dozen.

Note: Can use non-aluminum baking powder or sea salt (available at any health food store) as substitutes in recipe.

Rosaland K. White (Jackson, Mississippi)

QVC sends camera crews all over the world filming whatever may help enhance a product. The golf scene (shown right) where Barbara and Gwen met (they still discuss cookbooks and recipes between shots) may not make the cut—the camera almost didn't make it either! On the third take of the drive-off scene, Gwen forgot to set the wheel to turn and came within a hair of running smack into it!

Next Best Thing to Tom Selleck Cookies

My family likes the Girl Scout mint cookies and this is a close match. It's a favorite at Christmas and they freeze well. When I serve these, someone is sure to ask for the recipe.

1 (12-ounce) package chocolate
   chips
1½ cups brown sugar
¾ cup margarine
2 tablespoons water
2 eggs

2½ cups flour
1¼ teaspoons soda
1½ teaspoons salt
2 boxes chocolate mints (wrapped
   rectangles)

Melt chocolate chips. Remove from heat. Mix in sugar, margarine, and water till smooth. Beat in eggs. Add dry ingredients. Refrigerate for at least 1 hour.

Roll into balls. Bake on foil-lined cookie sheets for 10 minutes at 350°. (While cookies are baking, unwrap mints.) Remove cookies from oven. Place a mint on top of each cookie. Let melt and then spread. Make sure the top is "frosted" with the melted mint. You may even need more than 2 boxes of mints, depending on the size you make the cookies. Allow to "set" till candy hardens (if they can wait that long!).

Carol Visher (Madelia, Minnesota)

Butterscotch Potato Chip Cookies

1 cup sugar
1 cup brown sugar
1 cup shortening
2 eggs
2½ cups flour

1 teaspoon baking soda
¼ teaspoon baking powder
6 ounces butterscotch morsels
2 cups finely crushed potato chips
1 teaspoon vanilla

Cream sugars and shortening. Stir in eggs. Sift dry ingredients together and add to mixture. Stir in butterscotch morsels and potato chips. Add vanilla. Drop by spoonfuls onto cookie sheet. Bake at 375° for approximately 11 minutes. Makes about 8 dozen.

Becky Norsworthy (Broken Arrow, Oklahoma)

Peanut Butter Lovers' Cookies

3 cups all-purpose flour
2 teaspoons baking soda
½ teaspoon salt
2 teaspoons baking powder
2 sticks margarine, softened

1 (18-ounce) jar peanut butter
½ cup sugar
1 cup dark brown sugar
2 eggs
2 teaspoons vanilla

Preheat oven to 350°. Sift flour, soda, salt, and baking powder together; set aside. In large mixer bowl, cream margarine and peanut butter together till smooth. Add sugars one at a time and blend well. Add eggs and vanilla; blend well with mixer on low. Blend in flour mixture, gradually.

This dough is not like other peanut butter cookies. It will not roll in a ball. Use a small ice cream scoop or melon baller to put dough on cookie sheets. Do not grease sheets. Use fork dipped in ice water to criss-cross top. Bake 10–12 minutes or until a small amount of brown appears on edge of cookie.

Dawn Hardin (Plymouth, Indiana)

Ricotta Cheese Cookies

We've always made these for Christmas, but they are great for bridal and baby showers, and graduation parties, too. Just change the color of the icing to fit the occasion. This icing is great on any cookie.

2 sticks margarine, softened
2 cups sugar
1 (1-pound or 15-ounce) container
  whole milk ricotta cheese
2 eggs, beaten

2 teaspoons vanilla
4 cups flour
1 teaspoon baking soda
1 teaspoon salt

Cream margarine and sugar together. Add ricotta cheese until thoroughly blended. Add eggs and vanilla. Combine flour, baking soda, and salt. Gradually add to cheese mixture. Dough may be sticky. Refrigerate several hours, or overnight.

Preheat oven to 350°. Drop dough by rounded teaspoons onto ungreased cookie sheet. Bake for 15 minutes, or until lightly browned. Cookies will be cake-like in texture. Cool completely on racks and cover with Icing.

ICING:
1 (16-ounce) box powdered sugar
1 tablespoon cream cheese
½ teaspoon vanilla

3 tablespoons milk
Food coloring and decorative
  sprinkles (optional)

Combine Icing ingredients until blended well. Food coloring may be added to Icing. Ice cookies and decorate with colored sugars or sprinkles, if desired. Makes approximately 3–4 dozen cookies.

Coleen Kalafut (Wilkes-Barre, Pennsylvania)

Welsh Griddle Cookies

My husband's great-grandmother brought this recipe with her when she immigrated from Wales in the late 1890s. These cookies are such a favorite that the first couple of dozen are eaten as soon as they are removed from the griddle. My husband and son can't wait until the cookies cool. They are soft and delicious!

1½ cups sugar	1 teaspoon nutmeg
2 eggs	¼ teaspoon cream of tartar
1 cup margarine, softened	¼ teaspoon baking soda
⅓ cup milk	1 cup raisins which have been
4 cups flour, divided	boiled in 1 cup water, drained,
3 teaspoons baking powder	and cooled
1 teaspoon salt	

In large bowl, combine sugar, eggs, and margarine; mix well. Add milk and 2 cups flour; mix well. In a separate bowl, combine remaining dry ingredients. Gradually add dry ingredients mixture to first bowl until well blended. Batter will be very sticky. Fold in drained raisins. Refrigerate dough for at least 1 hour; dough is easier to handle when very cold.

    Only remove a small portion of dough at a time to roll out; leave remaining dough in refrigerator. Keep rolling surface and rolling pin floured well, as dough is very sticky. Roll dough thinly to about ¼-inch thickness; cut out cookies using a 2-inch round cookie cutter. Cookies are baked on an ungreased griddle on top of the stove. (I have a burner that is thermostat-controlled and I bake the cookies at 350° for 3–4 minutes on each side, until golden brown.) Remove to wire rack to cool.

Sheila M. Riffle (Wintersville, Ohio)

 More than 25 million individual customers have made at least one purchase from QVC or QVC.com.

Mom's Chocolate Delights

One of the best presents we received as kids during Christmas was not found under the tree. It was Mom's cookie tin which could be found in the refrigerator! It's true that great gifts come in small packages!

1 pound semisweet chocolate chips	1 cup chopped pecans
2 (1-ounce) squares unsweetened baker's chocolate	1 cup chopped dates
	5 cups cornflakes
	¼ teaspoon salt

Melt chocolate over hot water. Add all other ingredients. Mix well. Drop by teaspoonful onto waxed paper. Let stand in refrigerator or cool place, until firm. Enjoy!

Dee Scecchitano Fleming (Hopewell Junction, New York)

Butterscotcheroos

My grandmother is a great cook, especially desserts! This is one of the family's favorites. It's so fast and easy that I bring it to all the potluck dinners (and never bring any home). I even had a friend (who was in the hospital) ask me to make them for her husband's birthday!

1 cup sugar	6 cups crisp rice cereal
1 cup white corn syrup	½ cup chocolate chips
1 cup peanut butter	½ cup butterscotch chips

Combine sugar and syrup; heat till sugar melts. Remove from heat and stir in peanut butter till melted. Fold in cereal till mixed well. Press into 9x13-inch cake pan. Melt the chips. (I use the microwave by putting them in a microwavable dish and heating on HIGH 1 minute at a time until melted.) Then spread the melted chips onto the crispy treats. Put in refrigerator to set.

Terry L. Carter (Crossett, Arkansas)

Pecan Graham Layer Cookies

2 sticks margarine	1 egg
1 cup graham cracker crumbs	1 cup coconut
1 cup sugar	1 cup chopped pecans
½ cup milk	1 box whole graham crackers

Melt margarine. Add cracker crumbs, sugar, milk, and egg. Bring to a rolling boil. Stir constantly to keep from sticking. Remove from heat and add coconut and nuts. Line a 9x13-inch pan with whole graham crackers. Pour cooked mixture over the whole crackers. Place another layer of whole crackers over mixture. Allow mixture to cool and frost with Cream Frosting.

CREAM FROSTING:

¾ stick margarine	1 tablespoon milk
2 cups powdered sugar	1 teaspoon vanilla

Melt margarine and mix with powdered sugar; add milk. Stir in vanilla and additional milk, if needed. Spread over top layer of whole crackers and sprinkle with chopped nuts, if desired. Chill for 2 hours before serving. Cut into squares to serve. Keep refrigerated.

Connie Bullins (Germanton, North Carolina)

Through 25 features along the QVC Studio Tour, guests can learn more about QVC's beginnings, successes, and growth into a $3.8 billion preeminent electronic retailer. Visitors can catch a glimpse of the live broadcast from five studio views where monitors feature state-of-the art, pullback cameras in eight different locations within the studio.

Chocolate Cracker Candy

I work in a large elementary school as a secretary and we frequently have "coffee ands . . ." I used to make these all the time and they always disappeared.

½ box saltine crackers
2 sticks plus 2 tablespoons
  butter, divided
1 cup granulated sugar

1 (12-ounce) package chocolate
  chips
6–8 shortbread cookies (or ½ cup
  chopped pecans or walnuts)

Line large cookie sheet with sides with tin foil; butter foil well with 2 tablespoons butter. Place enough saltines to cover entire cookie sheet end to end. Melt the 2 sticks butter with sugar. Heat until bubbly and frothy; pour over saltines. Bake at 350° for about 8 minutes. Remove from oven and sprinkle chips over saltines; spread as they melt. Crush cookies and sprinkle these and/or chopped nuts over chocolate. Refrigerate several hours until chocolate is set. Cut into small squares. Keeps well in cookie tin lined with waxed paper.

Jo Anne Montanari (Toms River, New Jersey)

Gem Dandies

A yummy candy recipe . . . this one is a keeper!

1 (14-ounce) can coconut
1 can sweetened condensed milk
2 (5-ounce) cans whole almonds

1 (12-ounce) package milk
  chocolate chips
¾ bar paraffin

Mix coconut and condensed milk well. Spray a 9x13-inch glass casserole dish with nonstick spray. Pour coconut mixture in and bake at 300° for 10–15 minutes. Remove from oven. When cool enough to handle, dip out by tablespoons and roll into balls. (Dust hands with powdered sugar as needed.) Press an almond on top, slightly flattening ball. Put on cookie sheets and freeze.

Melt chocolate chips and paraffin in top of a double boiler. Dip each ball and place on wax paper to allow chocolate to harden. Can be stored in airtight container and kept for up to 2 weeks.

Lillie H. Byrum (Ridgetop, Tennessee)

Peppermint Pleasure

I brought the first batch of these into the Customer Service Department to share with some of the nice ladies there. By the end of the day I had lots of requests; four for the recipe, two for dates, and one marriage proposal. Just kidding. But if this candy can't open a person's heart, it may get you into their kitchen.

1 egg white	6–7 cups powdered sugar
7 tablespoons heavy cream	12 ounces semisweet chocolate
1 teaspoon peppermint extract	

In a medium bowl, beat egg white lightly. Add heavy cream and peppermint extract; then, slowly add powdered sugar till it forms a firm dough. Dust rolling surface with powdered sugar. Roll dough to about ¼-inch thickness. Cut dough into squares, or any shape desirable. Place cut-outs on cookie sheet lined with wax paper and leave to dry for 8 hours minimum. Turn candies over once about halfway through drying time.

Melt chocolate in double boiler over barely simmering water. Remove from heat and allow to cool slightly. Dip patties into chocolate with a fork, then return to wax paper to dry. Store in airtight container.

Gerard J. Medvec, QVC Employee (West Chester, Pennsylvania)

Nana's Christmas Candy

My mother used to make these as Christmas presents for all of my brother's and my teachers.

1 (14-ounce) can sweetened condensed milk	4 cups chopped pecans
1 cup flaked coconut	1 small (6-ounce) package chocolate chips
1 stick butter, softened	¼ pound paraffin
1½ (1-pound) boxes powdered sugar	

Mix first 5 ingredients and shape into balls the size of walnuts. Chill covered overnight. Melt chips and paraffin in double boiler. Remove from heat and leave over water. Stick toothpick into candy balls and dip in chocolate mixture. Place on wax paper to dry. Makes about 75 pieces.

Norlene Trice (Bonaire, Georgia)

Peanutty Heavenly Hash

**12 ounces semisweet chocolate
   chips**
11 ounces butterscotch chips

½ cup chunky peanut butter
16 ounces miniature marshmallows
1 scant cup dry roasted peanuts

Combine chocolate chips, butterscotch chips, and peanut butter in heavy pan over very low heat. Stir occasionally until just melted. Remove from heat. Fold in marshmallows and peanuts until well combined. Spread mixture in buttered 9x13-inch glass pan. Refrigerate until set. Cut into squares and enjoy.

Nikki N. Tsangaris (Indianapolis, Indiana)

North Pole Peanut Butter Fudge

I would like to thank my family, friends, and co-workers at the Santa Claus House for being such willing guinea pigs while I perfected this recipe.

½ cup milk
2 tablespoons butter
1½ cups sugar

3 tablespoons cocoa
1¼ cups peanut butter
1 cup marshmallow creme

In saucepan, combine milk and butter over medium heat. Sift sugar and cocoa into milk mixture. Mix well. Bring to a boil and turn heat down to medium low; cook for 8 more minutes, stirring often. Remove from heat.

Add peanut butter and marshmallow creme. Stir until combined. Put in buttered 8x8-inch pan. Refrigerate for at least 2 hours. Best if refrigerated overnight.

Dawn Jaksons (North Pole, Alaska)

 QVC is closed only one day of the year, Christmas Day.

Color-Me-Orange Cream Fudge

1½ sticks margarine
⅔ cup evaporated milk
3 cups sugar
1 (12-ounce) package white
  chocolate chips

1 (7-ounce) jar marshmallow
  creme
3 teaspoons orange extract
12 drops yellow food coloring
9 drops red food coloring

In saucepan, combine first 3 ingredients and bring to a boil. Lower heat and cook for 7 minutes, stirring constantly. Remove from stove. Take out 1 cup and set aside. Add chips and marshmallow creme to saucepan; mix well.

    To reserved 1 cup, add orange extract and yellow and red food coloring. Butter a 9x13-inch casserole dish. Pour white mixture in buttered dish. Pour reserved cup on top of white mixture. Take knife and swirl through both layers. Let set till firm.

Mary Meszaros (Baltimore, Maryland)

Peanut Butterscotch Fudge

My grandmother always made this fudge. It's different, but tastes great....a family favorite!

1 large or 2 small packages
  butterscotch pudding and pie
  filling (not instant)
2 cups sugar

1 cup firmly packed brown sugar
1 cup evaporated milk
2 tablespoons butter
⅔ cup peanut butter

In a 2-quart saucepan, combine pudding, sugars, milk, and butter. Cook over low to medium heat until mixture forms "soft ball" stage on candy thermometer. Remove from heat; stir in peanut butter until blended. Pour into a 9x9-inch pan. Let cool.

Beatrice Plumley (Wellsboro, Pennsylvania)

Chocolate Trail Mix

½ cup margarine, melted
2 tablespoons cocoa
3 tablespoons sugar
4 cups round oat cereal
4 cups square wheat cereal
1 cup peanuts (no skins)

1 cup golden raisins
1 (12-ounce) bag white chocolate
    chips
1 (6-ounce) bag milk chocolate
    chips

Preheat oven to 250°. Stir margarine, cocoa, and sugar together in small bowl. Mix cereals and nuts in large bowl. Add margarine mixture to cereal mixture and toss to coat. Put into a 9x13-inch baking pan. Bake for 1 hour; stirring every 15 minutes. Cool completely. Stir in raisins and chips after mixture is cool. Store in airtight container in a cool dry place. Enjoy!

Ronda J. Johnson (Hastings, Nebraska)

Baseball Bats

My two sons named these. A must at Christmastime.

1 package pretzel rods
1 package caramels
1½ cups semisweet chocolate
    chips

½ cup milk chocolate chips
2 squares premium white chocolate

Break rods in half. Melt caramels according to directions. Dip rods into caramel about half way. Place on greased cookie sheet. Freeze about 15 minutes to set. Mix both kinds of chips and melt; dip cold rods into chocolate to cover caramel. Place on greased cookie sheet. Melt white chocolate and drizzle over chocolate rods. Refrigerate to set.

Susan L. Anderson (Fort Madison, Iowa)

Gridiron Popcorn Nut Crackle

Coming from a family as the only girl surrounded by brothers, I have acquired a true love of the gridiron game of football, and have become a die-hard Cleveland Browns' fan. On Sundays, my mom would always try to come up with different snacks for all of us football-loving folks. When I became old enough to share the kitchen with my mom, I started creating or recreating snack recipes for those sport Sundays. This recipe is actually a basic popcorn ball recipe that was my grand-mother's. I added my own cooking knowledge and revamped it into popcorn nut crackle. So I guess this recipe is a new classic.

½ cup unpopped gourmet
  popping corn, or 2 packages
  plain microwave popcorn
2 cups dry roasted peanuts
2 teaspoons salt
½ cup water

2 cups sugar
4 tablespoons white corn syrup
2 tablespoons butter or
  margarine
¾ teaspoon baking soda

Pop popcorn as you would normally. Sift out hard and unpopped kernels. Place popped corn into large roaster pan. Sprinkle the peanuts and salt over popcorn. Do not blend. Set aside.

In a Dutch oven, combine water, sugar, syrup, and butter. Bring to a boil on high heat, stirring constantly with a wooden spoon. Boil until mixture turns a light to medium brown. (Do not boil any longer or crackle will have a scorched taste.) Remove from heat, still stirring. Stir in baking soda. Mixture will turn darker and increase in size. Stir vigorously, approximately 5 seconds, for maximum volume, and pour over salted popcorn and nuts. Allow to cool for approximately 1 hour.

Break apart into small chunks. Can be stored in sealed containers or plastic bags in a cool, dry place. DO NOT refrigerate.

Jeannette E. Rood (Toronto, Ohio)

Pies and Other Desserts

*Presentation is important to selling a product. On all-day cook shows,
the food prep area is filled with beautiful dishes. It is a tricky and skillful business
to have it all looking like it just came out of the oven (it did!), or the freezer
(it did!), and looking "photo-licious" for the camera.*

No-Bake Chocolate Truffle Cheese Pie

CRUST:

9 ounces chocolate wafers ¼ cup butter, melted

Crumble chocolate wafers and combine with melted butter. Press into pie pan. Refrigerate for 1 hour.

FILLING:

12 ounces heavy cream ⅓ cup sugar
1 (12-ounce) package semisweet 1 teaspoon vanilla extract
   chocolate
1 (8-ounce) bar cream cheese,
   softened

Heat heavy cream; pour over chocolate to melt. Stir with rubber spatula to combine. Let stand for 10 minutes, then refrigerate for 30 minutes.

Remove from refrigerator, and whip with a whisk until it begins to form peaks and is slightly lighter in color.

In a separate bowl, mix cream cheese, sugar, and vanilla with electric mixer on medium speed until well blended. Fold cream cheese mixture and whipped chocolate mixture together; pour into chocolate crust. Refrigerate 1 hour, then make Glaze.

GLAZE:

6 ounces heavy cream 6 ounces semisweet chocolate

Heat heavy cream and pour over chocolate. Stir to melt chocolate. Let stand 10 minutes. Remove pie from refrigerator and pour Glaze over pie. Return pie to refrigerator; chill for 3 hours. To serve, you can pipe whipped cream on top or serve as is.

Louise M. Porreca (Glen Riddle, Pennsylvania)

QVC's Prep Kitchen (opposite page) is quite often a very busy place. With several cooktops, ovens, sinks, and lots of counter space, cooking is made as convenient as possible. There is a walk-in refrigerator and freezer, plus several commercial-sized ones to accommodate all the dishes that must be prepared in advance by oftentimes a dozen cooks and chefs. The all-day cook events put all the chefs and equipment to the test . . . and they pass every time.

Chocolate Angel Strata Pie

2 eggs, separated
½ teaspoon vinegar
¼ teaspoon salt
½ teaspoon cinnamon, divided
¾ cup sugar, divided
1 (9-inch) pie crust, baked

¼ cup water
1 (6-ounce) package chocolate
  chips, melted
2 cups whipping cream, divided
Grated chocolate for garnish

Beat egg whites with vinegar, salt, and ¼ teaspoon cinnamon until soft mounds form. Gradually add ½ cup sugar, beating until meringue forms glossy peaks. Spread on bottom and sides of baked pie crust and bake at 325° for 15–18 minutes. Cool completely.

Combine the 2 slightly beaten egg yolks with ¼ cup of water. Add this to melted chocolate chips. Spread 3 tablespoons of this mixture over cooled meringue in shell and cool the remainder.

Combine ¼ cup sugar, ¼ teaspoon cinnamon, and 1 cup whipping cream. Beat until stiff and spread ½ of this mixture over chocolate in pie crust.

Combine remaining cream mixture with chocolate mixture and spread over cream in pie crust. Chill for 4 hours.

Beat remaining 1 cup of cream until stiff and spread over top of pie. Top with grated chocolate.

Mary A. Duckett (Mountaintop, Pennsylvania)

Peanut Butter Parfait Pies

These delicious pies can be made ahead and frozen until ready for use.

1 (18-ounce) jar crunchy peanut
  butter
2 (8-ounce) packages cream
  cheese, softened
1 (16-ounce) container whipped
  topping, divided

1 (16-ounce) box powdered
  sugar
1½ cups chocolate chip morsels
2 (6-inch) chocolate pie crusts

Cream together peanut butter and cream cheese. Stir in 12 ounces of whipped topping. Slowly fold in powdered sugar, mixing well. Stir in chocolate chip morsels. Pour mixture into pie crusts. Spread remaining 4 ounces whipped topping on pies. Serve chilled.

Hint: Before spreading whipped topping on pies, place pies in freezer for approximately 1 hour. Pie fillings will stand approximately 1 inch above crusts.

Marla D. Carriger (Johnson City, Tennessee)

Peanut Butter Meringue Pies

Times were tight when this recipe was created. It has been in the family for two generations. Children and grandchildren fight over these pies at Christmastime.

1 cup sugar
4 tablespoons self-rising flour
1 (8-ounce) jar smooth peanut
  butter
1 tablespoon vanilla flavoring

3 cups milk
5 egg yolks (reserve whites for
  meringue)
2 (8-inch) pie shells, baked

In saucepan, mix sugar, flour, and peanut butter. Add remaining ingredients except pie shells. Cook on medium heat, stirring constantly till it begins to thicken. Pour into baked pie shells.

MERINGUE:
5 egg whites
½ cup sugar

1 teaspoon vanilla

Beat egg whites till stiff. Gradually mix in cup sugar and vanilla; stir well. Spread over pies and brown in 375° oven (about 10 minutes).

JoAnna W. Harrell, QVC Employee (Rocky Mount, North Carolina)

Peanut Butter Turtle Pie

This is my family's hands-down favorite dessert. This recipe evolved over time to incorporate everyone's favorite flavors. The crunchy chocolate crust is mounded with a billowy mousse-like peanut butter filling and topped with gooey caramel and toasted pecans. The crowning glory is the glaze of rich chocolate which gilds this glorious lily. Decadent and so delicious.

1 (8-ounce) package cream
  cheese, softened
1 cup creamy peanut butter
1 cup powdered sugar
1 tablespoon butter, softened
1 teaspoon vanilla
1 (8-ounce) carton whipped
  topping, thawed

1 ready-made chocolate pie crust
1 cup caramel sauce, room
  temperature
2/3 cup pecan pieces, preferably
  toasted
1/2 cup chocolate chips
1/3 cup heavy cream
3 tablespoons sugar

Beat together cream cheese, peanut butter, powdered sugar, butter, and vanilla until smooth. Fold in whipped topping. Spoon into prepared crust. Smooth top of filling with back of spoon. Place in freezer 10 minutes. Pour caramel sauce over top of pie, spreading evenly. Sprinkle with pecans. Return to freezer for an additional 10 minutes.

Meanwhile, place chocolate chips, cream, and sugar in top of double boiler. Cook over medium-low heat until chocolate is just melted. Quickly pour chocolate mixture over top of chilled pie, spreading evenly. Refrigerate 2 hours, or until serving. Makes 8–10 servings.

Edwina Gadsby (Great Falls, Montana)

 On November 28, 1999, QVC.com, the QVC website, reported its first million-dollar day.

Lite and Lovely Peanut Butter
Ice Cream Pie

Since I'm always watching calories, I took the peanut butter pie idea and cut fat every place I could. It tastes great! I've served it to guests who have no idea it's a reduced-fat dessert.

CRUST:

8 large low-fat graham crackers, finely crumbled

2 tablespoons sugar
¼ cup margarine, melted

Mix cracker crumbs, sugar, and melted margarine. Press into 9-inch pie plate. Set aside.

FILLING:

½ cup non-fat frozen whipped topping, thawed
4 cups low-fat vanilla or chocolate ice cream, softened

½ cup reduced-fat peanut butter
Chocolate sauce for garnish (optional)

Blend whipped topping, softened ice cream, and peanut butter. Pour into crust. Freeze for at least 2 hours before serving.

To serve, drizzle chocolate sauce on plate, then place pie slice on plate. Chocolate sauce can also be drizzled on the pie slice itself. Yum! Serves 6–8.

Carla Link (Vancouver, Washington)

QVC transmits live retail programming 24 hours a day, seven days a week, to more than 80 million homes in the United States. QVC UK, a joint venture with BSkyB, which was launched on October 1, 1993, reaches 8.2 million households throughout the United Kingdom and the Republic of Ireland, broadcasting live 17 hours a day (from 9:00 a.m. to 2:00 a.m.). QVC Germany, which was launched on December 1, 1996, reaches more than 27 million households in Germany and broadcasts live 19 hours a day (from 7:00 a.m. to 2:00 a.m.). QVC Japan, which was launched on April 1, 2001, reaches more than 4.6 million cable and satellite households in Japan and broadcasts live 15 hours a day.

Coconut Dream Pie

This is the best coconut pie you will ever eat. Anytime I make this dessert for company, they request the recipe and have seconds. My nieces and other family members always request this pie when they come to visit. So easy to make and it goes quickly, so you better make two!

CRUST:

1¼ cups flour	**½ cup shortening**
1 teaspoon salt	**3 tablespoons cold water**

In medium bowl, mix flour, salt, and shortening. Using a pastry cutter or 2 butter knives, cut shortening into flour until it becomes crumbly. Adding 1 tablespoon of cold water at a time, cut into the flour mixture until all water has been added. Keep cutting until large clumps appear. Try not to handle the dough too much or it will toughen. Gather up the dough and make into a large ball. Roll out onto a floured board, then place into a pie plate. Cut off excess dough, flute, and bake at 425° for 20 minutes, or until light golden brown. Remove from oven and cool completely.

FILLING:

1 large package instant vanilla pudding	**1 cup milk**
1 cup heavy cream	**1 teaspoon coconut extract**

Using an electric mixer, beat all the Filling ingredients for 5 full minutes or until extremely thick. Spoon into cooled pie crust.

TOPPING:

1 envelope dry whipped topping	**½ teaspoon coconut extract**
½ cup milk	**½ cup shredded coconut**

Using electric mixer, whip dry whipped topping with the milk and coconut extract until thickened (it resembles whipped cream). Spread over Filling. Sprinkle the entire surface of the pie with shredded coconut. Chill for at least 1 hour before serving.

Rebecca Swift (Redding, California)

Grandma's Apple Pie

This is my grandmother's most popular pie! She actually makes her own pie crust from scratch, but wants to keep that a family secret.

6–7 medium-size baking apples	1 teaspoon ground cinnamon
2 ready-made pie crusts	½ teaspoon salt
2 tablespoons flour	2 tablespoons water
¾ cup sugar	2 tablespoons milk

Preheat oven to 400°. Peel, core, and slice apples; set aside. Line pie plate with 1 ready-made pie crust. In small mixing bowl, combine flour, sugar, cinnamon, and salt; mix well. Alternating apples and flour mixture, layer inside pie shell. Moisten fingers in water and dab along edge/rim of pie crust. Place top pie crust over pie plate and pinch edges of both crusts together. Cut slits in top crust; brush with milk and bake at 400° for 20 minutes. Reduce temperature to 375° and bake approximately 30 minutes.

Patti Reilly, QVC Host (West Chester, Pennsylvania)

Patti Reilly has a variety of hobbies and interests, including crafting and gardening. She is an animal lover, and has a black lab named Piper. Patti graduated in speech communications from the University of Rhode Island.

Coffee Pumpkin Pies

This is a recipe that is loved by all and has become a family favorite!

PIE SHELLS:

³⁄₄ cup shortening
¹⁄₄ cup boiling water
1 tablespoon milk

2 cups all-purpose flour (sifted
  once before measuring)
1 teaspoon salt

Put shortening in medium-sized mixing bowl. Add boiling water and milk and break up shortening with fork. Tilt bowl, and with rapid cross-the-bowl strokes, whip until mixture is smooth and thick (like whipped cream) and holds soft peaks when fork is lifted. Sift flour and salt together onto shortening mixture. Stir quickly, with round-the-bowl strokes, into a dough that clings together and "cleans" the bowl. Pick up and work into a smooth dough; shape into flat round. The dough is now ready to divide and roll into 2 pastries, either between waxed paper, or on a pastry cloth or board. Bake pie shells in 425° oven for 7–8 minutes, or until they begin to brown lightly.

FILLING:

1 (14-ounce) can sweetened
  condensed milk
¹⁄₂ cup milk
¹⁄₂ cup coffee liqueur

3 teaspoons pumpkin pie spice
1 (30-ounce) can pumpkin pie mix
4 medium eggs

Beat both milks, coffee liqueur, and pumpkin pie spice together until blended. Stir in pumpkin pie mix. Beat eggs and add to rest of mixture. Stir or beat on low until smooth. Stir Filling and pour ¹⁄₂ into each pie shell. Add any pastry decorations to top, if desired. Reset oven to 350° and continue baking till Filling is barely set in center, about 55–70 minutes. Cool on wire racks. Serve with Coffee Cream Topping.

COFFEE CREAM TOPPING:

1 cup heavy cream
1 tablespoon powdered sugar

1 tablespoon coffee liqueur

Beat cream with powdered sugar just until stiff; stir in coffee liqueur.

Penny Lyn Kane (Waterford, Michigan)

Just Like Grandma's
Pumpkin Custard Pies

This is the pie my grandmother made when I was growing up. After a miserable attempt to make a pumpkin pie soon after I got married, my husband asked me to call my grandma to get her recipe. The only problem was she didn't have a recipe. She said you use several eggs, a little of this, some milk—you get the picture. But finally, after a little trial and error, I got it! Here is the recipe for a pie like hers. Enjoy!

4 eggs, slightly beaten	**2 tablespoons cornstarch**
1²/₃ cups sugar	**2 cups milk**
Pinch of salt	**1 (14-ounce) can evaporated milk**
¹/₂ teaspoon nutmeg	**2 (9-inch) pie crusts, unbaked**
1 (1-pound) can pumpkin	**Cinnamon**

Beat eggs and sugar thoroughly. Add salt, nutmeg, pumpkin, and cornstarch, beating well. Add both milks (skim milk may be used). Place pie crusts on oven rack in middle of preheated 375° oven. Fill, using a dipper or pitcher, as mixture is very runny.

Sprinkle tops with cinnamon, covering pies. Very carefully, push oven rack in. Bake at 375° for 1 hour, or until edges of custard start to crack. Makes 2 pies. Cool and keep in refrigerator.

Ellen Midlam (Potomac, Maryland)

Grandma Hunt's Butterscotch Pie

This recipe has been passed through our family for about 100 years. Needless to say, it's a family favorite. This was originally done in a cast-iron frying pan.

1 stick butter	2 eggs
1 cup packed brown sugar	⅓ scant cup of flour
1 (12-ounce) can evaporated milk, divided	1 (9-inch) baked pie shell

Melt butter in pan. Add brown sugar and cook while stirring until mixture becomes waxy looking (a minute or two). Add ½ can of evaporated milk and stir (a whisk works best). Turn heat to low. In a blender, mix the rest of the milk with the eggs and flour. Mix thoroughly (if there are lumps, the mixture should be strained). Slowly add this to the ingredients in the pan while stirring constantly. Turn heat to medium and cook until thickened, stirring constantly. Pour into cooled pie shell and cool in the refrigerator. Serve with whipped cream.

Virginia A. Wood (Richmond, Michigan)

Transparent Pie

A Kielman family recipe. We sell these pies faster than we can make them at our restaurant!

4 eggs	1 teaspoon vanilla
2 cups sugar, minus 2 tablespoons	1 stick butter or margarine
2 tablespoons white corn syrup	16 baked tarts or 1 (9-inch) pie shell, baked*
1½ teaspoons vinegar	

In a heavy saucepan, mix and cook eggs, sugar, syrup, vinegar, and vanilla over medium heat. Cut butter in small slices and drop into mixture; cook till butter is melted. Pour mixture into tarts or pie shell. Bake for 17 minutes at 350°.

*If you make a pie instead of tarts, bake at 350° for 10 minutes. Then turn oven down to 300° and cook till all is firm except a small place in center of pie (about the size of a small egg); take it out of oven and let set, as it will finish cooking. Serve and enjoy!

Lovella Herrington (Maysville, Kentucky)

Outstanding Cantaloupe Pie

This is our family's original recipe for cantaloupe pie. The sweet aroma in the kitchen is awesome. I'm the third generation making cantaloupe pie. I updated the pie 30 years ago by using tapioca pudding because the pie was so juicy. After the first bite—faces look like they've just gone to heaven.

½ (3-ounce) package tapioca cook-n-serve or instant pudding mix (not granules)	½ medium cantaloupe
	¼ cup sugar
	½–¾ teaspoon cinnamon
1 frozen pie crust, defrosted	½ stick butter

Sprinkle tapioca in pie shell. Peel and slice cantaloupe into quarter-inch-thick long slices, just like an apple. Lay slices into defrosted pie shell starting on outside and going towards the center. Sprinkle sugar over cantaloupe. Sprinkle cinnamon over sugar (depending on how much you like cinnamon). Slice pats of butter and lay on top of pie. Bake at 325° for 1 hour. Pie is super delicious warm and can be served with a scoop of vanilla ice cream.

Jeanette Dornak (El Campo, Texas)

Easy Ice Cream Cocoa Crust Pie

This easy recipe combines our three favorite desserts: cheesecake, ice cream, and pie! It also works well with other ice cream flavors or frozen yogurt.

2 cups cocoa crispy rice cereal	1 quart strawberry cheesecake ice-cream, softened
¼ cup margarine, melted	
½ cup white chocolate chips	

Spray a 9-inch round deep-dish pie plate with nonstick spray. In large bowl, combine cereal with melted margarine. Stir well to mix. Press ⅔ of mixture into bottom and up the sides of pie plate. Refrigerate 10 minutes. Place chocolate chips in microwave-safe dish. Microwave for 1–2 minutes, or until chips are melted, stirring once. Drizzle white chocolate over chilled crust. Return to refrigerator for 5 minutes. Spoon softened ice cream evenly into crust. Sprinkle with remaining cereal mixture. Place in freezer for at least one hour before serving.

Maya Kline (Boise, Idaho)

Sweet Potato Cobbler

4–5 medium sweet potatoes,
  peeled and sliced ¼ inch thick
1½ cups sugar
¾ stick margarine

1 teaspoon vanilla flavoring
1 teaspoon cinnamon
1 teaspoon nutmeg
2 cups water

Place potato slices in a large saucepan. Add sugar, margarine, vanilla flavoring, cinnamon, and nutmeg; cover and cook on very low heat until it forms a syrup. Add water and turn heat to medium high. Cover and cook until tender. Meanwhile, prepare pastry.

PASTRY:
2 cups all-purpose flour
1 teaspoon salt

⅔ cup shortening
⅜ cup ice water

Preheat oven to 350°. Mix flour, salt, and shortening well with dough blender. Add ice water. Mix dough until you can handle it with your hands without it being too sticky. Form into a round ball.

Roll out dough on a cutting board using a rolling pin to ¼-inch thickness. Cut 6–8 pieces of pastry and drop into potato mixture for dumplings. Let cook about 5 minutes. Place potatoes and dumplings in a deep 9x13-inch glass dish. Cut the remaining dough into ½-inch strips; arrange on top of cobbler using basket weave design and bake for 45 minutes, or until golden brown.

Cheryl P. Barton (Brewton, Alabama)

 In 2000 alone, QVC shipped more than 79 million packages to 8.2 million worldwide customers.

Cran-Apple Cobbler

This cobbler is a favorite at our senior center potluck dinners.

2 (21-ounce) cans apple pie
    filling
1 (16-ounce) can whole cranberry
    sauce

1 small (1-layer) cake mix
1 stick margarine
½ cup chopped pecans

Mix apple pie filling and cranberry sauce. Pour into 9x13-inch baking dish. Sprinkle cake mix on top. Cut margarine into pats and place on cake mix. Sprinkle on pecans. Bake at 350° for 30 minutes. Cobbler should be bubbling and golden brown.

Nancy Henley (Glencoe, Alabama)

Microwave Pudding Delight

A quick dessert—an old favorite with a new twist!

1 (12-ounce) can evaporated milk
½ stick margarine
3 eggs, beaten
1 cup sugar

1 teaspoon vanilla
8 slices broken bread
1½ teaspoons cinnamon
½ cup raisins (optional)

Using a glass dish with lid, microwave milk and margarine 5 minutes on HIGH. Mix eggs, sugar, and vanilla and add to heated milk and margarine. Stir in bread, cinnamon, and raisins, if desired. Cook, covered, on HIGH for 3 minutes and then stir. Cook again for 1½ minutes. Be sure to cook with lid on dish and enjoy! Serves 8.

Note: You may have to adjust cooking time according to your microwave.

TOPPING (OPTIONAL):
½ cup powdered sugar
½ teaspoon vanilla

1 tablespoon lemon juice, or more

Sift powdered sugar and then whisk in vanilla and enough lemon juice to make sauce. Drizzle over pudding.

Carol J. Galuppo (San Antonio, Texas)

Chocolate-Covered Coffee Custard

3 eggs, beaten   ¼ cup coffee liqueur
¼ cup sugar   1¼ cups milk
1 teaspoon vanilla extract   ½ cup chocolate syrup

In a bowl, stir together the first 4 ingredients. Place milk in a 2-cup glass measuring cup; microwave on HIGH for 2–3 minutes, or until milk is scalded (do not boil).

Gradually stir about ¼ of hot milk into egg mixture; add the remaining hot milk, stirring constantly. Pour mixture into 4 (6-ounce) custard cups. Place cups in a circle in microwave oven and microwave on MEDIUM power (50% power) for 6–10 minutes, or until almost set in center; rearrange cups every 2 minutes. Chill thoroughly.

Invert custard onto serving plates. Spoon 2 tablespoons chocolate syrup over and around each custard. Serves 4.

Vivian Levine (Oak Ridge, Tennessee)

No Fuss Chocolate Mousse

6 ounces chocolate chips   2 whole eggs
2 tablespoons coffee liqueur   1 teaspoon vanilla extract
1 tablespoon orange juice   ¼ cup sugar
2 egg yolks   1 cup heavy whipping cream

Melt chocolate in the coffee liqueur and orange juice over very low heat. Put egg yolks and whole eggs in blender with vanilla and sugar. Blend for 2 minutes at medium-high speed. Add the cream and blend for another 30 seconds. Add the hot melted chocolate mixture (this will cook egg yolks) and blend until smooth. Pour into serving bowl or small individual cups. Refrigerate. Makes 4 servings.

Gail Black (Omaha, Nebraska)

Easy Spanish Flan

This is a Spanish custard which has been a family favorite for years. My mom, now 81 years old, always looks forward to eating this and it always blesses me. It really is a fast, easy, and elegant treat.

1 cup sugar	1 can sweetened condensed milk
1 (8-ounce) package cream cheese, softened	1 teaspoon vanilla
	¼ teaspoon salt
1 can evaporated milk	5 eggs, beaten

Heat a pan of hot water (large enough for Bundt pan to be set in) in 350° oven.

In a saucepan over medium heat, cook sugar down to liquid form (melted). Immediately remove from heat and pour quickly into bottom of greased Bundt pan. Turn to coat bottom. Set aside.

In a blender, add all remaining ingredients except eggs. Blend till creamy and smooth. Place creamed mixture and eggs in large bowl. Stir until incorporated. Pour mixture into Bundt pan (on top of melted sugar). Place Bundt pan in a preheated 350° water bath for 1 hour. Insert knife to loosen edges, if necessary. Turn out while still slightly warm (otherwise caramel re-hardens).

Sandria Gutierrez (Kresgeville, Pennsylvania)

This Green Room (actually painted beige) provides a comfortable place for on-air guests to relax before and after their appearances. Guests can monitor their sales on computers which provide up-to-the-minute information. They can also enjoy a cold drink, coffee, or snack, call home, or of course, watch QVC. There are three Green Rooms.

Banana Dessert Salad

This recipe has been in the family for 60 years. It is always requested at family gatherings and I have to double the recipe! Family members fight over who is going to get the first bite!

1 egg	1½ teaspoons vanilla
⅔ cup sugar	7 small bananas
2 heaping tablespoons flour	1 (8-ounce) carton whipped
1 cup milk	topping
¼ cup heavy cream	⅓ cup chopped peanuts
1 tablespoon butter	Mini-marshmallows (optional)

Beat egg. Add sugar and flour. Stir in milk and cream. Cook and stir in heavy pot on low heat until thick. Stir in butter and vanilla. Cover and refrigerate until ready to slice bananas. Slice 3 bananas and place in casserole dish; cover with half of the pudding mixture. Layer with half the whipped topping. Repeat layers. Garnish with sliced banana around edge of dish. Sprinkle peanuts and marshmallows over top.

Marsha Newland (Indianapolis, Indiana)

Just Delicious Dessert

¾ cup chopped nuts	1 (12-ounce) carton whipped
1⅓ cups flour	topping, divided
1⅓ sticks butter, melted	2 (3-ounce) packages instant lemon
1 (8-ounce) package cream cheese	pudding
1 cup powdered sugar	3 cups milk

Mix nuts, flour, and melted butter. Press into 9x13-inch baking dish and bake at 350° for 15 minutes. Let cool completely.

Beat cream cheese, sugar, and 1 cup whipped topping. Chill for 15 minutes. Beat puddings with milk for 2 minutes. Spread cream cheese mixture over cooled crust. Spread lemon mixture over cream cheese mixture. Top with remaining whipped cream.

Mary A. Duckett (Mountaintop, Pennsylvania)

Frosty Cool Strawberry Squares

Great for a bridal or wedding shower, or when you've just stepped out of the pool!

1 cup flour	**½ cup butter, melted**
¼ cup brown sugar	**½ cup chopped nuts**

Stir ingredients together. Spread into a 9x13-inch baking dish. Bake 20 minutes at 350°, stirring occasionally to make crumbs. Coat the bottom and sides with mixture, saving a little for topping.

TOPPING:

2 egg whites	**2 tablespoons lemon juice (fresh**
1 cup sugar	** is best)**
1 (10-ounce) package frozen	**2 cups whipped topping**
** strawberries, thawed, not**	**1 teaspoon almond flavoring**
** drained**	

Beat egg whites, sugar, strawberries, and lemon juice on high speed for 10–15 minutes. Mixture will be somewhat stiff, much like divinity. Fold in the whipped topping and almond flavoring. Spoon onto baked crumbs in pan and top with remaining crumbs. Freeze at least 6 hours. Cut into squares and serve with fresh sliced strawberries . . . and champagne!

Annette Miller (Oklahoma City, Oklahoma)

Welcome Home Chocolate Dessert

This recipe has been in our family since the 1940s and 1950s. Whenever any of us was away at school or college, our first night home, this was always requested as the dessert of choice.

½ cup butter	2 egg whites, beaten until stiff
2 squares unsweetened	peaks form
chocolate	12 graham crackers (6 squares),
1 cup powdered sugar	crumbled
2 egg yolks	Vanilla ice cream

Melt butter and chocolate over medium heat in a double boiler. Remove and add powdered sugar. Add egg yolks one at a time. Fold in beaten egg whites. Put ½ of graham cracker crumbs in bottom of 8-inch square pan. Pour chocolate mix over crumbs, and then add remaining graham cracker crumbs on top. Let chill for 4–8 hours, or overnight. Serve with a scoop of vanilla ice cream on top.

Melissa S. Hess (Black Diamond, Washington)

Chocolate Chip Tiramisu

1½ tablespoons instant coffee	1 (12-ounce) container frozen
granules	whipped topping, thawed
¾ cup warm water	½ cup mini-chocolate chips
1 (10¾-ounce) frozen pound	Ground cinnamon
cake, thawed	
1 (8-ounce) package mascarpone	
or cream cheese, softened	

Stir coffee and warm water together until coffee is dissolved. Cool. Cut pound cake into approximately 12 slices; then slice diagonally.

Place first layer of cake in a see-through bowl. Drizzle with coffee. In mixer, blend mascarpone or cream cheese with whipped topping for about 1 minute. Fold in chocolate chips. Add ½ whipped topping mixture as second layer. Repeat with one more layer of cake drizzled with coffee, ending with remaining whipped cream mixture. Sprinkle top with ground cinnamon. Enjoy! (Pictured on cover.)

Cheryl Hoffman (Coconut Creek, Florida)

Dipsy Doodle Noodle Kugel

1 (8-ounce) package cream
   cheese
¼ pound (1 stick) margarine
   or butter, softened
½ cup sugar

4 eggs
1 teaspoon salt
2 cups milk
1 (8-ounce) package wide egg
   noodles, cooked, drained

TOPPING:
½ teaspoon cinnamon
½ cup sugar

½–¾ cup cornflake crumbs

Beat together cream cheese and margarine well. Add sugar, eggs, salt and milk. Fold in cooked noodles. Put in buttered 9x13-inch casserole. Sprinkle on Topping mixture. Bake at 375° for 1 hour. Serves 8–12.

Brenda Berger (Las Vegas, Nevada)

Lemon Bisque

This recipe was given to me by a woman who was my landlady; I thought of her as a second mother. My family has this dish at every holiday dinner.

1 (12-ounce) can evaporated milk,
   well chilled
1 (6-ounce) package lemon gelatin
   (no substitute)
1½ cups boiling water

⅛ teaspoon salt
¾ cup sugar
3 tablespoons lemon juice
1 small can crushed pineapple,
   drained

Be sure milk is well chilled, at least 4 hours. Dissolve gelatin in boiling water. Add salt, sugar, and lemon juice. Chill gelatin mixture till syrupy. Whip chilled milk. Add gelatin; whip again. Fold in pineapple. Chill again.

Amelia Belson (Hannibal, New York)

Editors' Extra: Evaporated milk doesn't whip stiff—it is very light.

Floating Clouds Lemon Fluff

Years ago when I created this recipe, I was a busy mother of four children and teaching. I wanted a good lemon dessert, especially for summer, that didn't take as much time to prepare as lemon meringue pie, but would feed a lot of people. I came up with this, and now I get more requests for this recipe than anything else I make!

1 large angel food cake
2 (4-serving) boxes lemon
   pudding and pie filling

½ teaspoon pure lemon extract
4 egg whites
½ cup sugar

In a large trifle bowl, place a layer of angel food cake pieces; set aside. Prepare lemon pudding mix according to directions for lemon pie. Add lemon extract and set aside. Make meringue by beating egg whites till foamy, then adding sugar gradually, beating till stiff.

Very slowly fold hot lemon pudding into meringue (the hot pudding will cook the raw egg whites). Fold until no white shows. Pour enough lemon mixture over cake pieces to cover. Add additional cake pieces to make another layer. Top with remaining lemon mixture. Fill to the top, (mixture will drop when it is absorbed by cake). Cover bowl with plastic wrap and refrigerate for at least 3 hours. Decorate with fresh mint leaves. Serves 10–12.

Ellen Hughes (Washington, Pennsylvania)

This handy mobile lift can be easily maneuvered down wide hallways and then lift workers, like Eric Godfrey, to greater heights for light and set adjustments.

Toasted Coconut Lemon Angel Pie

My grandmother ran a boarding house and tea room in the fifties. One day she decided to experiment with eggs for a pie. I was a teen at the time and worked with her until this pie came out right. We now serve it at birthday parties instead of cake. Our daughter loves it because it is so light.

4 eggs, separated	**³/₄ cup toasted coconut**
¹/₄ teaspoon cream of tartar	**1¹/₂ pints heavy cream**
1¹/₂ cups sugar, divided	**2 tablespoons powdered sugar**
3 tablespoons lemon juice	

Beat egg whites until frothy. Add cream of tartar. Continue beating until whites are very stiff, gradually beating in 1 cup sugar. Spread in large pie tin that has been well greased, making it look like a pie crust with a small indentation in the middle for the filling. Bake 1 hour at 250°.

Beat egg yolks until thick. Beat in ¹/₂ cup sugar and lemon juice. Cook over hot water until thickened. Spread on cooled meringue crust.

Toast coconut in baking pan in oven (or toaster oven) at 400° until brown (takes only a few minutes, so watch).

Beat heavy cream until thick, gradually adding powdered sugar. Spread on top of filling, then sprinkle coconut on top. Chill. Eat! Enjoy!

Shirley Williams (Auburn, New York)

Summer Lemon Pies

I have a very large family (six children) and am always trying to bake economically, simply and fast. No one has tried these pies who didn't absolutely want more! At church socials or at home, it is so loved at both! No leftovers.

1 (14-ounce) can sweetened condensed milk	**1 (12-ounce) container whipped topping**
1 (12-ounce) can frozen lemonade (or limeade)	**2 graham cracker crusts**

Mix first 3 ingredients. Pour into graham cracker crusts; chill until firm.

Doris Miller-Brinson (Swainsboro, Georgia)

Easy Lemon Freeze

I take this to all family gatherings, and there is never any left at all!

1 cup graham cracker crumbs
1 tablespoon sugar
2 tablespoons margarine
1 (21-ounce) can lemon pie filling

1 cup sweetened condensed milk
½ cup concentrated lemon juice
1½ cups whipped topping

Mix graham cracker crumbs with sugar, reserving 1 tablespoon of mixture for topping. In a small saucepan, melt margarine and stir in graham cracker mixture. Pat on bottom of 8x8-inch pan. Set aside. In a large bowl, mix lemon pie filling, sweetened condensed milk, and lemon juice. Mix until smooth. Spread into pan. Top with whipped topping. Sprinkle reserved graham cracker crumbs on top. Put in freezer for minimum of 3 hours. Take out just before serving. To double the recipe, use a 9x13-inch pan and leave in the freezer a minimum of 4 hours.

C. L. Johnson (Kansas City-North, Missouri)

Graham Cracker Ice Cream

My mother-in-law has been making this ice cream since the 1940s and doesn't remember where she got the recipe. We make different kinds of homemade ice cream, but this is everyone's favorite. Very easy and delicious.

2 cups sugar
2 cups finely crushed graham
   crackers

5 cups 2% milk
3 cups heavy cream
1 tablespoon vanilla

Mix sugar and cracker crumbs (you can put the graham crackers into a zip-lock bag and use a rolling pin to crush, or put into a food processor). Add milk, heavy cream, and vanilla. Mix well and pour into ice cream freezer container. Mix according to manufacturer's directions on ice cream freezer. Enjoy.

Marie Delzer (Ashley, North Dakota)

Natural Home-Made
Doggy Biscuits

There are so many recipes out there already for us people to enjoy, I wanted to include something a little different. I met my wonderful wife, Kelly, because of Murphy, the Q-Dog. Kelly is Murphy's trainer and owner and we met on the very first day that Murphy came to be a part of our show. I owe that dog a lot, so this is how we reward him for his good deeds.

1 pound liver, blended　　　**2 teaspoons garlic salt (yes, dogs**
1 cup cornmeal　　　　　　　**love garlic just like people do)**
1/2 cup whole-wheat flour

Mix all together, adding just enough water to make a thick paste (not too much). Spread on a lightly greased cookie sheet. Bake at 350° for 20 minutes (do not allow to burn). Cut up into Doggy Biscuits while still warm and serve 1 or 2 after they have cooled.

Dan Hughes, QVC Host (West Chester, Pennsylvania)

Prior to joining QVC, Dan Hughes was a stand-up comedian, traveling the comedy circuit from Indianapolis to San Francisco. He also has worked as a motivational speaker, mainly addressing students and encouraging them to continue their education. Raised in Indianapolis, Indiana, Dan has a natural interest in car racing and its stars. In his free time he is an avid reader of more than 20 magazines and trade publications each week. Here is Dan with his daughter, Allison, and a basketful of puppies. Nothing like a schlurpy kiss behind the ear to get you going!

Index of Contributors

Not all of QVC's hosts are human. Murphy the Q-dog is a happy-go-lucky Golden Retriever. Always in the company of his trainer and companion, Kelly (who is married to host Dan Hughes), Murphy goes home to live with them in the country at the end of each day. Murphy is a registered, working animal with the American Humane Association.

■ ■ ■ *Contributors* ■ ■ ■

Hochevar, Liz 65
Hoersten, Lisa R. 230
Hoffman, Cheryl 279
Holt, Diana 96
Hostetler, Jaye Ann S. 76
Huchthausen, Kristine L. 149
Hughes, Dan 284
Hughes, Ellen 281
Hunt-Jones, Wilma 41

I

Ingle, Molly 57

J

Jaksons, Dawn 257
Johnson, C. L. 283
Johnson, Ronda J. 259
Jones, Gladys 218

K

Kalafut, Coleen 251
Kane, Penny Lyn 269
Kappner, Marcy 127
Keatley, Nanci C. 206
Kellogg, Susan M. 142
King, Dave 105
Kline, Maya 272
Kuhnle, Suzanne 62

L

Lack, Betty 176
Lafferty, Cheryl M. 84
Larsen, D. Arlone 72
Latusek, Glenda L. 48
Lehman, Linda 77, 160
Leistner, Marsha 165
Levine, Vivian 54, 275
Link, Carla 266
Lohr, Rita 181
Lomupo, Helen D. 126
Love, Kate 211
Lowman, Willena 68
Lyon, Leah 140

M

MacIver, Pam 24
Maffet, Marilyn 124
Mahler, Lola E. 116
Manko, Marianne 138
Mann, Sherry 157
Marlette, Vicki L. 186
Martin, Anita 144
Martin, Susan A. 128
Martinson, Nancy 171, 229

Matchett, Janelle 245
McCausland, Melanie 58
McDaniel, Becky 204
McDonald, Rosalie 97
McIlwain, Lena 13
McKane, Nancy 150
McKee, Lois 81
McKee, Mary 88
McLeod, Nancy E. 179
McMillian II, Jerry D. 66
McNair, Debra W. 166
McRae, Cheryl L. 228
Medvec, Gerard J. 256
Meszaros, Mary 258
Michael, Jean 95
Midlam, Ellen 270
Miehle, Cynthia J. 109
Miller, Annette 278
Miller, Ardis R. 93
Miller, Mary Lee McAbee 112
Miller-Brinson, Doris 282
Mitchem, Betty 155, 190
Mize, Amanda 171
Moe, Bev 168
Monroe, Jennie A. 144
Montanari, Jo Anne 255
Morales, Lauren Ann 162
Moran, Dorothy Tannahill 61
Murray, Carol 34
Myers, Julanne 216, 247
Myers, Lois J. 40

N

Nahajewski, Anna 15
Nava, Kathryn A. 189
Newland, Marsha 277
Norsworthy, Becky 250
Nugent, Carol 176

O

O'Bryant, Nancy 129
Odom, Janet 163
Olson, Charlene M. 188
Optekar-Dickman, Nancy 241

P

Palamara, Kathy 200
Palos, Jeanne 163
Palumbo, Bernadette 118
Paravisini, Linda 203
Parrish, Kim 91
Paviolo, Lynda 33, 153
Peluso, Barbara 172
Perkins, Rendy 84

Pin, Mary 117
Pitts, Christa 16
Plowman, Kay 151
Plumer, Sharee 80
Plumley, Beatrice 258
Poole, Kim 115
Porreca, Louise M. 262
Powers, Theresa R. 86
Presentati, Kristina 24
Probst, M. Ruth 36

R

Raleigh, Beverly 232
Ransome, Brett 170
Ransome, Laurie 123
Reed, Fran 159
Reichenberger, Heidi 239
Reid, Doris J. 80
Reilly, Patti 268
Reynolds, Carol 203
Rice, Joanne M. 131
Richard, Janice 72
Ridley-Pacicca, Joanne 85, 191
Riffle, Sheila M. 252
Roberds, Linda 108
Roberto, Mary 68
Robertson, Lisa 51
Robinson, Marilou 188
Robinson, Sandy 192
Robles, Chila 27
Roche, Monica 38
Rock, Elizabeth 103
Rock, Ralph 158
Roe, Mary Beth 180
Rogers, Rebecca A. 141
Roney, Steffie H. 125
Rood, Jeannette E. 260
Rosell, Karen J. 223
Runkle, Susan M. 152
Russell, Carol 178
Ryan, Camilla C. 111
Ryan, Mary Kay 237

S

Sack, Liz 200
Saint, Mary Ann 158
Salgado, Beverly 245
Sandal, Kristi L. 130
Saulnier, Lorraine M. 78
Savu, Julie A. 177
Saylor, Carol A. 168
Scates, Patsy 133
Schierloh, Phyllis 25
Schmitz, Wanda K. 153
Scobie, Anne Marie 98

QVC's beautiful atrium is its hub. Four major hallways and a stairwell with a bridge lead to its many offices, meeting rooms, studios and production areas throughout QVC's enormous complex. The cafeteria, the library, the bank, and the convenience store are all nearby.

Q

R

S

Index of Recipes